The New Shell Guides

The Lowlands and Borders of Scotland

The New Shell Guides

The Lowlands and Borders of Scotland

Roddy Martine

Introduction by Peter Maxwell Stuart
Series Editor: John Julius Norwich
Photography by David Ward

Michael Joseph · London

MICHAEL JOSEPH LTD

Published by the Penguin Group
27 Wrights Lane, London W8 5TZ, England
Viking Penguin Inc., 40 West 23rd Street, New York, New York 10010, USA
Penguin Books Australia Ltd, Ringwood, Victoria, Australia
Penguin Books Canada Ltd, 2801 John Street, Markham, Ontario, Canada L3R 1B4
Penguin Books (NZ) Ltd, 182–190 Wairau Road, Auckland 10, New Zealand

Penguin Books Ltd, Registered Offices: Harmondsworth, Middlesex, England

First published in Great Britain in 1989

Typeset in Linotron 10/11pt Plantin by Cambrian Typesetters, Frimley, Surrey
Colour reproduction by Scantrans, Singapore
Printed and bound by Kyodo-Shing Loong Printing, Singapore

A CIP catalogue record for this book is available from The British Library

Cased edition: ISBN 0 7181 2940 7
Paperback edition: ISBN 0 7181 3173 8

Front cover photograph: Traquair House (see p. 123)
Title-page photograph: Culzean Castle (see p. 39)

Contents

Introduction

PETER MAXWELL STUART
20th Laird of Traquair

That intrepid lady traveller, Celia Fiennes, who journeyed across England and Wales in the late 1680s, recorded in her memoirs on reaching the Borders that she had heard 'reports enough to discourage further progress northwards'. For the most part she had been told that persons who travelled there 'go from one Nobleman's house to another . . . those houses are all kinds of Castles and they live great, though in so nasty a way . . . one has little stomach to eat or use anything . . .'. She attributed it wholly to their sloth, 'for I see they sit and do little'. However, she appreciated the fish there and bought some, but insisted on taking it back for the English to dress it. Today at Eyemouth on the coast just above Berwick the quality of the fish is so good that it is regularly exported to the USA and to many European centres, notably Barcelona in Spain.

Other writers, not least of whom was Dr Johnson, wrote disparagingly about the Scots, and long after the Union in 1707 relations between England and Scotland were anything but friendly, even among the upper classes. Across the Border the Scots disliked everything English, while the English had a similar attitude to all things Scottish. Those who did go north regularly considered themselves intrepid travellers venturing into hostile and unknown country. Scotland was regarded as North Britain right into the next century, and even at my home at Traquair in the Borders printed stationery from the 1920s still bore the initials 'NB' under the address!

A world of difference

Over the three centuries since Celia Fiennes made a few tentative steps into the Borders, the picture of Scotland has changed naturally but not quite so quickly or dramatically as might be expected during such a long period. Visitors who enter the country, whether it be at Berwick-upon-Tweed on the A1, by the spectacular boundary at Carter Bar on the A68 or further west at Longtown or Gretna, soon find themselves in a very different world from the one they left in the south. 'A world of difference,' proclaims the Scottish Tourist Board in its advertising campaign to bring people north of the Border, and different it certainly is. First there are the people, kind and hospitable but fiercely independent and proud of their origins and local traditions. Then there is the language, the different country dialects which have survived four centuries of erosion by the English, opening up a whole new dictionary of words and phrases which will puzzle the visitor – messages (shopping), ken (know), lug (ear), tatties (potatoes), loons (boys), and so on. There are differences too in almost every aspect of life – from religion, in which the influence of the Kirk is now much less than in the past when it formed the main core of government, to the legal system, from food and cooking, licensing regulations and holidays to politics and architecture: the list is endless. Even the banknotes are different and, of course, the weather is always unpredictable except possibly to those

Borthwick Castle (see p. 113)

whose work keeps them close to the land. In the Borders, for instance, where you might expect a softer climate, you will probably need three sweaters and a raincoat in July.

This *New Shell Guide*, a fitting companion to the one already published which covers Northern Scotland and the Islands, tells the story of another Scotland which stretches from the North Sea in the east to the shores of the Solway in the west. It is indispensable to the traveller who wishes to pause awhile on his or her journey north, to avoid being drawn into the tourist trail and above all to enjoy the peace and quiet of some of the most beautiful and varied country to be found anywhere in Britain. It might also help to dispel the impression spread by some tour operators that Scotland begins not at the Borders but in Edinburgh or Glasgow, with all roads leading north to the Highlands.

Land of contrasts

In fact, the land lying between and to the south of these two cities is a microcosm of the whole country, full of contrasting scenery, rich in legend and history and full of surprises for the enterprising traveller. Berwick-upon-Tweed in the south-east, guarding the approaches to the North Sea (referred to, incidentally, in 19th-century guidebooks as 'the German Channel'), seems an obvious starting point. Possibly the best example of a fortified town in Europe, it is something of an enigma: geographically it is on the wrong side of the River Tweed, situated as it is on the north bank, politically part of Northumberland but also a Scottish royal burgh. During the Scottish Wars of Independence

Neidpath Castle (see p. 158)

from the 12th to the 16th centuries, it changed hands thirteen times, before becoming independent of both England and Scotland. Oddly enough, it is still at war with Russia, never having signed the peace treaty after the Crimean War. Its long and chequered history, characterized by the feuds and battles between the Scots and the English, forms a fitting introduction to similar events which swept the Border lands to the west.

It might be appropriate here to define the area known as the Scottish Borders; for the term can be slightly misleading since not all the counties 'march' (or border) with England. In local government terms there are four districts comprising the Borders Region: Berwickshire, Roxburgh, Ettrick and Lauderdale, and Tweeddale (which has the distinction of being the nation's highest county above sea level). As you journey further west into Dumfries and Galloway, finally reaching the Solway Firth, the region becomes progressively less attached to the traditions of the Borders.

A good method of exploring and following the history of the area is simply to trace the network of rivers and streams which weave their way across the region: Tweed, Eye, Yarrow, Jed, Blackadder, Gala and Ettrick, to name just a few. The greatest of these is, of course, the Tweed, flowing 97 miles from its source at Tweedsmuir in the Lowther Hills to the sea at Berwick. One of the great salmon-fishing rivers in the country, the Tweed has a magic which appeals not only to fishermen struggling to land a fine salmon or sea trout but also to tourists who enjoy other forms of outdoor activity such as walking, riding, photography and birdwatching.

Every mile of the river unfolds on some new scenic beauty. There are the hills: the Cheviots dominate the south, the Moorfoots and Lammermuirs to the north and west form the Tweed basin (converging on Tweedsmuir where the river rises) and, in the central area, the three Eildon peaks are constantly on the horizon. Everywhere there is evidence of volcanic movement and eruption, but with one or two exceptions – as in the upper Tweed – there is little similarity with the Highlands. Instead, here the hills have a soft, rounded quality; green is the predominant colour, emphasising the richness of the pastures in the valleys. Centuries ago, in the time of the Stuart kings who hunted here, much of this country was thickly forested and the rivers formed a natural barrier against intruders from the south, whether they were the common enemy, the English, or the Scots taking revenge on neighbours for stealing their cattle. Along the banks of the Tweed, particularly in Peeblesshire (which is now reverting to its old name of Tweeddale), fortified towers (or peels) can still be found perched on commanding heights, within sight of each other so that their occupants could communicate by means of smoke signals. Neidpath just below Peebles is a good example; others are Elibank, Horsburgh, Cardrona and, further afield, Newark and Smailholm. My own home of Traquair was also one of these until the 1st Earl in 1640, with time on his hands (he was confined to his estates at that period), thought the comfort and security of his own house more important than its function as a fortress, so he simply had the river moved away from the house to a position known as the New Water. Afterwards came the Civil War in which the Stuarts were heavily involved, and later the Jacobite Risings – although the latter left little mark on the area, the Lowlands being somewhat apathetic to the cause of the Stuart Restoration.

Abbeys, churches, houses and castles

The Borders has more than its fair share of ruined buildings, a testimony to the bloody conflicts which swept the country up to the early 1600s. The imposing ruins of the Border abbeys of Dryburgh, Jedburgh, Kelso and Melrose stand as a reminder of the attempts by the English to subjugate the Scots. They are well worth visiting, for the authorities who look after them are beginning to realize their potential in new methods of display. The town of Jedburgh, the first Scottish town that greets visitors after crossing the border at Carter Bar, is particularly outstanding. Its recently restored centre and its historic buildings, such as Queen Mary's House and the Castle Jail, are fine examples of what can be done to combine the old with the modern in terms of town planning and architecture.

From the remains of once-active monastic settlements it is rewarding to explore further afield for the smaller churches which form the focal point of their community. Examples which spring readily to mind may be found in Roslin, Midlothian; Stobo and Lyne, Tweeddale; Edrom, Berwickshire; Bowden, Ettrick and Lauderdale. In contrast to the old, a completely new building has been erected in the form of a modern monastery, the splendid Tibetan centre, at Eskdalemuir high up in the Eskdale Hills (which, incidentally, has one of the highest rainfalls in the British Isles). It has a wonderfully peaceful atmosphere with a great spirit of hospitality. The numerous crafts carried on under its roof parallel monastic activities of centuries ago.

After things spiritual, look at other buildings of a historical nature, notably the great country houses; and the Borders Region is particularly fortunate both in their scope and variety. Many of these are family houses inhabited by people

Dryburgh Abbey (see p. 53)

Queen Mary's House, Jedburgh (see p. 126)

whose ancestors have lived in them for many generations; many too are situated conveniently close to each other. Over in Berwickshire by Duns is Manderston, a perfect example of an Edwardian house true to the 'upstairs-downstairs' tradition, whose original owners spared no expense when building it at the beginning of this century. In contrast, my own home, Traquair in Tweeddale, is the oldest inhabited house in Scotland. Once a royal hunting lodge, it has close associations, like many other places in the region, with Mary Queen of Scots and Bonnie Prince Charlie. He was the last person to pass through its

The Bear Gates, Traquair House (see p. 123)

famous Bear Gates, in 1745; they were then closed against a world which rejected a Stuart Restoration.

Over the hills near Selkirk is Bowhill, home of the Duke of Buccleuch, with its superb collection of Old Master paintings. Further afield, at the other end of the Borders north of Dumfries (near Thornhill) is another Buccleuch house, Drumlanrig; it has a wonderful setting and boasts an equally fine collection of treasures and paintings. Not far from Selkirk and overlooking the Tweed is Abbotsford, which was Sir Walter Scott's home, now a shrine to the memory of a man who did so much to give Scotland a name in the world of literature and poetry. Another famous house, also overlooking the Tweed, is the Duke of Roxburghe's impressive Floors Castle, the largest historic house in the country. Not far away, near Earlston, famed as the birthplace of the famous Thomas the Rhymer, is Mellerstain, a wonderful example of Adam architecture, one of the great Georgian houses of Scotland.

Finally, at Lauder is the ancient Border stronghold, the sixteenth-century Thirlestane Castle, which guarded the approaches to Edinburgh. Lauder is reputed to have the most unspoilt pre-Victorian high street in Scotland, having escaped the worst effects of the industrial revolution when the growing textile and woollen industries left their depressing mark on many Border towns; indeed, its streets still conform closely to the pattern laid out in medieval times. If you happen to be there on the first Saturday in August, you will be met by hundreds of horsemen followed by bands and crowds of townspeople singing and dancing along the High Street. This is Lauder Common Riding, one of a series of similar events which are held in nearly every Border town from May to September.

Festivals and activities

These annual festivals on horseback are an exciting feature of Border life dating from the days when Borderers rode out to preserve their boundaries and protect them from encroachment. The one held at Selkirk, the largest in the region, has the oldest origins, dating back to the times when only one survivor returned from the Battle of Flodden in 1513. Go there at 6am on the first Friday in June and enjoy the unique and unforgettable experience of suddenly finding yourself in the middle of what seems to be the town's entire population who, with arms linked, move in procession to the water's edge of the River Tweed at the foot of the town, singing the traditional song. There is a certain mystique surrounding these festivals which will puzzle the visitor; remember, however, that they are not laid on as tourist attractions but exist for the benefit of the local inhabitants who treasure their traditions. The visitor will find a little prior research into local customs worthwhile to enable full appreciation of the proceedings: learn the meaning of such terms as souter (standard bearer), bussin (the colours), cornet (youngest cavalry leader in a troop), sour plums (originating from the time when a raiding party of English were surprised and defeated by citizens of Galashiels after suffering from the effects of eating unripe plums), callant (best of the young men) and whipman (one responsible for driving the cattle at an agricultural show). They all emphasise the importance of the horse and there are few places where riding is so universal as the Borders.

In addition to the Common Ridings, the other activities usually associated with the horse enjoy popularity – hunting, trekking, eventing and, of course, the shows. If you wish really to get to grips with the spirit of the Borders and to experience the feel of the country, there is no better way than to mingle with the crowd at one of the many agricultural shows held throughout the summer months. Each has its own distinctive character and there is much competition between the different towns and districts. This rivalry now finds friendly expression on the rugby field, and the Border Sevens season is famous.

The countryside also opens up great opportunities for the walker and with a few exceptions (such as the Grey Mare's Tail near St Mary's Loch) the hills are relatively gentle. The Forestry Commission has been specially enterprising in laying out forest trails and walks. If you are very ambitious, you can attempt the whole length of the recently opened Southern Upland Way, a 212-mile footpath between Portpatrick on the west coast and Cockburnspath on the east. It passes through Dumfries and Galloway, Strathclyde and, in its eastern section, through the heart of the Borders. Alternatively, you can limit yourself to a short stretch, enjoying the use it makes of many pre-existing paths and tracks, some of them hundreds of years old, including drove, military and forest roads, lochside paths and the track beds of disused railways.

For the motorist access to the region is not difficult with two major motorways at each side, the A1/A1(M) in the east and the M5/M6 in the west via Carlisle and Dumfries. Unlike in the Highlands, where the choice is progressively limited as one goes further north, here in the Borders there is a great network of small country roads which cover the area from east to west, bringing a sense of pleasure and adventure to the traveller. Many of these roads follow routes which have been travelled for centuries, such as the stretch on the A68 running from Darlington to Edinburgh which follows the line of the

Near Haddington

original north road built by the Romans. Apart from a few peak weekends in the summer, these routes are relatively uncrowded.

Most people who cross the Border aim not unnaturally for the capital city, but it is a matter of choice whether they want to get there in the shortest time or linger in that part of the Borders Region already described. If they take the eastern route after Berwick-upon-Tweed, the Lothian Region of the south-east is well worth a diversion, with Edinburgh, sitting at the foot of the Pentland Hills, providing its heart. Some of the richest farmland in Scotland is here, and as long as you do not expect to find hills as you will further east, the country is full of interest, particularly in the field of conservation. There is the Muir Country Park near Dunbar, many attractive villages such as Gifford, and Haddington, one of the finest remaining 18th-century towns in Scotland and particularly worth visiting. Above all, the region is a great place for golf, with eighteen courses including the world-famous Muirfield at Gullane. As in many other parts of Scotland, a game of golf can be played with a choice and freedom which is lacking in the south. Nine- and eighteen-hole courses may be found within reasonable distance of most towns in the Lowlands and, charging very reasonably, they are always well patronized.

Literary heritage

This introduction to the Lowlands would not be complete without some mention of the rich literary heritage associated with the region. Sir Walter Scott's great contribution to Scotland, giving the country a place in international literature, has already been mentioned; but his protégé, James

Hogg, the Ettrick Shepherd, brought up on a Border farm near Yarrow, is not so widely known. Like Scott he was one of Scotland's literary giants, but his roots lay very much in the countryside where he lived and worked, a fact which is reflected in his writings, *Confessions of a Justified Sinner* being his greatest achievement. Recently a Hogg Festival was held with great success; for the Borders still preserve a strong tradition in the arts, both drama and music.

Other famous names with a Border background include Mungo Park the explorer; William Chambers the publisher and historian; Andrew Lang the poet and writer; Tom Scott the painter; and the writer John Buchan, later Lord Tweedsmuir. It is not difficult to imagine Richard Hannay, or indeed any of Buchan's characters, striding out across the hills near Broughton where the writer spent much of his childhood and where there is now a John Buchan Centre.

Then, of course, there is that great figure of the Scottish literary landscape who hailed from the Lowlands, Robert Burns. The 'Ploughman's Poet' is revered by Scots the world over, and at home with a fervour that surprises many first-time visitors to his country. It is said that he gave Scotland 'her sweetest song and earth her saddest story'. His short lifespan of thirty-seven years was in fact not untypical of many of the rustic population of that time. Burns was a poet of the people, sharing their poverty and hardships, hopes and ambitions, vices and virtues in the harsh countryside of two hundred years ago. Today that country can be explored by the visitor who, helped by the numerous heritage trails, will have no difficulty in tracing his life and the places in which he worked and visited. Burns Country extends from Ayrshire in the north down to Dumfries and Galloway in the south-west; here it is well worthwhile making a

The Auld Brig O'Doon, Alloway *(see p. 23)*

diversionary expedition to the beautiful 200-mile coastline along the Solway.

It was in Galloway that Scotland saw the beginnings of Christianity and from there that Robert the Bruce started out to fight for Scottish independence. In this part of the country the effects of the Gulf Stream bring a warmer climate than further east, and in May and June five to six hours of sunshine are not unusual. August and September are warm, but you may expect rain on one in every three days and you must beware of midges. There is plenty to see and explore: attractive whitewashed villages, planned towns built in the 18th century and remote country – New Abbey, dominated by the warm stone of Sweetheart Abbey; Kirkcudbright, a favourite haunt of artists; Gatehouse of Fleet; and New Galloway, the smallest royal burgh in Scotland, to mention only a few. Finally, at the far western tip of Wigtownshire lies an area largely overlooked by tourists; it ranges from the coastal towns of Port Logan and Portpatrick to the tropical gardens of Ardwell and Logan.

Two great cities

In the same way that visitors to the eastern Borders make for Edinburgh, in the west they aim for Glasgow on their way to the western Highlands. During the depression years following the Second World War when the traditional industries were in decline, harsh critics said that the best thing about Glasgow was the ease with which you could escape from it by the network of newly built roads which cut a swathe through the centre. Today those critics are silenced by the transformation which has overtaken the city under the inspired leadership of 'Glasgow's miles better' Provost Michael Kelly, his successor Robert Gray and an enlightened city council. A new spirit pervades the city which has secured it the nomination of European City of Culture in 1990. In 1988 it was the scene of the highly successful Garden Festival.

Glasgow is bustling with every form of activity, cultural, sporting and commercial. In the Glasgow Museum and Art Gallery at Kelvingrove there is possibly the best municipal collection of pictures in Britain, and the Burrell Collection in its inspired setting is also of international stature – an impressive tribute to one of Scotland's greatest cultural benefactors. The annual Mayfest (of comparatively recent origin) cannot as yet rival Edinburgh's Festival, but it is an example of Glasgow's enterprise in the world of entertainment, music and drama. Scottish Opera has its well-deserved home here and there are exciting developments in the world of the arts.

Good shops in imaginative surroundings in the heart of the city, modern hotels, the largest conference centre in Scotland and some of the best restaurants to be found anywhere have made Glasgow a place with a great future. Architecturally, with its associations with Charles Rennie Mackintosh, it is of outstanding interest and has inspired the design of many buildings in cities all over the world, notably in Chicago and Melbourne. No wonder Sir John Betjeman called it the finest Victorian city in the world.

I always think that the best thing about Glasgow is its people. Lose your way – not difficult if you are a motorist – and you will soon experience the warmth and humour and kindness of the true Glaswegian.

Statue of Queen Victoria, George Square, Glasgow (see p. 97)

From Glasgow an easy drive of about an hour along the motorway takes you to Edinburgh, where this journey through the Lowlands must come to an end. Spare the time if you can for a diversion through the Clyde Valley, where there is much well worth seeing. New Lanark is a unique industrial village established in 1785, the site of Robert Owen's radical social and educational experiment. Not far away are the spectacular Falls of Clyde within the Scottish Wildlife Trust's Reserve. Near Hamilton, situated in a country park at Chatelherault, is a beautifully restored 18th-century hunting lodge of the Dukes of Hamilton, and at Blantyre is the David Livingstone Centre. The little town of Biggar, further afield, is also worth a visit. It has not only one of the best rural museums in the country, Gladstone Court (converted like so many of its kind from an ironmonger's shop), but also Green Hill Covenanter's House, Moat Park Heritage Centre, the oldest surviving gasworks in Britain (built in 1839) and a superb, completely equipped Victorian puppet theatre.

And so to Edinburgh. It is difficult, in so few words, to do justice to this showplace of Scottish history and tradition, this noble city born out of strife and built like Rome on seven hills. As Robert Louis Stevenson aptly remarked, 'Edinburgh pays cruelly for her high seat by having one of the vilest climates under heaven.' The visitor is advised, therefore, to be prepared for the worst, particularly a cutting wind even in summer. Another speciality of the Edinburgh weather is a damp raw haar (or mist) creeping in from the Forth, and occasionally isolating the city from the surrounding country which more often than not is bathed in sunshine. At times like these, little imagination is needed to conjure up images of the dark deeds, mysteries and hauntings that are so much a part of Edinburgh's history and folklore. The city then seems to hang suspended as the mist unfolds like some ghostly curtain, slipping down through the narrow wynds (or closes) below the castle.

In contrast to its rival Glasgow, which looks forward to the future, Edinburgh looks back on its past, reflecting the glories and disasters of Scottish history with a well-deserved pride and not a little unconcealed satisfaction. To the tourist Edinburgh is, of course, the castle, majestically overlooking the superb panorama of the city. The gardens below lead to Princes Street, always crowded, with flashes of tartan at every corner. The tourist trail inevitably leads the visitor from the castle down the High Street past St Giles, along the Royal Mile to Holyrood Palace. Beyond the familiar landmarks, however, there is another side of Edinburgh which invites exploration: the New Town, Dean Village and Stockbridge, Newhaven, Leith and Portobello, Morningside, Corstorphine, Cramond, Queensferry and so much more. It is also worth getting to know the Edinburgh of the Festival, the Tattoo and the Fringe – all packed into a relatively short period and giving the city in August almost a foreign air of cosmopolitan gaiety. When these are over, Edinburgh slips quickly back into its more dignified and stately role.

It is here in the capital that your journey should end, so pause for a while, if you can escape from the crowds, and contemplate your Scottish experience, an experience that might inspire you to take an alternative route back south, east or west to recapture more of the magic and beauty of the Lowlands of Scotland.

Edinburgh from Arthur's Seat (see p. 58)

Abbotsford, home of Sir Walter Scott

Note on using the Gazetteer
Entries in the Gazetteer are arranged in alphabetical order. 'The', if part of the name, follows the main element: **Eildon Hills, The** (alphabetized under E).

Entry headings consist of the name of the place or feature in **bold** type, followed by the region's name in *italics* and a map reference in parentheses: **Haddington**, *Lothian* (3/D1). The figure 3 is the map number; D1 is the grid reference, with D indicating the across and 1 the down reference.

If a name mentioned within the text of an entry is printed in capital letters – i.e. PAISLEY – this indicates that it has its own entry in the Gazetteer.

Bold type is used for certain places, buildings or other features of interest or importance referred to within Gazetteer entries.

Every effort has been made to ensure that information about the opening to the public of buildings, estates, gardens, reserves, museums, galleries, etc., and details of trails, walks and footpaths, and of ferries, were as accurate and up to date as possible at the time of going to press. Such particulars are, of course, subject to alteration and it may be prudent to check them locally, or with the appropriate organizations or authorities.

Gazetteer

Abbey St Bathans, *Borders* (4/A3)
Located on a particularly beautiful stretch of the Whiteadder Water, which flows through Berwickshire to join the River Tweed, this is a small village where once stood a 13th-century priory dedicated to St Bathan, a follower of St Columba. A major attraction nowadays is the trout farm which is open to the public and incorporates an interpretive centre describing the history and life of the valley from prehistoric to modern times.

Abbotsford, *Borders* (3/D5)
Renowned as an example of architectural eccentricity, this great house was the home that Sir Walter Scott built for himself and it is still owned by his descendants. Close to MELROSE, on the right bank of the River Tweed, the site was originally associated with a crossing place used by monks travelling to and from Melrose Abbey. Sir Walter bought the farm here in 1881 and the creation of this most individual of houses occupied the last twenty years of his life. In 1822 he demolished the old farmhouse and built the main block of the building which can be seen today. When soaring costs led him towards bankruptcy, his creditors joined ranks and presented Abbotsford to Sir Walter in appreciation of his services to the Scottish people. Abbotsford remains a mixture of styles reflecting Sir Walter's whims and tastes – a mock Tudor baronial complex of turrets and gables. The porch was modelled on that of Linlithgow Palace and the screen on the east side of the court was copied from details in the cloisters at Melrose Abbey. The house contains original fragments commemorating Scotland's romantic but often violent past – the door of the Old Tolbooth, for example, and a 1668 panel from the Guild House of the Soutars of Selkirk. The Armoury here contains fine pistols, relics of Waterloo and the noble Marquis of Montrose's

Sir Walter Scott's study at Abbotsford

sword. In the Library are Rob Roy's purse, Sir Henry Raeburn's portrait of Scott and a drinking glass used by Robert Burns whom Scott met as a young boy.

Aberlady, *Lothian* (4/C1)
This attractive village is a popular place for retirement and is within commuting distance of EDINBURGH. It was once the port of HADDINGTON, but the bay is heavily silted over. A small trestle bridge over the Peffer Burn leads to Aberlady Bay Nature Reserve, famous for its colony of pink-footed geese, mammals and butterflies. The dunes along the wide, sandy beach are preferably approached from GULLANE so the wildlife is disturbed as little as possible, but the area is generally popular with walkers and sunbathers who want to get away from the crowds during the summer months.

North-east of the village is Luffness House, privately owned by the Hope family. It is of ancient date and stands within a fortalice constructed by the French general De Thermes in 1549. The house itself was built in 1584, but has been much restored and renovated. The Myreton Motor Museum nearby, open daily, accommodates vintage cars, commercial vehicles and bicycles. The Scottish novelist Nigel Tranter has his home on the outskirts of Aberlady.

Gosford House lies south-west of Aberlady on the road to Longniddry. Designed by William Adam in 1790, it is the home of the Earls of Wemyss and March. It has a fine marble hall and double staircase and there are some spectacular paintings.

Ailsa Craig, *Strathclyde* (1/A9 – not shown)
Ten miles offshore from GIRVAN and situated in the Firth of Clyde, this plug of an extinct volcano lies about 13 miles south of the Isle of Arran and is sometimes called 'Paddy's Milestone' because it is half-way between Belfast and GLASGOW. In Gaelic it is known as 'Fairy Rock', and in medieval times renegade monks were sent here in exile from Crossraguel Abbey.

The granite from Ailsa Craig was used in the manufacture of curling stones of a fine quality. Today the island provides a spectacular focal point from the coast road to BALLANTRAE and all along the Ayrshire coast, and it has become a sanctuary for seabirds.

Airdrie, *Strathclyde* (2/B3)
In the heart of Scotland's industrial belt, this has

Ailsa Craig in the Firth of Clyde

become in part a dormitory suburb for GLASGOW. It dates from the late 17th century when Robert Hamilton, who had bought the farm here, engineered an act of parliament creating Airdrie a market town. It became a burgh in 1821.

Alloway, *Strathclyde* (1/C7)
Birthplace of Robert Burns on 25 January 1759. The poet lived his first seven years here in a cottage built by his father in 1757. In 1766, the family moved to the farm at Mount Oliphant. Burns incorporated Alloway kirk into his fictional poem 'Tam O' Shanter' and it was from here that the witches' orgy was observed. Opposite the church, which was ruined even in Burns' time, is the Land O' Burns Centre which has visual displays showing the eventful life of the poet. The Burns Monument (open from April to mid-October), designed as a Grecian temple, was erected in 1820, a rather unlikely tribute to Scotland's bard. In the gardens there are lifelike statues by James Thom of Burns' characters. Below here is the Auld Brig O' Doon which also features in 'Tam O' Shanter'.

Just to the north is Rozelle House, an 18th-century mansion altered in the 1830s by David Bryce and which is the headquarters of Kyle and Carrick Museums and Gallery Service. Regalias of former district burghs are on display with other items of historical interest. The stable block has been converted to form the four Maclaurin Galleries which house fine art, photography, crafts and embroidery. There is a Henry Moore bronze and other examples of outdoor sculpture.

Ancrum, *Borders* (3/E6)
Close to the River Teviot, on the curve of the River Ale, not far from JEDBURGH, this is a secluded village where the shaft of a 12th-century mercat (or market) cross stands on the village green. A woodland centre on nearby Monteviot Estate incorporates an interpretation exhibition featuring the different types of woodland and the care of timber.

On Peniel Heugh Hill stands the Waterloo Monument, erected by the Marquis of Lothian and his tenants to commemorate the end of the Napoleonic Wars. In 1545, at Lilliard's Edge on Ancrum Moor, an English force was overpowered by the Earl of Angus and Scott of Buccleuch and a party of Scots who included the Fair Maid Lilliard who, once her legs were cut off, fought on bravely on her stumps.

The Burns Monument, Alloway

Annan, Dumfries and Galloway (6/E5)
Situated near the mouth of the River Annan, which rises in the Moffat Hills and flows into the Solway Firth, this busy market town is close to the Scotland/England Border. Annan had connections with the de Brus family in the 12th century before they moved to Lochmaben. A Georgian moat house is located beside the original motte and bailey of their castle. In the town hall is the Brus Stone, associated with King Robert I.

Prince Charles Edward Stuart spent a night at the Buck Inn on his retreat from Derby in 1745. The Revd Edward Irving (1792–1834) was born in Annan. He formed the Catholic Apostolic Church for which he was defrocked but was later reinstated.

West of Annan lies the village of **Ruthwell** where, in the local church, can be seen the Ruthwell Cross, an early Christian monument. In 1810 the first savings bank was founded here by the local minister, Henry Duncan, who died in 1843. The building is now a museum.

Caerlaverock Castle, a stronghold of the Maxwell Earls of Nithsdale dating from the 13th century and now a ruin, is situated west-south-west of Ruthwell. The castle, which is open to the public, was captured by King Edward I of England in 1301, and capitulated to the Covenanters in 1638. In the churchyard here is buried Robert Paterson, the model for Sir Walter Scott's Old Mortality. Caerlaverock National Nature Reserve, which consists of 13,594 acres of saltmarsh and sand, extends along the coastline of the Solway Firth. This Wildfowl Trust reserve is open from mid-September until the end of April.

At **Ecclefechan**, north of Annan, Thomas Carlyle, the great 19th-century writer, was born. His birthplace, Arched House, stands in the Main Street and is now a museum containing his memorabilia and correspondence. His statue by Boehm stands at the top of the village and he is buried with his parents and brother in the churchyard. Archibald Arnott (1772–1885), Napoleon's doctor on St Helena, is also buried here.

Hoddom Bridge, built by Thomas Telford over the River Annan, stands about 1½ miles west of Ecclefechan near the 16th-century Hoddom Castle, a fortress built and held by the powerful Johnstone family; and a great Anglian monastery founded by St Kentigern once stood close by.

Arbigland (6/C6) *see* Dumfries

Ardeer (1/B4) *see* Irvine

Ardrossan, *Strathclyde* (1/B4)

This 19th-century town was planned by the 12th Earl of Eglinton, the Montgomery family having had a castle here in the 12th century. In its heyday, Ardrossan Castle must have been a fortress of considerable strength, protected as it was on the north side by a deep foss over which a drawbridge must have been thrown, and on the south by the steep rocks on which the building itself stands. Despite its seeming impregnability, Oliver Cromwell succeeded in sacking Ardrossan and used its stones to build his fort at AYR.

The town of Ardrossan became important as the terminus for passenger and freight traffic sailings to Belfast and to the Isle of Arran. It also grew into a popular holiday resort as a result of its fine sandy beaches and safe bathing. Off North Bay is a bird sanctuary. Across the South Bay is **Saltcoats**, whose name derives from saltworks established here by King James V in the 16th century and which shares North Bay's popularity with holiday makers. An interesting phenomenon can be seen in the harbour at low tide when a number of fossilized tree trunks become visible. The Martello Tower dates from 1800 and this masonry gun position can be found on the heights above Auchenharvie School. Originally two storeys high, it was built to protect the mines from attack by French warships during the French Revolutionary Wars.

Ardrossan has a Roman Catholic church, St Peter-in-Chains, Swedish in design. The town's former third parish church, which dates from the mid-1700s, now houses a collection of local history created by the late Owen Kelly. This North Ayrshire Museum is located off Hamilton Street and displays include an art exhibition, ship models, a replica of a 19th-century kitchen and a reconstruction of the Stevenston burial kist (or tomb).

Just inland of Saltcoats is **Stevenston**, where there was certainly a settlement as early as the 13th century and various archaeological finds in the neighbourhood indicate a much earlier community. Kerelaw Castle was once the seat of the Cunningham Earls of Glencairn and dates from the 15th century. It was partly destroyed by the Montgomeries who were at feud with the Cunningham family in 1488. The laburnum tree which stands in the middle of the ruin was sent to Kerelaw from Africa by the explorer David Livingstone.

Arniston, *Lothian* (3/B3)

This was the seat of the so-called 'uncrowned king of Scotland', Henry Dundas, 1st Viscount Melville, who 'managed' Scotland for the British prime minister, William Pitt. His family dominated the Scottish legal profession in the late 17th and early 18th centuries, but acquired lands at Arniston as early as the 16th century. William Adam was instructed to design the present house on the site of an older building. It is considered a characteristic example of the Scottish classical house of that period.

Caerlaverock Castle, which capitulated to the Covenanters in 1638. The Covenanters were so named because in a series of 'covenants' during the late 16th and 17th centuries they bound themselves to maintain the Presbyterian doctrine as the sole religion of Scotland, defying all measures to reinstate Roman Catholicism.

Athelstaneford, *Lothian* (4/D2)
Legend has it that the Picts and the Scots joined forces here to fight a great battle against the Northumbrian King Athelstane. Before the fighting began, the Picts and Scots saw a white cross of cloud against a blue sky and they vowed that should victory be granted to them, they would make St Andrew the patron saint of the land. This story was a favourite of King James VI (who was also King James I of England), although there is considerable confusion as to when the battle was and who actually took part in it. It is said that Athelstane was killed during the battle and buried near the ford of the 'Cogtail Burn', and certainly, in 1840, when a quarry was opened on the spot, a stone coffin was discovered. However, King Athelstane is recorded as having died in 940 and two later traditions suggest that he was either fighting Angus MacFergus, King of Picts (731–61) and Achaius (*c*733), or that he met his end at the hands of a Pictish king called Hungus (*c*815). Obviously neither of these versions can be correct; but because of this old fable King Kenneth II (971–995) is believed to have adopted the St Andrew's Cross as the flag of Scotland.

In 1965 a plaque was erected by public subscription in the parish churchyard to commemorate this significant, although uncertain, event. At night, the plaque and a St Andrew's flag are floodlit.

Sir David Lindsay, who lived in the 16th century and whose magnificent work – *Ane Satyre of the Thrie Estaits* – has twice been revived at the Edinburgh International Festival, is said to have been born here. The philosopher David Hume's friend, the Revd John Home, author of the drama *Douglas: A Tragedy*, held the living here until asked to resign because the clergy of the time did not approve of their ministers writing stage plays.

The village of Athelstaneford was laid out by the Kinloch family of nearby Gilmerton House. Inland from the Edinburgh to Berwick-upon-Tweed road, it is beautifully maintained and something of a showplace. To the north of Athelstaneford is the airfield of **East Fortune** where there is a Museum of Flight.

Auchencairn, *Dumfries and Galloway* (6/A6)
Seven and a half miles south of CASTLE DOUGLAS, this village on a hillside looks out across the bay in the Solway Firth from which it takes its name. Offshore is romantic **Hestan Island** associated with the McDowal and Balliol families and which, in the 14th century, was a refuge for King Robert I's brother, Edward Bruce. Hestan Island is referred to as 'the Isle of Rathan' in S. S. Crocket's stirring book *The Raiders*, and there are many real-life tales of smuggling adventures and secret caverns associated with it.

Auchinleck, *Strathclyde* (1/E6)
The Boswell family built two keeps here, the second dating from the 17th century, and the Edinburgh lawyer, Alexander Boswell, on becoming a judge, took the courtesy title of Lord Auchinleck. It was he who built the present fine mansion which is known in the district as 'Affleck Big House'. Lord Auchinleck was the father of James Boswell (1740–95), also a lawyer and the close friend of Dr Samuel Johnson whom he brought to stay at Auchinleck House. Dr Johnson was complimentary about the 'elegant modern mansion' and commented on the inscription on the front of the house –

Quod petis, hic est;
Est Ulubris; animus si te non deficit aequus.

('What you seek is here, even in Ulubrae, if your mind is firm.' Horace, *Epistles* I, xi, 29–30. Ulubrae was notable for its remoteness from Rome.)

The ancient parish church here has early Christian origins, was enlarged in the 17th century and now houses a Boswell Museum which is only open by arrangement, and those interested should contact Cumnock and Doon Valley District Council (Tel: 0290 22111).

Ayr, *Strathclyde* (1/C6)
A busy town on the Firth of Clyde, Ayr is popular with holiday makers because of its extensive sandy beaches, golf courses and other recreational amenities including racing and sailing. Both Romans and Strathclyde Britons had settlements here, and the town received its first charter from King William the Lion in the 13th century.

Ayr featured prominently in the resistance against King Edward I of England led by William Wallace (1270–1305) in 1297. The Wallace Tower in the High Street is Neo-Gothic in style and was designed by Thomas Hamilton in 1834 to replace a former tower. There is a statue of Wallace by local self-taught sculptor James Thom.

All that remains of the great Burgh Kirk of St John the Baptist is St John's Tower. Here, on 26 April 1315, the Scottish parliament met to discuss the Royal succession in the event of King Robert I's death. Ayr and the memory of the poet Robert Burns are inseparable. The Tam O'Shanter Museum was a brewhouse in Burns' time to which Douglas Graham of Shanter Farm supplied malted grain and it is said that this was the starting point for the fictional ride described in the celebrated poem. It now serves as a Burns museum run by Kyle and Carrick District Council.

The poet sometimes attended services at the Auld Kirk, also called the church of St John, situated off the High Street. A mort safe used to guard against bodysnatchers can still be seen. There are two bridges referred to by Burns in his poem 'The Twa Brigs' – the narrow, arched Auld Brig traditionally built with money donated by a spinster lady who had seen her lover drown at the ford here, and the New Brig designated for pedestrians only. A second new bridge was built in the 19th century.

The oldest house in Ayr is Loudoun Hall which dates from the early 16th century and was the home of the Campbells of Loudoun. It has been restored as a cultural centre and is used by local organizations for meetings and exhibitions.

One of Ayr's most famous sons is John Loudon McAdam, the road builder, who was born in the Sandgate in 1756. A monument with a plaque was erected in his memory in 1936 in Wellington Square Gardens; here there are statues of three other prominent Ayr men – General Neil, Sir James Fergusson of Kilkerran and the 13th Earl of Eglinton.

A fine example of Georgian architecture still remaining in the district is the Newton Steeple situated on the centre of a traffic island. It once formed part of the building used as the Council Chamber of the Burgh of Newton which amalgamated with Ayr in 1873.

A great annual event is the Ayrshire Agricultural Show which takes place in April. There is a Golf Week and an Arts Festival held in June, and a Bowls Week in August. Lying to the south is the Belleisle Estate where there are golf courses and beautiful gardens featuring an aviary, pets corner and a deer park.

To the south-west of the Heads of Ayr is **Dunure**, a tiny fishing village. Here the unfortunate Allan Stewart, commendator of Crossraguel Abbey, was roasted to death in 1570 by the 4th Earl of Cassillis who wanted to acquire the abbey lands. Dunure Castle, where this event took place, is now a ruin, as is Dunduff Castle, once owned by the Stuarts and then the Whiteford family. To the south of Dunure, on the road to GIRVAN, is the Electric Brae where the road appears to be descending when, in fact, it is rising. This optical illusion is brought about by the contours of the surrounding landscape. At the north end of Culzean Bay there are fine sands popular with bathers.

Ballantrae, *Strathclyde* (5/B2)

The name of this attractive seaside town will always be associated with Robert Louis Stevenson's novel *The Master of Ballantrae*, although it was not the setting he used for the plot. Sand and shingle beaches make Ballantrae popular with holiday makers and weekenders from Glasgow. In the vicinity are the ruins of various Kennedy strongholds – Ardstinchar Castle, visited by Mary Queen of Scots in 1563; and, up the valley, Kirkhill and Knockdolian. South of the town is Glen App, a finely wooded area of considerable beauty.

Three miles to the north at Benane Head on the coast is Sawney Bean's Cave, once the dwelling place of a notorious family of cannibals who would prey on passers-by.

Balmaclellan, *Dumfries and Galloway* (5/H3)

An attractive village close to NEW GALLOWAY and the northern end of Loch Ken. Sir Walter Scott modelled his character Old Mortality on villager Robert Paterson, a stonemason who travelled Scotland restoring the tombstones of Covenanting martyrs. Paterson's wife was a schoolmistress in Balmaclellan until her death in 1785.

Bargany (1/B8) *see* Girvan

Barrhead, *Strathclyde* (1/D3)

A healthy textile industry sprang up here in the 18th century, influenced by the location of the settlement between the Rivers Levern and Kirkton. For many years calico printing was the main occupation, but from the mid-19th century to the present it has been sanitary engineering.

Bass Rock, The (4/E1), *see* North Berwick

Bathgate, *Lothian* (2/E3)

The early fortunes of this town, which was created a burgh of barony in 1663, centred on

Scott's View at dawn

the weaving industry, then on coal mining. James Young (1811–89) first made paraffin for commercial use at nearby Whiteside and Bathgate's proximity to the M8 has attracted a wide range of manufacturing industries.

Sir James Young Simpson, discoverer of chloroform as an anaesthetic, was born here in 1811.

Three miles to the north is Cairnpapple Hill where there are burial cairns and a Neolithic sanctuary remodelled in the Bronze Age as an open-air temple in the form of a stone circle. It has been excavated and opened out.

Bedrule (3/D7) *see* Hawick

Beith, *Strathclyde* (1/C3)
A town which grew up in the 18th century with the linen and silk industry, Beith subsequently became famous for the manufacture of gloves and furniture. The Auld Kirk was built here in 1556 by Thomas Boyd, a minister, or, as he preferred to be known, 'the Reider at Baith'. A stone by the original bell is inscribed 1614.

Bellshill, *Strathclyde* (2/B3)
By all appearances this could be considered part of Glasgow, having grown up in the 19th-

century industrial boom, servicing notably the coal and steel industries. A unit of Lithuanian prisoners of war was stationed here after the Crimea conflict in 1855 and many remained, determinedly maintaining their ethnic identity and traditions with an extensive Lithuanian library and an active social club.

Bemersyde, *Borders* (3/D5)
The Haig family has lived on these lands since the 12th century, although the ancient prophecy of Thomas the Rhymer –

Tide, tide, what'er betide,
There'll aye be Haigs at Bemersyde

– was proved inaccurate in 1867 when the direct line died out and the property was sold. In 1921, however, Bemersyde was purchased and presented to Field-Marshal Earl Haig as a reward from the nation for his work during the First World War.

Nearby is Scott's View, which overlooks Old MELROSE, the River Tweed and the Eildon Hills, under which, according to Border legend, sleep King Arthur and his knights. Sir Walter Scott so loved this view that his funeral procession paused here momentarily on the way to his burial at Dryburgh Abbey.

Biggar, *Strathclyde* (2/E6)
A small town with a wide main street, landscaped with trees and greatly enhanced in appearance and interest by the dedicated work of the Biggar Museum Trust. The family of the British prime minister William Ewart Gladstone came from Biggar, his grandfather moving to Leith in the mid-18th century. The Gladstone Court Museum, open from Easter to October, features a 19th-century town – shops, a library and schoolroom. Greenhill Covenanter's House, once a sadly neglected farmhouse, is now a museum of 17th-century local life and recalls the Covenanting struggles of that time. The Moat Park Heritage Centre in a former church is also a museum of local history and the Gasworks Museum is the site of the Biggar Gas Light Company which operated until 1973. Typical of a small-town gasworks, this is the only surviving example in Scotland, and the oldest part dates back to 1839. In the High Street the 16th-century parish church of St Mary contains parts of the 12th-century church dedicated to St Nicholas. Close by is Biggar Water which, when in flood, is said to flow in two directions at once, westwards into the River Clyde and eastwards into the River Tweed.

The crowning of the Fleming Queen, a ceremony held in July, celebrates Mary Fleming from nearby Boghall Castle, who was one of the four Marys who attended Mary Queen of Scots. The Flemings were responsible for the defence of the town. At Puppet Tree House on the BROUGHTON road there is a Victorian puppet theatre with tearoom, gardens, games and car park where the Purves Puppets perform.

Blantyre, *Strathclyde* (1/F3)
This village sprang up with the cotton-spinning industry, influenced by the Glasgow industri-

alist, David Dale. Blantyre's most famous son is David Livingstone, the explorer, who was born here in 1813, and the 'one-room' dwelling in which this event took place has been restored, along with the adjoining houses in Shuttle Row, to form a museum in his honour. Among other exhibits, a sculpture by Pilkington Jackson commemorates Livingstone's last journey when his devoted native bearers carried his body 1500 miles to the coast of Africa for transportation to England and burial at Westminster Abbey.

Bolton (3/D1) *see* Haddington

Bonchester Bridge, *Borders* (3/D7)
Set in the middle of Wauchope Forest country, which is part of the Border Forest Park, this is a small village on the Rule Water, below Bonchester Hill, which rises to the east. Remains of a hill fort and other foundations indicate that there was an early settlement here. Greenriver House is an early 19th-century mansion nearby.

Bonnyrigg, *Lothian* (3/B2)
The villages of Bonnyrigg, Redrow, Polton Street, Hillhead and Broomieknowe came together in 1865 to form the present town which, under the terms of the Local Government (Scotland) Act 1929, was joined with **Lasswade** which had been created a police burgh in 1881. The town lies on the ridge of land between two rivers, the North Esk and South Esk. Monks from the nearby abbey of NEWBATTLE are believed to have ploughed there in the 18th century, thus starting agricultural activity for which the area is noted, but it was the water from the North Esk which brought prosperity, notably with the paper-making industry. An industrial estate established in the 1970s provides various manufacturing jobs and the town centre has been redeveloped. An open-air market takes place on Thursdays.

Bonnyrigg and Lasswade have been twinned for over twenty years with St Cyr l'Ecole, 14 miles from Paris; this was the home of the French Military Academy until it was destroyed by enemy action in 1944.

Sir Walter Scott lived at Lasswade Cottage for the first six years of his married life. A cottage at nearby Polton, formerly called Mavisbush House but now De Quincey Cottage, was occupied by the Victorian writer and opium addict Thomas de Quincey during his final years until his death in 1859.

The ruins of Bothwell Castle

The village of Cockpen to the south-east is associated with the ballad about its laird. A church opened in 1820 stands close to the ruins of an older church which was consecrated in 1242. Dalhousie Castle, originally a 15th-century tower, besieged unsuccessfully by King Henry IV of England in 1400, belonged to the Ramsay family and is now an hotel.

Bothwell, *Strathclyde* (2/A4)
In 1398 Archibald 'the Grim', 3rd Earl of Douglas, founded the Church of St Bride here: a few fragments of the original remain in the much restored building. The ruins of Bothwell Castle, maintained by the Historic Buildings and Monuments division of the Scottish Office, loom beside the River Clyde, north-west of the town. Erected during the reign of King Alexander II for the Sheriff of Lothian, it was captured by the English and used as a base during the Wars of Independence. Through marriage the land passed to the Douglas family who held it until their downfall in the reign of King James II. Bothwell Castle was presented to Patrick Hepburn, Earl of Bothwell, by King James IV, but was later exchanged for lands at Liddesdale and Hermitage belonging to the 5th Earl of Angus, another member of the Douglas family. The north-east tower was dismantled to provide building materials for a fine 18th-century mansion demolished earlier this century. It was in this new house that Sir Walter Scott wrote his ballad 'Young Lochinvar'.

There is a monument commemorating the Battle of Bothwell Brig fought in 1679, after which 1200 Covenanters were sentenced to five months' imprisonment at Greyfriars Churchyard in EDINBURGH.

Bowden (3/D5) *see* St Boswells

Bowhill (3/C6) *see* Selkirk

Bridge of Weir, *Strathclyde* (1/C2)
Situated on the Gryfe Water, this is a fashionable residential area and commuter dormitory for GLASGOW, enhanced by excellent golfing facilities. The village dates from the 18th century, founded on the cotton industry and moving on to the tanning of leather.. To the north-west are the Quarrier's Orphan Homes founded in 1871 by William Quarrier, a prosperous self-made man who himself had been born into poverty.

Broughton, Borders (2/F6)
This is a pretty village standing on Biggar Water ¾ mile above its junction with the Tweed. The celebrated author John Buchan, who became governor-general of Canada and 1st Lord Tweedsmuir, grew up in the town where his grandfather was minister. There is, consequently, a John Buchan Centre in the United Free Church. A popular Scottish ale brewed here is called Greenmantle after one of Buchan's most successful novels. One of the houses in the main street has an outstanding garden; it is not open to the public but is clearly visible from the road.

On the edge of the town is Broughton Place, designed by Sir Basil Spence for Professor and Mrs Elliott in 1938. It is in the 17th-century Scottish baronial style and the present owners have incorporated an art gallery which they open to the public during the summer months. Once these lands belonged to the Borders Murray family, great supporters of the Stuart cause. The original house was burned to the ground in 1775 and the estate bought by Lord Braxfield, the 'Hanging Judge', in 1780.

Follow the road to MOFFAT along the River Tweed as it snakes towards its source and you come to Tweedsmuir. Here the Crook Inn (now an hotel) is a famous posting house visited by Robert Burns. A former Jacobite landlord, captured at Culloden in 1746, escaped down the steep slopes of the Devil's Beef Tub on the way to his trial at Carlisle. The Devil's Beef Tub is an extraordinary hollow, naturally formed in the hills, where the Border Reivers (the name given to cattle rustlers in this area) often took refuge and hid their stolen beasts.

At Tweedhopefoot is the Border Collie and Shepherd Centre, situated on a small hill farm

Hay field near Broughton

commanding marvellous views of the surrounding hills and valley. There are sheepdog demonstrations, a museum and craft shop.

Broxburn, *Lothian* (2/E2)
A manufacturing town which once prospered from the shale-oil industry. Broxburn could certainly never claim to be pretty, but there is a certain character about the place and some fine houses such as Houstoun House along the road to Uphall, formerly the home of the Lindsay family and now a hotel. One point of interest is the 'solar stone' located west of the town at Kirkhill Farm. This was raised in the 18th century by the 11th Earl of Buchan, founder of the Society of Antiquaries in Scotland.

Caerlaverock Castle (6/D5) *see* Annan

Cairnryan, *Dumfries and Galloway* (5/B4)
On the shores of Loch Ryan, this was a strategic port during the Second World War, and across the loch on the opposite shore, which is called Wig Bay, was a flying-boat school. In the summer, the whitewashed cottages sparkle in the sun and it is a popular holiday spot. In the centre of the village is Lochryan House, an 18th-century house set in beautiful grounds.

Outside the town, on Laight Moor, are the Taxing Stone and Long Tom standing stones.

Canonbie, *Dumfries and Galloway* (6/G4)
Two miles north of the Border. A tract of land between the Rivers Sark and the Esk became known as 'the Debateable Land', an area of lawlessness where neither Scotland nor England could enforce good behaviour. The 16th-century Gilnockie Tower, otherwise known as Hollows, was a stronghold of Johnnie Armstrong of Gilnockie, a Border Reiver of note. In 1530 King James V decided that he should make an example and demanded to meet Armstrong. On doing so, he immediately hanged him and thirty-six of his followers at Teviothead. In 1542 the priory of Canonbie was destroyed by the English, and in 1552 the Scots Dyke was constructed to create a recognized boundary between England and Scotland.

Carfin, *Strathclyde* (2/B4)
North-east of MOTHERWELL, this village was settled by large numbers of Irish after the potato famine and Poles in the mid-19th century, both groups attracted by the local mining operations. There is a grotto which was dedicated in 1922 to Our Lady of Lourdes and which consequently attracts large numbers of pilgrims. It was built by unemployed Catholic men of the district.

Carlops, *Borders* (2/F4)
Situated on the North Esk River on the EDINBURGH to BIGGAR Road, Carlops was inhabited in the 18th century by weavers. It is a popular place for walkers: paths lead into the Pentland Hills, notably one past North Esk Reservoir to the Bore Stone. Allan Ramsay refers to this area in his pastoral comedy *The Gentle Shepherd* which was published in 1725; he was one of a group who regularly visited the mansion of Newhall nearby.

Carluke, *Strathclyde* (2/C4)
In the 17th century this town was a burgh called Kirkstyle, which consisted of a few cottages. With the cotton-weaving boom in the 19th century, Carluke was born, but probably the area has always been best known for the growing of fruit. The tower of an 18th-century church still stands and there is a memorial to the Revd

Peter Kid, minister in the 17th century, who was a Covenanter and imprisoned on the BASS ROCK.

To the south-west at Milton Lockhart a plaque at Milton Lockhart Farm marks the birthplace of Major-General William Roy in 1729. Roy, who died in 1790, is known as 'the father of the Ordnance Survey of Great Britain' which derived from one of his military maps.

Carnwath, *Strathclyde* (2/D5)

The shaft of the 16th-century market cross incorporates various road distances. Some nearby ruins indicate the location of Cowthally Castle, ancient stronghold of the Somerville family, where Scottish Stuart kings came to dine. The lands of Carnwath, however, were held by the Lockhart family from the 17th century and, although they had acquired Lee in 1272, the present castle was rebuilt in the 19th century. Up in the hills near **Dunsyre** is the sculpture garden of Ian Hamilton Finlay who describes himself as a 'concrete poet' and has contributed to some of the major art collections in the world. The Lang Whang, an old drove road, leads through the Pentland Hills to EDINBURGH.

Carrington (3/B2) *see* Gorebridge

Carstairs, *Strathclyde* (2/D5)

Famous for its railway junction for EDINBURGH, GLASGOW and London, Carstairs is now best known for its state hospital specializing in forensic medicine. The old village lies about a mile away and has a village green and an 18th-century church.

In the village of **Thankerton** near the River Clyde, 5 miles south of the junction, is an old tollhouse. Crawford House on Tinto Hill, formerly called Westmains, is the home of the chief of the Crawford family. The original mansion is ruined, but there are plans for the Crawford Family Trust to restore it as a Clan Society Centre. Located in the post office at Thankerton is the Clyde Valley Tartan Centre

Philip Law near Carter Bar (see p. 34)

which sells items of clan interest, tartan, crest badges and information relating to the Douglas, Home, Armstrong, Lockhart and Carmichael families.

Covington, 1 mile away from Thankerton, has a church which dates from the 15th century but was a religious site from early times.

Carter Bar, *Borders* (3/E8)

The gateway to Scotland high up in the Cheviot Hills, where the motorist can enjoy spectacular scenery. The last positive Borders conflict between the Scots and the English took place in 1575 with the Raid of Reidswire and a stone commemorates this event. The Romans had a great camp known as Ad Fines spread across this often bleak moorland, and there are Roman and Iron Age earthworks in the area. The road here follows the line of the Roman Dere Street which leaves the Cheviots and crosses the River Tweed near MELROSE.

Castle Douglas, *Dumfries and Galloway* (6/A5)

Situated above Carlingwark Loch, this town was once called Causewayend after an ancient causeway which led from an artificial island dwelling (or crannog) built on a wooden platform on the loch. Later the name was changed to Carlingwark, and then in 1789 the land was purchased by William Douglas, a merchant who had made a fortune in America and who renamed it Castle Douglas when developing a cattle market.

Long before, however, these lands were controlled by the Douglases at Threave Castle, a formidable tower stronghold built by Archibald the Grim, 3rd Earl of Douglas, who died here in 1400. In 1455 it was the last Douglas castle to surrender to King James II of Scotland who sought to destroy Douglas power, and the capitulation took place only because the King brought in cannon to batter the walls.

Threave Gardens and a Visitor Centre are open to the public. The gardens cover 60 acres of the original 1,490-acre estate, and are a real delight. The Victorian house here is used by the National Trust for Scotland for their School of Gardening. In spring, nearly two hundred varieties of daffodil provide a dazzling display, but the garden can be enjoyed throughout the year. Threave Wildfowl Refuge on the River Dee provides a roosting and feeding place for

Opposite: Threave Castle
Below: Clatteringshaws Loch, north-west of Castle Douglas

many species of wild geese and duck and is also open to the public.

Clovenfords, *Borders* (3/C5)
On the Caddon Water, which flows into the River Tweed, this little hamlet is settled deep into the rolling Border hills. Nearby, in 1868, the head gardener of the Buccleuch estates established the Tweed Vineries. John Leyden, the poet, was schoolmaster here in 1782, and William and Dorothy Wordsworth visited the village in 1803, inspired by the beauty of the surrounding countryside. Outside the inn is a statue of Sir Walter Scott, who lodged here before moving to live at Ashiestiel in his capacity as sheriff of SELKIRK.

Clydebank, *Strathclyde* (1/D1)
Not much more than one hundred years ago Clydebank was farmland. In 1871, however, James and George Thomson came here from Govan and launched their first ship in 1872. In 1899 John Brown and Co. acquired Thomson's and the famous ships which have been launched from this great yard opposite the mouth of the River Cart include the *Lusitania*, the *Queen Mary*, the *Queen Elizabeth* and the *QE2*. Extensive bombing severely damaged the town during the Second World War, but a great spirit was maintained. Since then Scottish shipbuilding has suffered from powerful international competition and the future remains uncertain.

Coatbridge, *Strathclyde* (2/B3)
A large industrial town which grew up around successful ironworks. Once the Monkland to Kirkintilloch railway passed through the town, and in the 19th century an experimental venture sought to employ umbrellas and windpower for traction. Summerlee (Industrial) Heritage Park is designed around the excavated core of the Summerlee Ironworks. Permanent displays of working exhibits of the traditional iron, steel and heavy engineering industries can be seen, reflecting the pre-eminence of Coatbridge in the 19th-century iron industry.

Drumpellier Country Park and Visitor Centre has 500 acres of woodlands, lowland heath, freshwater lochs, an eighteen-hole golf course, football and rugby pitches and part of the Monkland Canal, constructed in 1770–81 for the purpose of carrying coal to GLASGOW. The

Clydebank (Scottish Development Agency)

Visitor Centre, which overlooks Lochend Loch, houses displays of park wildlife.

Coatbridge has excellent outdoor and indoor leisure centres and a popular indoor bowling club. Its most distinguished son is Lord Reith, the first director-general of the BBC, who was born here in 1889.

Gartsherrie Church is an important monument to the early days of the iron industry since it was provided by the Baird family for their workers; the Gartsherrie Ironworks were one of the only two works whose furnaces were not in operation on Sundays. The church was opened in 1839 and is of Gothic style with a clock tower and steeple. The interior was renovated in 1926.

Cockburnspath (4/A2) *see* Coldingham

Cockenzie (3/C1) *see* Prestonpans

Coldingham, *Borders* (4/C3)
Mostly an 18th-century town, but the priory, which is now the parish church, was founded in 1098 by King Edgar. Built to replace a nunnery on St Abbs Head which had been destroyed by the Danes in 870, this priory was burnt by the Earl of Hertford in 1545 and eventually blown up by Oliver Cromwell in 1648.

Coldingham Bay

In nearby **Cockburnspath**, a seaside village on the edge of the Lammermuir Hills, a 14th-century church incorporates an interesting round tower. Cockburnspath Tower is now a ruin, but the early 17th-century mercat cross is worth a glance, being crowned with a thistle. This is dramatic coastal scenery with cliffs dropping down to sandy beaches. Pease Bay is particularly popular for swimming in the summer; nearby stands the ruined Norman Church of St Helen. Follow a little farm road on to the clifftops and after a brisk walk along a winding track you can reach the ruins of the 16th-century Fast Castle, once a formidable stronghold held first by the Homes and later by Logan of Restalrig, who inherited it through marriage. There is a tradition that treasure from the Spanish Armada ships is buried nearby. Pease Bridge was built over the Coldingham Road in the late 18th century and spans 300 ft. When constructed it was said to be the highest bridge in the world.

North of Cockburnspath is Dunglass estate where the Collegiate Church, founded by Sir Alexander Hume in 1450, with a richly embellished interior, has been partly restored. It was attacked by the English in 1544. Dunglass

Culzean Castle

House, which stands on the Dean Burn, occupies the site of the Home fortress, and part of the ancient keep is incorporated in the present building.

Coldstream, *Borders* (4/B6)
Invading armies, the Scots into England and the English into Scotland, crossed the River Tweed here. In 1513 the flower of Scotland's manhood, led by King James IV, went to die at the Battle of Flodden, and each year this tragic event is commemorated at Coldstream.

In 1766 a five-arched bridge, spanning 300 ft, was erected by John Smeaton, and a plaque commemorates a visit by Robert Burns to England in 1787. Couples used to come to Coldstream from England to be married in the same way that many also travelled to Gretna.

In 1659 General Monk raised the Coldstream Guards for Oliver Cromwell at a house here,

long ago demolished, but a museum now stands on the original site. At the east end of the town stands an obelisk in memory of Charles Marjoribanks, first member of parliament for Berwickshire after the 1832 Reform Bill.

The Hirsel, a mansion with fine gardens and a small loch, is the home of Sir Alec Douglas-Home, the former British prime minister (now Lord Home). The Homestead Museum housed in old farmstead buildings has an integral craft centre, and exhibitions show the history of the estate, old tools and natural history. There is a famous rhododendron wood and walks in the Leet Valley are very popular.

Six miles to the west is **Eccles**, which stands between the Rivers Leet and Tweed. Henry Home (1696–1782) was born here; when he was raised to the Scottish bench as a judge in 1752, he took the courtesy title of Lord Kames after a local place-name.

Colmonnel (5/C2) *see* Girvan

Covington (2/D5) *see* Carstairs

Creetown, *Dumfries and Galloway* (5/F5)
A pretty little village, once known as Ferrytown of Cree, which supplied granite to Liverpool docks. Sir Walter Scott called it Porton Ferry in his novel *Guy Mannering*, and there is a fascinating rock and gem museum here which attracts many visitors. The clock tower commemorates Queen Victoria's Diamond Jubilee.

The ruins of 16th-century Carsluith Castle stands 4 miles to the south. Nearby Barholm Castle was once used by the reformer John Knox as a refuge.

Crossraguel Abbey (1/B8) *see* Maybole

Culzean, *Strathclyde* (1/B7)
Overlooking the Firth of Clyde and set in 565 acres, Culzean Castle is considered Robert Adam's masterpiece. The castle, built for the 10th Earl of Cassilis in the late 18th century, was erected around the tower of an ancient Kennedy castle. Today Culzean is the jewel in the crown of the National Trust for Scotland (NTS), having been made over to that organization by the 5th Marquis of Ailsa and the Kennedy family in 1945. Apart from the magnificent interior, there is a walled garden, a camellia house and aviary, and in 1973 the grounds were designated Scotland's first countryside park.

In 1973, the farm buildings were opened as the Home Farm Centre which incorporates a shop, restaurant and rangers' offices. An interpretation centre shows the life and times of Culzean Castle, illustrating its development from a simple tower house to the present day. In recognition of his services to Britain during the Second World War, President Eisenhower of the USA was presented with the lifetime use of a flat at Culzean in 1946. An exhibition traces the General's career and his association with the castle.

Above and opposite: Cumbernauld (Cumbernauld Development Corporation)

Cumbernauld, *Strathclyde* (2/B2)
It must be accepted that once a new town has been in existence for over thirty years, it should cease to be thought of as 'new'. Cumbernauld Development Corporation was set up in 1956 to create an 'overspill' town for Glasgow. Since then, with various phases of development, it has become a model example of its kind with second- and third-generation citizens. The eventual target population for Cumbernauld is 70,000, but it currently fluctuates around 50,000.

The enormously successful film 'Gregory's Girl' was based on Cumbernauld and accurately depicts a way of life with great humour and sensitivity. There is a real sense of community nowadays with a popular theatre and local diversions. Cumbernauld House, the headquarters of Cumbernauld Development Corporation, was built in the neo-classical style by William Adam in 1731. The parklands and policies were once owned by the Fleming and Livingstone families, and latterly by the Burns family. The enormous clock in the town shopping centre originally belonged to St Enoch Station in Glasgow and was donated by a businessman. Throughout the town centre there are examples of contemporary art and sculpture.

Cumbrae, Isles of, *Strathclyde* (1/A3)
Great Cumbrae and Little Cumbrae (privately owned) lie in the Firth of Clyde between the Island of Bute and the mainland. An ancient church on Great Cumbrae was replaced in 1612 and again in the early 19th century. On Little Cumbrae there was a castle sometimes used by King Robert II as a royal residence, of which the Hunters of Hunterston were hereditary keepers until the 16th century. It was attacked by Oliver Cromwell in 1653 and only ruins now remain.

On the south side of Great Cumbrae lies the fashionable holiday town of **Millport**. Here is the Cathedral of the Isles which boasts that it is the smallest cathedral in Europe. Standing in the middle of the town is Garrison House, built by Captain Crauford of the famous cutter *The Royal George* as a barracks for his crew in 1745. This is now the Museum of the Cumbraes and features regularly changing exhibitions.

At Keppel is the Marine Biological Station and Museum, opened for scientific research in 1887 and extended in 1903. There is a fine aquarium and it is open to the public.

The highest point on the island, at 417 ft, is the Glaidstane. From this spot one of the finest and most comprehensive views of Scotland may be enjoyed. A plaque on the stone indicates places of interest.

Cumnock, *Strathclyde* (1/E6)
A market town on the Lugar Water in the heart of coal-mining country, Cumnock was once famous for manufacturing snuff boxes, but now industry here is spread generally. There is a bust of James Keir Hardie (1856–1915), a founder of the Labour Party and its first Member of Parliament, who lived in the town when he was Secretary of the Miners' Federation. The other notable monument is the Mercat Cross which was originally erected in 1509 at Townhead Street, but moved to its present position at the Square in 1769 and restored. The 1891 Baird Institute bequeathed to the town by a local draper, John Baird, mounts temporary exhibitions of Victorian pottery, wooden souvenirs and Ayrshire embroidery.

At Airds Moss, not far away, a great defeat was inflicted on the Covenanting army in 1679. Two viaducts span the River Lugar, one at Templand standing 175 ft high and one at Glaisnock standing 75 ft high. Ironworks were founded at Lugar in 1846, but closed in 1928. The Adam mansion, Dumfries House, lies to the west.

Changing Landscape

THE DUKE OF BUCCLEUCH AND QUEENSBERRY KT

The old maxim about beauty being in the eye of the beholder applies as much to scenery as to anything else. A raging mountain torrent is exhilarating to some, but can mean vertigo or claustrophobia to others. Between that and a prairie, there is much to please (or displease) everybody! To sample them all, it would be necessary to travel the globe; but, in providing a range of most alternatives within a short distance of each other, the British Isles excel. An especially compact example of a richly varied landscape may be found in the south of Scotland, comprising the Edinburgh and Glasgow central belt and the southern uplands and extending to the Border with England.

This landscape changes as you move around it, with limitless satisfying variations, or if you simply wait and watch: thanks to Scotland's northern latitude, the sun never rises so high in the sky as to diminish the long, colourful and ever-moving shadows. Here in the south of Scotland there is everything from the rich arable lands bordering the Forth and Tweed, the wild geese flats by the Solway, the infinitely varied intermediate countryside with such spectacular views as the Eildon Hills, the Pentlands and the Cheviots, to the really rugged mountains of Galloway with their circling eagles.

The Eildon Hills (see p. 85)

Nature has indeed been generous to southern Scotland but, as well as this, many generations of landowners proved to be inspired landscape artists, achieving on three dimensions of spacious hills what 'Capability' Brown and Repton struggled to accomplish in flat confined parkland. So skilfully have the woodlands been blended with natural contours and the folds of the hills that much that is man-made might be assumed to be natural. What finer tribute could a landscape consultant wish for than that! Even today's landowners are adding new woodlands that will still further enhance the scenery to be enjoyed by future generations.

Many first-time visitors tend to think that Scotland begins at the Edinburgh/Glasgow level and stretches northwards from there. Those who come by air may have some excuse for so thinking; and a few motorists might be excused, too, if they have taken the fastest route, the A74, through some of the least enticing countryside. But what they do miss! For those who travel in the hope of seeing lovely scenery – which includes most of us – the A68, A7 and A75/76 can provide some breathtaking glimpses of the Border counties, the Lothians or Dumfriesshire. Even if commitments prevent a pause in the Borders, the approach to Edinburgh from the high ground to the south provides one of the most magnificent panoramas in the world. The heather-clad Pentland Hills stretch far away to the west, while Edinburgh with its remarkable skyline is set against the glittering background of the Firth of Forth and the hills of Fife beyond. As you draw closer, those well-known features of the Castle and Arthur's Seat spring into focus, acting as a beckoning finger all the way into the heart of the capital.

There is probably no better place to pursue a discussion on landscape than Edinburgh itself. Quite often Nature is complimented for providing a lovely landscape and man condemned for spoiling it; but not so in Edinburgh, where the Old and the New Towns in the centre show an almost miraculous marriage between natural and man-made features. The Castle, on its jagged rock, might have been cast by a magician's spell, while the tall four-hundred-year-old stone tenements, clinging to the contours of the many hills

Edinburgh Castle (see p. 59)

of the Old Town around it, blend perfectly with their setting. St Giles' Kirk, dating mainly from the 15th century and with its crowned tower of 1495, has been, and still is, the focal point of innumerable national events. It dominates the Royal Mile (the High Street) which, after several decades of skilful restoration, is a delightful place to wander, peering into closes and alleyways until reaching the Palace of Holyroodhouse at the bottom. The present palace, some three hundred years old, seems quite young compared with the abbey beside it, founded some five hundred and fifty years earlier. It is still the official residence of the monarch on state visits, at least once a year, and of the lord high commissioner of the Church of Scotland, as well as being a fitting setting for garden parties and military pageantry that overflow on to the threshold of Arthur's Seat towering majestically above.

Across the great divide to the north, once a loch and then a railway, lies Princes Street, marking the southern boundary of the New Town. Owing to much mixed architecture, Princes Street itself is better looked *from* than looked *at*, but as you proceed northwards you come upon one of the most remarkable and successful examples of comprehensive town planning executed anywhere. Covering the period 1770 to 1850, this was an age of beautiful architecture, inspired by such famous figures as Robert Adam, Sir William Chambers, Sir Henry Raeburn and William Burn. The scale of the development is such that a car is necessary to explore it unless you are a really energetic walker with many hours to spare.

In the late 18th and early 19th centuries, Edinburgh was hailed as the cultural centre of Europe, attracting men of letters, writers and artists. Sir Walter Scott, with his promotional talent, would have rivalled any present-day tourist board director. Art galleries sprang up, among them William Playfair's National Gallery of Scotland, which is not only satisfying to behold; it contains one of the most exquisite collections of paintings to be found anywhere.

It may seem strange to lavish such praise on Edinburgh's cultural achievements when, for 1990, it is Glasgow that has been designated the International City of Culture. This is a great tribute to the citizens of Glasgow and successive governments who have been gradually transforming this great industrial and commercial centre with almost double Edinburgh's population, once renowned for its smoky rivet-clanging shipyards where giant *Queen* liners were built, and for the infamous slums of the Gorbals. It is now blossoming into a fine city with a good blend of Georgian, Victorian and modern architecture, while landscaping of a large derelict area for the 1988 Garden Festival has been widely acclaimed. Though man once failed to enhance the landscape here, the situation is being rapidly retrieved. Glasgow has a spectacular art gallery at Kelvingrove, to say nothing of the Burrell Collection of art treasures of every description, situated on the south side of the city. The outstanding modern architecture of the collection's new home is well worth seeing, quite apart from its contents.

Both Edinburgh and Glasgow share another advantage seldom enjoyed by cities of comparable size: their proximity to really magnificent countryside which can be reached with extraordinary ease and speed. In the case of Edinburgh there is a lovely foreshore, and all around the city lie such treasure-filled historic houses as Dalmeny and Hopetoun to the north, Gosford House and Lennoxlove to the east and the beautiful parkland of Dalkeith House with its fine Adam bridge to the south. To the west are the Pentland Hills and even the dry ski slope now blends into the landscape. All the way along the A702 to Biggar there are outstandingly well-landscaped woodlands adorning curvaceous hills.

Golf enthusiasts, of course, head east from

Galloway Forest Park (see p. 87)

Edinburgh and they at least can be in no doubt that they are well and truly in Scotland on reaching such celebrated courses as Gullane and North Berwick.

Glasgow allows rapid escape to Loch Lomond and the Highlands, though many of the world's top golfers go south-west to Turnberry. On their way they can hardly avoid the spell of Robert Burns, his Alloway home and his country that stretches all the way south to Dumfries. However, before setting off on the Burns trail, Culzean Castle and Country Park should on no account be missed. This is one of the National Trust for Scotland's prime attractions and, as an example of a blending of the best work of man, in the form of the finest of Adam architecture, with that of nature, in the form of a sheer cliff and crashing Atlantic breakers below, it is hard to beat. The elegant interior includes the Eisenhower Suite; and the Stables, with their display centres, give a fascinating insight into rural life over the last two hundred years. Not far from here, Blairquhan Castle and Gardens are also well worth a visit.

To the south of Ayrshire lies Galloway with its huge tract of very beautiful and unspoilt country. Much of this is reminiscent of the Highlands, with eagles and red deer abounding. The landscape has changed little in the last two centuries, though some large man-made forests were created by the Forestry Commission in the years following the Second World War. These have mainly passed through the unattractive adolescent stage and now provide fine recreational opportunities for lovers of wildlife and the great outdoors. They will be constantly changing in the years ahead as the first generation of trees grows up and is gradually harvested, to be replaced by a second generation.

Following the A77 coast road to the Mull of Galloway, pausing at Penkill Castle, there are several famous gardens that welcome visitors. The acid soil and the moist, mild climate (a benefit of the Gulf Stream) make it one of the finest areas in the UK for temperate plants as well as rhododendrons and azaleas. Castle Kennedy has a remarkable avenue of 100-ft tall monkey puzzles as well as a noteworthy garden. Logan near Stranraer and, further east, Threave and Arbigland are also renowned. All along the south side of Wigtownshire and Kirkcudbrightshire there are charming and attractive small towns and villages, with a reputation for friendly hospitality. Yet one is never far away from the really rugged and wildly beautiful countryside further inland.

By driving north, past some magnificent stands of Douglas fir, up the A762 and A713 to

Landscape near Biggar (see p. 28)

Dalmellington, it is possible to rejoin the Burns trail at New Cumnock. Only in 1984 was it discovered that this was a route used by the Romans on their way to the Clyde from Hadrian's Wall nearly two thousand years ago. Thanks to the severe drought that year, aerial photography was able to reveal numerous forts along the line of the A76, together with a previously unknown camp for a thousand Roman soldiers in the park of Drumlanrig Castle.

The A76 leads southwards through Sanquhar, where it is possible to post a letter in the first post office opened in Britain. If time allows, a diversion up the B797 to Wanlockhead is another rare experience.

The road winds through a conservation area of natural scrub woodland to an open landscape of smooth, steep hills upholstered in heather. Near the summit of the Lowther Hills is the unexpected remote village of Wanlockhead – the highest in Scotland, some 1500 ft above sea level. Gold, silver and lead were mined here for over four hundred years until the 1930s; but now the industrious community has been replaced by those seeking holiday cottages and retirement homes. However, an enterprising mining expert has breathed new life into the village by opening a unique mining museum, together with access to some of the old workings and machinery.

Leadhills, a similar former mining village, lies over the watershed in Lanarkshire and a right turn on to the B7040 leads to the hamlet of Elvanfoot, close to the source of Scotland's two greatest rivers, the Forth and the Clyde. Another right turn at the A702 leads through the Dalveen Pass, which can look alternately beautiful and daunting. The steep, treeless hills have a satisfyingly velvety appearance as a result of close cropping by hardy sheep, which provide man's livelihood. Yet it requires some 2000 acres of this sort of terrain, carrying eight hundred breeding ewes, to keep one shepherd. On some of the more heathery areas the red grouse, unique to Scotland and northern England, with rare variations in Ireland and Norway, can be encouraged to co-exist alongside them, thereby attracting sportsmen from all over the world.

As you head towards the Nith valley, civilization becomes apparent in the form of charming, whitewashed farmsteads and the little village of Durisdeer, nestling in the folds of the hills. Its three-hundred-year-old church contains a white marble mausoleum and a tomb that would not look out of place in St Peter's, Rome. Its occupants' father, James Douglas, Duke of Queensberry, built one of the most exquisitely beautiful castles – pale pink Drumlanrig – just 4 miles further on across the River Nith in the 1680s. He was my direct ancestor, and subsequent generations can claim credit for the beautiful wooded landscaping that adorns Nithsdale for miles around, some of it planted to resemble the shadows cast by cumulus clouds on a sunny day.

Back on the Burns trail, the A76 passes by Ellisland Farm and thence to Dumfries, both of which hum with Burns memorabilia and atmosphere. From here it is a short drive to the Solway, with Peter Scott's Nature Reserve of wild geese and, close by it, the romantic shell of ancient Caerlaverock Castle. For those seeking history or culture, Rammerscales, not far from Lochmaben, has Jacobite relics and links with Flora MacDonald; quite close is Ecclefechan, where Thomas Carlyle was born in 1795.

Turning towards the Scottish Borders, a quick visit to Gretna might appeal to those with romantic memories of the days when marriages forbidden in England could be performed here.

Travelling north-east, parallel to the Border with England, the visitor passes through the 'Debatable Lands' which were bitterly disputed with the English and fought over for centuries. Some small peel towers like Gilnockie remain as reminders of those grim days, but none is more effective in this than Hermitage Castle, dominating the route that linked Newcastleton in Liddesdale to Langholm in Eskdale, or to Hawick over the watershed.

Today the A7 leads on to Hawick, the largest of the ancient Border burghs and, like most of them, rich in history, tradition and talent, for it is in these places that world-famous names in knitwear are to be found. Now the same skilled hands that worked in woollen manufacture are expanding the new key industry of electronics on which local prosperity increasingly depends.

The Border counties of Roxburghshire, Selkirkshire, Peeblesshire and Berwickshire offer an abundance of attractions for the visitor. Not only is there a rich variety of scenery, but in no part of the United Kingdom is there so great a concentration of eight-hundred-year-old abbeys (Melrose, Dryburgh, Jedburgh and Kelso), historic houses (Neidpath, Traquair, Bowhill, Abbotsford, Mellerstain, Thirlestane, Manderston, Ferniehurst, Floors and Ayton Castles) and outstanding gardens (Dawyck, Kailzie, Mertoun and The Hirsel). There is a matching variety of places to stay, from the renowned Peebles Hydro to enchanting holiday cottages. But above all

Jedburgh Abbey (see p. 125)

Traquair House (see p. 123)

these tantalizing attractions, there is the atmosphere of romance inspired by such authors as Sir Walter Scott of Abbotsford and James Hogg, the Ettrick Shepherd, who brought alive the folklore, wizardry and magic that have mysteriously evolved in these parts since, and possibly before, the Roman occupation of the remarkable triple Eildon Hills nearly two thousand years ago. In novels, verse and opera the tales of 'the Scott country' have spread across the world, stirring the hearts and minds of man.

A choice of routes can complete the last stage of this anti-clockwise circuit of southern Scotland, back to the starting point in Edinburgh. The wildest and most rustic route is up the Ettrick Valley, past the remote farm where the genius James Hogg struggled with nature, to St Mary's Loch. Pass over the watershed and, pausing at Scotland's highest waterfall, the Grey Mare's Tail, continue through Moffat, a popular holiday centre, up past the Devil's Beef Tub and then downhill from where it is possible to step across the River Tweed, almost all the way to Edinburgh.

Shorter routes to the capital either follow the Tweed to Peebles and thence over the hills to Penicuik, or pass through Galashiels on the A7, or make use of the A68 through Lauder over Soutra Hill and down through Dalkeith.

For those with more time, there is much to be seen on the more civilized route following the Tweed down to its mouth at Berwick, thence along the A1 through the good arable lands of East Lothian and past famous names in the world of golf. Landmarks like North Berwick Law and the Bass Rock, whitened by thousands of gannets, enliven an otherwise more peaceful landscape than is to be found in so much of southern Scotland.

Although the scenery is forever changing and although dialects may differ, there is one tradition that all Scots are proud to share and that is their reputation for warm-hearted hospitality.

Dalbeattie, *Dumfries and Galloway* (6/B5)
In the wooded vale of the Urr Water, grey granite was used to build this town; it was this very granite, quarried in the area, which founded the town's fortunes, being used, for example, to build London's embankment. Although the surrounding countryside is very pleasant, the town is austere in appearance. Two miles north-west of Dalbeattie on the B794 is the 12th-century Motte of Urr. This large earthwork with its 80-ft-high circular mound is the most extensive motte and bailey castle in Scotland. King John Balliol was born in the Castle of Buittle in 1249, but this was later dismantled and, in the 16th century, some of its stones were used to build the tower of the farmhouse of Buittle Place which exists today.

Four miles south-west of Dalbeattie is Orchardton Tower, a circular tower house built in the middle of the 15th century by John Cairns before passing to the Maxwell family. It is in remarkably good order and can be visited by applying to the custodian who lives in a nearby cottage.

Orchardton Tower

Dalkeith, *Lothian* (3/B2)
The most probable origin of the name of this town, situated on a peninsula between the North and South Esk Rivers, is the Gaelic *Dal-Ceath*, (or narrow vale). Dalkeith once stood on a Roman road and today remains on the major routes south from Edinburgh. In the past its proximity to the Cistercian NEWBATTLE Abbey was important, but this later became the home of the Marquises of Lothian and is currently an educational college.

In the reign of King David I, the manor of Dalkeith was given to William de Graham. In the 14th century the property passed through marriage to the Douglas family. Cardinal Beaton was held prisoner here in 1543 and the castle yielded to the English after the Battle of Pinkie in 1547. In 1575 Regent Morton rebuilt and transformed the castle into a palace where King James VI came to stay. In 1642 the 9th Earl of Morton sold the property to the 2nd Earl of Buccleuch, who passed it on to his daughter Anne, wife of the ill-fated Duke of Monmouth, a natural son of King Charles II and Lucy Walter, a descendant of King Edward I of England. (Anne and Monmouth had been married when she was twelve years old and he fourteen.) As Duchess of Buccleuch in her own right after Monmouth's execution for rebellion in 1685, she commissioned Sir John Vanbrugh to restyle the palace. Prince Charles Edward Stuart stayed here for two nights in 1745 and both King George IV and Queen Victoria came to Dalkeith Palace on their visits to Scotland. It is currently leased out as office accommodation by Buccleuch Estates.

The 19th century brought industrial prosperity to the area – bricks, textiles and particularly coal mining. Dalkeith became a popular shopping centre and many residents moved to the spacious Georgian suburb of Eskbank.

A pleasant walk is through Dalkeith Park and along the river. There is an 18th-century bridge and orangery and a nature trail. The park (not the palace) is open to the public daily from March until the end of October. On the outskirts of the town is Thornybank, a privately owned industrial estate, where firms are engaged in printing and bookbinding, wool spinning and electronics. A cattle market takes place in Dalkeith on Mondays. For over twenty-five years Dalkeith has been twinned with Jarnac, a town in south-west France.

Dalmellington (1/D8) *see* Maybole

Above: Dirleton Castle
Overleaf: Drumlanrig (see p. 53)

Dalry, *Strathclyde* (1/B4)
Situated on the River Garnock north of Kilwinning, the town of Dalry developed as a weaving town in the 18th century. Nearby Blair House dates from the 14th century, but incorporates a 15th-century keep. In the glen there is a well-known stalactite cave and the Dawn Water flows through the estate.

On the B781 to West Kilbride is Blackshaw Farm Park where there is a working farm. Visitors can see real farming techniques at first hand and enjoy demonstrations of activities such as sheep shearing. There are also tractor and trailer rides and children's play areas.

Denholm (3/D7) *see* Hawick

Dirleton, *Lothian* (4/D1)
Houses and a 17th-century church front on to a green and look over towards the freestone ashlar ruin of Dirleton Castle, built by the Norman de Vaux family in 1225 and passing through marriage to the Halyburtons and Ruthvens. Patrick Lord Ruthven and Dirleton was grandfather of John, Earl of Gowrie who conspired against King James VI. It appears from letters of the time that Dirleton was the bribe for Logan of Restalrig's involvement in the plot, but after Gowrie's death and forfeiture, Dirleton was granted to Sir Thomas Erskine who was created Lord Dirleton in 1603, later Viscount Fenton and Earl of Kellie. In 1298, Dirleton Castle held out against the invading King Edward I of England, but eventually surrendered to the Bishop of Durham. When Cromwell invaded Scotland in 1650, the castle was, after a gallant defence, taken and dismantled.

The castle is, nevertheless, open to the public. In the grounds is a 17th-century bowling green. A dovecot dates from the same period. Dirleton is a popular holiday resort with a well-known hotel, the Open Arms. Close by are sandy beaches and some of Scotland's best golf courses.

Douglas, *Strathclyde* (2/C6)
Extensive mining work over the years was found to have damaged the foundations of 18th-century Douglas Castle, owned by the Dukes of Hamilton, and it had to be dismantled in the 1940s. The chapel, however, survived and the tombs of famous Douglas chiefs – Sir James 'the Good', who took King Robert I's heart on the

Crusade against the Moors in Spain; and Archibald, 5th Earl of Angus – can be seen in Old St Bride's Church here. King James III had surrounded himself with low-born favourites, much to the disgust of the Scottish nobles. In 1482, spurred on by Lord Gray who had recounted the fable of the mice (who agreed that it would be a good thing to 'bell the cat'), Angus took the lead when they had difficulty in deciding who would actually do it. At Lauder, in front of the king, Angus and his conspirators seized Robert Cochrane (the king's Master of the Artillery) and others and hanged them. Thereafter, Angus was known as 'Bell-the-Cat'.

The church tower is believed to have been given by Mary Queen of Scots in 1565 and there is a monument commemorating the raising of the Cameronian Regiment.

Drumelzier, *Borders* (2/F6)
A prophecy attributed to Thomas the Rhymer locates the grave of Merlin the magician close to the confluence of the Drumelzier Burn and the River Tweed. This Merlin of Scottish Arthurian legend is said to have wandered off crazed after a great battle in the Caledonian Forest. At Drumelzier he encountered some particularly unfriendly shepherds who stoned him to death, and he is believed to have been buried under a thorn tree.

Tinnis Castle was the 16th-century stronghold of the Tweedie family who held their lands here for three hundred years until they were confiscated in the reign of King Charles I, terminating a long-standing feud with the Geddes family during which a James Geddes was murdered in Edinburgh. The ancient burial vault of the Tweedies is in Drumelzier church, but only ruins of the castle remain.

This is fine sheep-farming country with rolling hills and the River Tweed snaking towards its source beyond Tweedsmuir. Marching with Drumelzier is the Agricultural Research Station at Stanhope, also Dawyck Estate rich with daffodils in the spring. The woods of Dawyck contain tall Douglas firs, Chinese rhododendrons and a pinetum. Various trees were introduced in the 18th century by the one-time owner, Sir James Naesmyth.

A restored Norman church is a feature of the small village of **Stobo**, on the road towards PEEBLES. The castle, restored in the 19th century, is now a popular health spa.

Chimneys and turrets at Drumlanrig

Drumlanrig, *Dumfries and Galloway* (6/B2)
The 1st Duke of Queensberry built this romantic castle between the years 1679 and 1690 and it stands on the site of an earlier Douglas castle. Sir William Bruce was involved with the original plans, but it was James Smith, son-in-law of the King's master mason, Robert Mylne, who was the architect. Although Drumlanrig is particularly Scottish in feeling, it was a great departure from the traditional medieval concept. It is said that the Duke was so appalled at the cost of this venture that he spent only one night at Drumlanrig after it was completed.

The Queensberry titles merged with the dukedom of Buccleuch and the present Duke opens Drumlanrig to the public during the spring and summer months. Within is the finest collection of furniture, paintings, silver and china in Scotland. Not least among the treasures on display are items inherited through the marriage of Anne, Duchess of Buccleuch, to the Duke of Monmouth. There are also craft workshops and an adventure playground.

The tiny moorland village of **Durisdeer** has a 17th-century church in which are fine effigies by the Flemish artist Van Nost of the 2nd Duke and Duchess of Queensberry. There is also a stone in memory of a Covenanter shot in 1685. To the north-east is the well-preserved outline of a Roman fortlet of the Antonine period and traces of an earlier Roman road.

Dryburgh, *Borders* (3/D5)
A small village stands close to the ruined abbey which was founded in 1150 for Premonstratensian monks on the left bank of the River Tweed by Hugo de Morville, Constable of Scotland. Sir Walter Scott (1771–1832) and Field Marshal Earl Haig (1861–1928) are buried here. In 1834, the 12th Earl of Buchan erected a statue to commemorate Sir William Wallace and this stands nearby, overlooking the river.

Dumfries, *Dumfries and Galloway* (6/C4)
Created a royal burgh by King David I, this handsome town on the River Nith has become a centre for commerce and industry. It was at Greyfriars Monastery in Dumfries that Robert the Bruce stabbed his cousin and rival, the Red Comyn, in 1306. Although it was Bruce's followers, notably Sir Roger de Kirkpatrick, who ensured that Comyn was dead, the deed gave Bruce's opponents the opportunity to have him excommunicated from the Church of Rome, although this did not sway him from the cause of Scotland's freedom from English domination. A plaque on a building in Castle Street records the event.

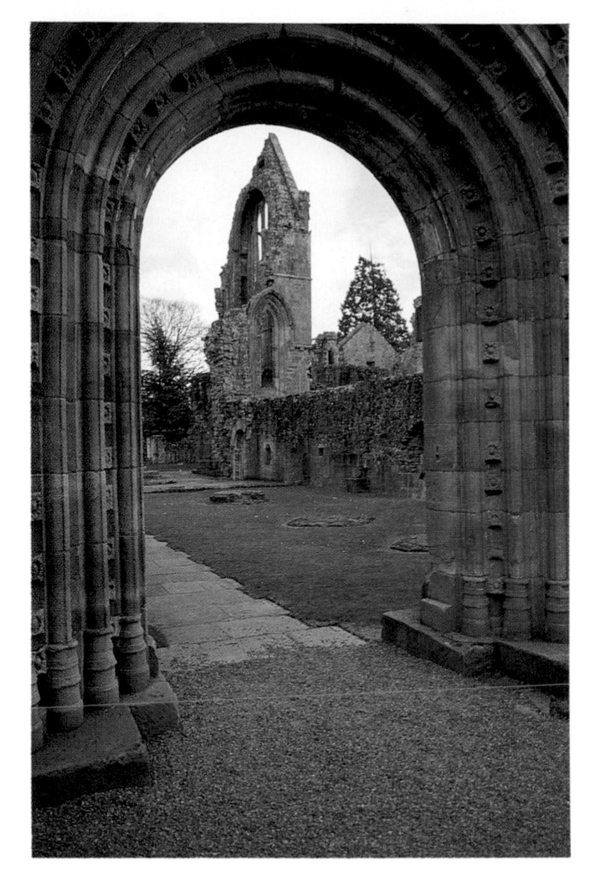

Dryburgh Abbey

In 1791 Robert Burns came to live in Dumfries where he was employed as an exciseman. He lived first in a flat in what is now Bank Street, but later moved to a larger house in Burns Street as it is now known. Today this is a Burns Museum and contains manuscripts and memorabilia. An imposing statue of the bard was erected in front of the modern Greyfriars Church but he is buried in the graveyard of the Church of St Michael where he and his family worshipped. The old town mill on the west bank of the River Nith is now a Robert Burns Centre with a permanent exhibition and an audio-visual theatre.

Dumfries Academy has a distinguished reputation and past pupils have included Sir James Barrie and Sir Robin Philipson, painter and president of the Royal Scottish Academy. The Guid Nychburris Festival is held in Dumfries annually in early summer. Across the River Nith, which is spanned by five bridges, is

Sweetheart Abbey

Maxwelltown which amalgamated with Dumfries in 1929. Here there is a town museum with a camera obscura. Nearby is Dumfries Priory Christian Heritage Museum.

Just north of Dumfries are the remains of Lincluden College – a collegiate church and the accommodation for its canons. The church was built by the Duke of Tourain, son of the Douglas Earl, Archibald the Grim, and his wife Margaret Stuart, daughter of King Robert III. Their tombs lie in the church.

Four miles to the south is Kirkconnel Flow, designated a National Nature Reserve. At **New Abbey**, 7 miles to the south, is Sweetheart Abbey, now ruined. Built in the 13th and 14th centuries as a Cistercian abbey, this was founded by the Lady Devorguilla (or Devorgilla), Lady of Galloway and a great heiress. She married John Balliol, and together they founded the college named after them at Oxford. It was their son who, through her, claimed the throne of Scotland and became King Edward I of England's 'puppet king'. Sweetheart Abbey was so named because Devorguilla built it in memory of her husband whose embalmed heart she carried with her after his death until she herself died sixteen years later. She was buried in the abbey, together with the heart in its ivory casket. New Abbey also has a restored working corn mill and a delightful Museum of Costume in Shambellie House.

At **Arbigland**, near Kirkbean, 12 miles to the south, the founder of the American Navy, John Paul Jones, was born in 1747. The gardens of Arbigland House are open to the public during the summer and Paul Jones' cottage can be seen in the estate grounds.

North of Dumfries, a road leads up to Glenkiln Reservoir amid lonely hills and dramatic scenery. Here the Keswick family, associated with the Hong Kong-based company of Jardine Matheson, created a Sculpture Park featuring works by Jacob Epstein and Rodin, and Henry Moore's 'King and Queen'.

Dunbar, *Lothian* (4/F1)

An ancient fishing port and coastal royal burgh on the edge of wealthy farming country renowned for its rich red soil and fine potatoes. Dunbar remains a popular holiday resort, boasting more sunshine hours than any other location in Scotland. Belhaven Beach to the west and the White Sands to the east are the main sea-bathing attractions. Fossil hunters and archeo-

Sculpture at Glenkiln

logists find their way to Barns Ness with its limestone rockfaces.

The Earl of Bothwell abducted Mary Queen of Scots in April 1567 and, prior to their marriage in May, took her to Dunbar Castle. The ruins can still be seen in the harbour area. This was the scene in 1338 of a spirited defence against the English led by 'Black Agnes', wife of the 9th Earl of Dunbar and a daughter of Thomas Randolph, 1st Earl of Moray.

The 17th-century town house has a six-sided tower and, in the High Street, the birthplace of John Muir (1838–1914), the father of American conservation, is open to the public in June, July, August and September (not Saturdays). The parish church, rebuilt in 1821 and which incorporated a monument to George Home, Lord High Treasurer of Scotland who died in 1610, was badly damaged by fire in 1987. In 1650 a great battle was fought between Covenanters and Oliver Cromwell's General Leslie; a stone erected in 1950 recalls the event, in which the Covenanters were soundly defeated.

Dundonald, *Strathclyde* (1/C5)

North-east of TROON, this village grew up around the now ruined Dundonald Castle, built by King Robert II who died here in 1390. His son, King Robert III, also died here in 1406. The estates were bought by the Cochrane family from PAISLEY, who were raised to the peerage in 1647 as Earls of Dundonald, and they built the castellated mansion known as Auchans House which was visited by Dr Johnson in 1773. It is now a ruin.

Dundrennan (5/J6) *see* Kirkcudbright

Duns, *Borders* (4/A4)

This is essentially still a country market town of old Berwickshire, away from the main traffic routes and in the foothills of the Lammermuirs. On the summit of Duns Law above the town is a Covenanters' Stone commemorating the camp raised by General Leslie and his followers before they marched to Newcastle in 1639 in support of the Scottish Reformed Church. Duns Church itself dates back to the 19th century; and although the Hay family acquired the estate in the 17th century, Duns Castle, designed by Gillespie Graham and incorporating an old tower, is relatively modern.

Manderston House, which is open to the public, is a wonderful example of extravagance.

Staircase at Manderston House, the rails plated in silver

It was built by Sir James Miller, son of Sir William Miller of Leith who amassed a great fortune when trading with Russia. Sir James's intention was to impress his father-in-law, Lord Scarsdale, and the house was completed at the turn of the century. The staircase is a replica of that in the Petit Trianon at Versailles, the rails plated in silver. Silk damask wall coverings and drapes abound and the floors are marble. The stable block is considered one of the finest in Europe. The British world champion racing driver Jim Clark is buried at Chirnside parish church, but he grew up in Duns and, after his tragic death in Germany in 1968, a Jim Clark Museum was opened in the Burgh Chambers. There is also a memorial at Chirnside.

Duns claims to be the birthplace of Duns Scotus (1266–1308), a Franciscan who became a leading divine and one of the greatest medieval philosophers. Contradiction of his work after his death brought the word 'dunce' into the language.

Dunsyre (2/E5) *see* Carnwath

Dunure (1/B7) *see* Ayr

Durisdeer (2/C9) *see* Drumlanrig

Eaglesham, *Strathclyde* (1/E3)
This GLASGOW dormitory town became the centre of world attention when Hitler's deputy, Rudolf Hess, crash-landed his aircraft here in 1941. It was founded on the site of a former village by the 12th Earl of Eglinton in the 18th century. The parish church has an eagle weather-vane on its spire. In 1960 Eaglesham became the first village in Scotland to be permanently listed as a place of special historic architectural interest. To the west are the remains of Polnoon Castle, built by the Montgomerie family in the 14th century. Eaglesham Moor lies to the south-west.

Earlston (3/D5) *see* St Boswells

East Calder (2/E3) *see* Mid Calder

East Fortune (4/D1) *see* Athelstaneford

East Kilbride, *Strathclyde* (1/E3)
The first overspill new town for GLASGOW, built in the centre of renowned dairy-farming country, this is nevertheless one of the oldest villages in Scotland, dating from the 12th century but made a burgh of barony in the reign of Queen Anne. Notable sons of East Kilbride include the anatomists William and John Hunter who were born at Long Calderwood House in the 18th century, and there is a monument in their memory. The first meeting of the Scottish Society of Friends took place here in 1663. To the north is Mains Castle, which has been restored.

After more than twenty years there comes a point when a new town can no longer deserve its designation: East Kilbride is now an established commercial centre with second- and third-generation citizens.

East Linton, *Lothian* (4/D2)
The River Tyne flows here through a little gorge, crossed by a 16th-century bridge. The National Trust for Scotland (NTS) owns 17th-century Preston Mill which is still in working condition and of great beauty. John Rennie, the engineer who built the old Waterloo Bridge in London, was born at Phantassie House in 1761 and there is a memorial to him nearby. Phantassie

Doocote, a fine example of its genre, is also maintained by the NTS. Earlier this century, this appealing corner of East Lothian attracted artists such as Martin Hardie, Robert Noble and John Pettie.

At Prestonkirk to the north is the 18th-century parish church which incorporates a 13th-century chancel. Two miles to the south-west are the ruins of Hailes Castle, once a Gourlay stronghold and later held by the Hepburn family. The Earl of Bothwell brought Mary Queen of Scots here in 1567 after their escape from BORTHWICK Castle. It was eventually dismantled by Oliver Cromwell during his 1650 invasion. To the south, amid scenery dominated by Traprain Law, once stood a Celtic town, and Roman silver unearthed in the area can be seen at the Royal Museum of Scotland in EDINBURGH.

Four miles away is Whittinghame House, built in the 19th century and where, in 1848, A. J. Balfour (later the Earl of Balfour), British prime minister, was born. He is buried in the grounds and nearby is Whittinghame Tower which dates from the 15th century. Two miles south-east is one of Scotland's only two lakes, Pressmennan Lake, created in 1819 (the other is Menteith).

Preston Mill, East Linton

East Saltoun (3/C2) *see* Pencaitland

Ecclefechan (6/E4) *see* Annan

Eccles (4/A5) *see* Coldstream

Eddleston, *Borders* (3/A4)
Situated in the Valley of Eddleston Water, this small village is shielded by Blackhope Scar rising 2,137 ft to the east and by the Lower Cloic Hills to the west. The prehistoric Milkieston Rings lie nearby. The Black Barony Hotel recently opened here was once owned by the Murrays of Elibank and known as Darnhall. South of the village is a monument erected in memory of George Meikle Kemp (1795–1844), a Pentland shepherd's son who designed the fantastic Scott Monument in EDINBURGH. Sadly, he was drowned before his masterpiece was completed.

Edinburgh, *Lothian* (3/A1)
It was Thomas Jefferson, America's third president, who said of Scotland's capital that it was a city 'that no place in the world can pretend to compete with'. That was at a time when Edinburgh dominated the Age of Enlighten-

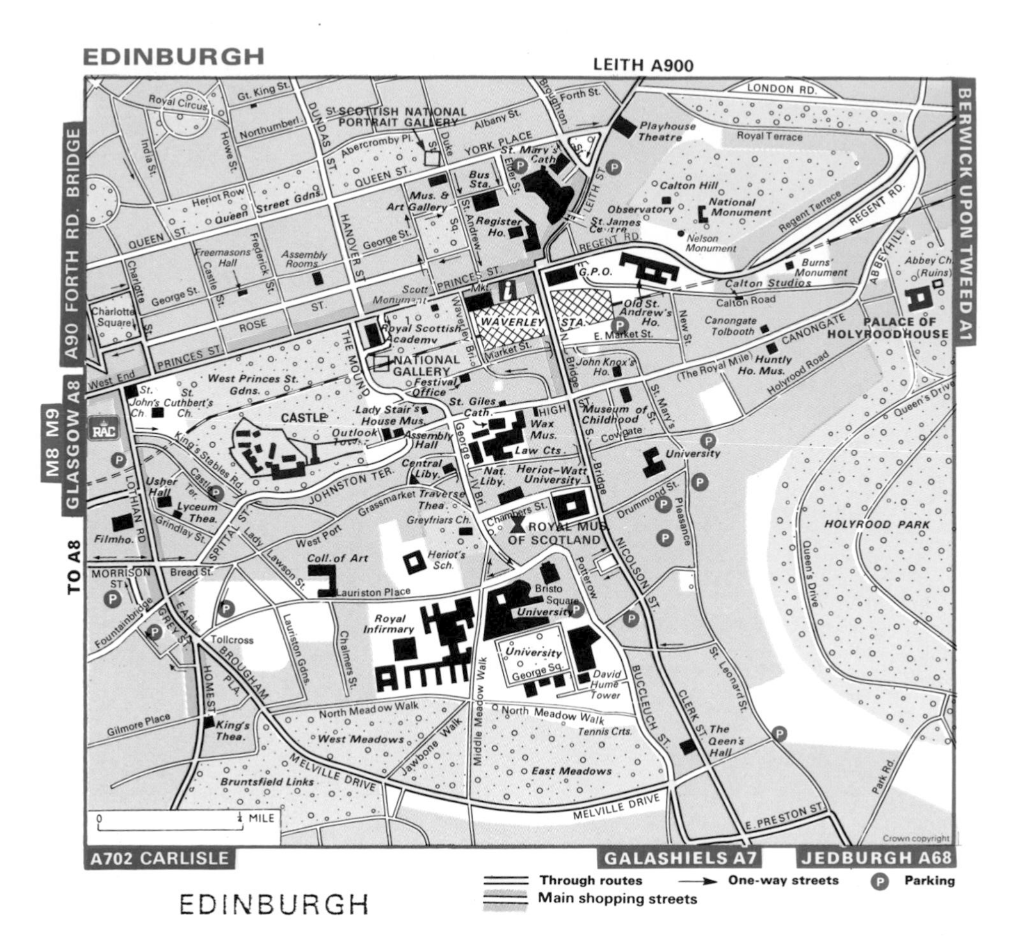

ment, when it was the seat of learning, medicine, law and literature. Much has changed in the world since the turn of the 18th century when men of the calibre of the philosopher David Hume, the economist Adam Smith, Dr Johnson's biographer James Boswell, the chemist James Black, the mathematician John Playfair, not to mention Sir Walter Scott, could be encountered in the elegant streets of Europe's most admired new town. Yet Edinburgh remains gracious, sophisticated and independent, and is undergoing something of a resurgence more subtle than that of its great west-coast rival, GLASGOW.

Edinburgh, like Rome, is built on seven hills, and at the centre is the castle rock, a volcanic plug. Scottish Arthurian legend suggests that this was the site of ancient Camelot, a long-ago prince of Strathclyde being named Arthur and having his fortress either here or on that other volcanic outcrop known as Salisbury Crags, with Arthur's Seat at the centre of the royal park of Holyrood. Be that as it may, Edinburgh rises out of the low ground sloping towards the coastline of the Firth of Forth and there has been a castle on a rock here for over one thousand years.

In the 7th century, a king of Northumbria called Edwin gained possession of whatever fortification existed at that time, and the encampment he created became known as Edwin's Burgh. But it was St Margaret, Queen to Scotland's King Malcolm III, who first saw the real potential of Edinburgh. This remarkable woman, a Saxon princess and granddaughter of the English King Edmund Ironside, had fled to Scotland to escape the Norman invasion of 1066. Capturing the heart of a rough and ill-educated king, she brought new ideas of government and the Roman religion to Scotland, supplanting the old Celtic faith. Although the King preferred his court to be at Dunfermline, she built her little chapel of worship on the highest point of Edinburgh Castle rock in 1076, and of the buildings of that time, mostly destroyed in 1313 by Sir Thomas Ranulph, Earl of Moray, this is all that remains.

Queen Margaret's youngest son, King David I, founded the Abbey of the Holy Rood, named after the fragment of the cross of Jesus held by his mother ('rood' means 'cross'). In the centuries that followed, the town of Edinburgh grew up, straddling the sloping rock which descended from the castle to the abbey, and in the 16th century King James IV built the first palace.

The Old Town

From its dominant position on the top of the castle rock, Edinburgh Castle has witnessed all the great events in Scotland's history. Across the modern drawbridge and gatehouse, the visitor is confronted by the great parapet of the Half-Moon Battery, built in 1574. The path then leads towards the Portcullis Gate, constructed by the Regent Morton in the 16th century. Much rebuilding and restoration has obviously taken place over nine hundred years, St Margaret's Chapel itself being restored in 1853.

They say that you can always tell citizens of Edinburgh because, no matter where they are, at one o'clock precisely they glance at their watches in keeping with the gun fired daily from the castle battlements. 'Mons Meg', the massive cannon used at the siege of Norham, and which until recently stood on the summit known as King's Bastion, is now displayed indoors. In the same room is an interesting illustrated exhibition about its manufacture, history and capabilities as an artillery piece. It weighs 5 tons and is capable of hurling an iron ball to a distance of 1500 yards.

In April 1566 Mary Queen of Scots was persuaded to move into the royal lodging in Edinburgh Castle in preparation for the birth of her child. The heir to the throne was born on 19 June in a tiny room with one small window overlooking a precipice above the Grassmarket. There is a story that the Queen lowered her infant son out of this window in his cradle to be smuggled to safety, but historians are sceptical.

In the nearby Crown Room are the Honours of Scotland. The Scottish crown is one of the oldest in Europe, said to date from the reign of King Robert I but with arches which belong to an even older crown. The sceptre was a gift from Pope Alexander VI to King James IV in 1494, and the sword of state a present to that same King from Pope Julius II. When Oliver Cromwell occupied Scotland in 1651, the Scottish regalia were hastily taken to Dunnottar Castle on the coast of Kincardineshire for safe keeping. When Dunnottar came under siege, a servant girl smuggled the items out in a flower basket and they lay buried in a churchyard until the

Edinburgh beyond Salisbury Crags

Edinburgh Castle

Restoration when they were returned to Edinburgh Castle and sealed up in a room for over one hundred years. It was Sir Walter Scott who, in 1818, prompted by the proposed visit of King George IV to Edinburgh in 1822, made a search and rediscovered them so that they can now be seen by everyone.

The Scottish United Services Museum illustrates Scottish military and naval history with a large collection of exhibits ranging from uniforms to ship models. Another building here is the Scottish National War Memorial, designed by Sir Robert Lorimer to blend into the historic surroundings.

On the Esplanade each autumn is held the Edinburgh Military Tattoo, one of the great attractions of the annual Edinburgh International Festival. This military spectacle, which takes place in the open air, is one of the most dramatic and moving experiences Britain has to offer.

From the castle a road known as the Royal Mile slopes down to the Palace of Holyroodhouse. For generations much of this street was made up of slum tenements, so much so that Queen Victoria refused to travel along it. The subsequent restoration has been a laudable success with the rejuvenation of all the dark little closes and wynds (or narrow alleys) which make up the very fabric of Edinburgh's past. At the head of the Mile is the Scottish Whisky Heritage Centre and opposite is the Outlook Tower, designed by Patrick Geddes, which houses a camera obscura. Nearby is Gladstone's Land with fine painted ceilings, Lady Stair's House with its collection of Burns, Scott and Stevenson memorabilia, and Deacon Brodie's Close, recalling a citizen whose double life of respectable burger by day and burglar by night scandalized his contemporaries and brought him to the gallows. As you cross from the Lawnmarket to the High Street (both part of the Royal Mile), the High Kirk of St Giles stands to the right, the City Chambers through arched entrances to the left.

St Giles' Kirk was first dedicated in 1243, but was largely destroyed by the English in 1385. In 1829 a 'Gothic' restoration took place, but the bulk of the structure dates from the 15th century. The interior, however, where John Knox preached his first sermon in 1559, retains much of its former atmosphere with four great Norman-style pillars supporting the crown steeple, recently beautifully restored. In the south-east corner is the splendid Thistle Chapel, completed for the Knights of the Most Ancient and Most Noble Order of the Thistle by Sir Robert Lorimer and dedicated in 1911.

The Royal Mile, once a clutter of residential buildings, is now, at street level, a parade of tourist shops, although generally of a high standard. Parliament Square next to St Giles' has a fine statue of King Charles II on horseback; here are the law courts, Parliament Hall where the Scots Parliament met until the 1707 Act of Union, and the Advocates and Signet Libraries.

Towards the bottom of the High Street, before you enter the Canongate, are various houses of interest. A 16th-century dwelling is known as John Knox's House, although it is almost certain that the reformer lived here for only a short time. The lower floor is occupied by the royal kiltmakers, Kinloch Anderson Ltd, and the upper galleries have been lovingly restored three times by the Church of Scotland who are the owners. The most recent restoration in 1987 was with the co-operation of the Historic Buildings Council and the City of Edinburgh District Council. Moubray House, next door, was built by the family of that name in the 1470s and it is currently occupied by the Moubray House Press.

Across the road there is the Museum of

P. 62: Lady Stair's House
P. 63: The Tolbooth, Canongate (see p. 65)

ESTAB. 1820
TOLBOOTH TAVE

Opposite: St Giles' Kirk (see p. 61)

Childhood, featuring toys, dolls and model railways, and recreating the joys and tribulations of childhood. The Edinburgh Wax Museum is a mini-Madame Tussauds, but with a distinctly Scottish flavour. The Netherbow Arts Centre provides exhibitions and theatre facilities, and down Fountain Close is the headquarters of the Saltire Society, founded in the 1930s to promote Scottish culture in its widest sense. In Tweeddale Court is the Scottish Poetry Library.

Where the High Street meets the Canongate is the site of the Netherbow Port, which is traced in brass on the causeway. Important rehabilitation schemes have now taken place in the Canongate. Huntly House, a museum run by the district council, displays fascinating artefacts relating to the history of Edinburgh; the Tolbooth, dating from 1591, which formerly served as a courthouse and a prison, is also a museum. Next door is Canongate Church, built as a replacement for the Abbey Church of Holyrood. In the graveyard here lie many famous names – Adam Smith; Horatius Bonar, the hymn writer; and the young poet Robert Fergusson, so much admired by Robert Burns that he erected a stone over his grave. In 1988 the Saltire Society placed a small plaque here in memory of three great Scottish poets, the three Roberts – Fergusson, Burns and Stevenson.

At the foot of the Canongate are the gates of the Palace of Holyroodhouse. Originally the palace was no more than a guest house for the abbey. At the time of the Earl of Hertford's invasion in 1544, it was a high turreted building, but after the Restoration King Charles II decided to rebuild it with Sir William Bruce as architect and Robert Mylne as master mason. A full survey of the palace as it existed in 1663 led to the Privy Council's allocating £30,000 for the repair. Work began in 1671, and by 1672 the Earl of Lauderdale, as commissioner for parliament, took up residence in the north-west tower. However, kings and queens did not come again to Holyrood until 1822 when King George IV visited Edinburgh and held a levee; although a bed was placed in the bedchamber of the Great Apartment, he chose to sleep at DALKEITH Palace. He cannot have been impressed with Holyrood, for before he left he ordered more repairs, and it was only the influence of Sir Walter Scott which ensured that 'Queen Mary's apartments should be preserved sacred from every alteration'. Thus we can see her bedchamber, her small dining room and the spot where her Italian secretary David Rizzio was murdered in an outer chamber.

Queen Victoria first visited Holyrood in 1842, but its real restoration as a royal house took

P. 66: Terraced houses near the castle
P. 67: John Knox's House (see p. 61)
Below: The Palace of Holyroodhouse

AS·YI·SELF·

Left: Greyfriars Bobby
Opposite: Princes Street

place in 1911 when King George V and Queen Mary began to make regular visits, and in 1920 the forecourt was reconstructed to be grander and more austere. There are some fine paintings and interesting historic items on show at Holyrood – regalia worn by King George IV, Lord Darnley's suit of armour, suspiciously small for a man of 6 ft, and King James VI's cradle. The paintings are rather disappointing, although there are fine pictures of King George V and Queen Mary and a portrait of Her Majesty Queen Elizabeth II wearing the robes of the Order of the Thistle, by David Donaldson. The portraits of Scottish kings and queens through the ages in the picture gallery were all painted in the same period by Jacob de Wet, using King Charles II himself as a model for his ancestors.

Holyroodhouse is still used annually as a royal residence and for Scottish state occasions. A garden party is held each year in June.

The spread of Edinburgh from the narrow ridge of the Royal Mile began in the 14th century towards the south. The Cowgate was once a fashionable place to live and, now that an Old Town Association has begun to make its influence felt, may well be again. A notable pioneer in this area, which became badly rundown at the turn of this century, is the 369 Gallery, which promotes the work of young contemporary Scottish artists and allocates them exhibition space and studios. In Blackfriars Street, which runs up to the Royal Mile, is the Richard Demarco Gallery, also involved with contemporary but more international art.

The Cowgate runs into the open space of the Grassmarket, where the monks of the Greyfriars introduced cattle sales. Here stood the public gallows; executions took place here as late as the early 18th century. The Grassmarket has been attractively landscaped and a popular venue here is the Traverse Theatre, a small *avant-garde* playhouse founded by a group of Edinburgh enthusiasts in 1963.

On the corner of George IV Bridge and Candlemaker Row is the tiny statue of Greyfriars Bobby, the little Skye terrier who so faithfully visited his old master's grave each day. On the east side of the castle, fronting on to the slopes of the Mound, is the Assembly Hall of the Church of Scotland which has an imposing statue of John Knox in its forecourt. Close by is Ramsay Garden, the elegant dwellings restored by Patrick Geddes in the 19th century overlooking Princes Street Gardens. Ramsay Garden incorporates the house of that fine Scottish poet Allan Ramsay (1686–1758) and his distinguished painter son, also Allan Ramsay (1713–84). On the Edinburgh skyline, Ramsay Garden rises spectacularly at the very foot of Edinburgh Castle's esplanade.

The New Town

Mid-18th century Edinburgh, running along and behind a spine of rock, was a cramped, rather squalid place, quite out of pace with the aspirations of its citizens. It was not surprising therefore that the lord provost and magistrates began to consider regulations concerning building in 'the fields to the north', the land across the North Loch, which lay in front of the castle rock.

The concept, evolved as early as 1752, was to create a new town notable for 'the neatness and accommodation of its private houses; the beauty and conveniency of its numerous streets and open squares, of its buildings and bridges, its parks and extensive walks'. In 1767 architects and others were invited to 'give plans of a New Town marking out streets of a proper breadth, and by-lanes and the best situation for a reservoir, and any other public buildings which may be thought necessary'. The response was immediate. Six plans were submitted and within three months a young architect, James Craig, was given the most remarkable opportunity of his lifetime.

Much has been written in praise of Edinburgh's New Town. Naturally, the plan has also had its critics. But, when all is considered,

ROYAL BRITISH HOTEL

Craig's triumph lies in his brilliant use of the site rather than in the originality of his design. A main feature of this use of the site was the exposure of Princes Street towards the high rise of the castle rock. Princes Street, having buildings on one side only, must surely rank today as one of the most picturesque shopping streets in the world. But it was intended for a number of the rich and famous inhabitants of the overcrowded tenements at the heart of the Old City. And these residents moved on the understanding that 'no buildings were to be erected to the south of Princes Street', by which means the proprietors of houses on that street in particular would enjoy the advantages which they considered of greatest value – free air and an agreeable prospect. The original houses of Princes Street were plain with simple fenestration. Many had only a common stair, entered from a mews lane behind, and some of these buildings were only two storeys high. But the first feuars (who held the freehold of their houses but were obliged to pay an annual fixed fee to a feudal superior who owned the rights of the land on which their properties were built) came from cramped, unhealthy quarters and it must have seemed as if they were entering the open fields. Furthermore, they were men of wealth and influence who sternly opposed any development which they saw as threatening their new-found environment.

A further problem arose therefore when it came to joining up Princes Street with the Royal Mile and, for that matter, to building any roads leading to that side of town. Drainage of the North Loch began in 1759 with the object of creating pleasure gardens for the exclusive use of the residents of Princes Street. Surprisingly, there was no effective protest at the creation of the Mound, but this is probably because it came about more or less by accident. The Mound, as such, is constructed of rubble dug out of the foundations of the New Town, and by an Act of 1816 the town council was authorized to build on it according to a plan agreed in consultation with a group of feuars from Princes Street, with a subsequent guarantee that Princes Street Gardens should be preserved as an open space. But it was not until 1830 that a proper road was constructed.

Ironically, Princes Street was among the first New Town streets to show signs of decline. Until 1799, however, it remained predominantly a residential street. In 1799 residents included no fewer than twenty-two Writers to the Signet and seven advocates. By 1830 there were also six hotels, the Aberdeen Smack and Steam Packet Office, numerous tailors, furriers, booksellers, the Tax Office for Scotland and a bird stuffer.

The most significant innovation of the early 19th century was the arrival of the railway. By 1846 the line was open and the architect William Playfair given the task of concealing it with a stone wall and embankment. Edinburgh owes much to Playfair over this period, but his masterpieces were the Royal Scottish Academy of 1826 and the National Gallery of Scotland completed in 1857. These magnificent buildings, situated respectively on and at the foot of the Mound, the former surmounted by Steell's massive statue of Queen Victoria, are certainly his finest classical contributions to his native city. It is interesting to note that the National Gallery of Scotland has recently renovated its interiors to recreate the original magnificent impact of grandeur and colour, something which was lost over the years when art galleries fell into the mould of stuffy museums.

The building of the Scott Monument, that other feature of Princes Street, began in 1840, eight years after the death of Edinburgh's most famous citizen. One hundred and eighty feet high, its outrageous mix of pure romanticism and Gothic fantasy was conceived by an untrained joiner called George Meikle Kemp, winner of the open architectural competition. This unfortunate man never saw his vision completed as he was drowned in the Union Canal during its construction. The enclosed statue, by Sir John Steell, shows Sir Walter in shepherd's plaid with his beloved staghound at his feet. The exterior of the construction incorporates over sixty statuettes of characters from the author's books. It is open to the public for those willing to climb 287 steps.

At the east end of Princes Street stands the General Post Office, the work of Robert Matheson, built on the site of the former Theatre Royal. The foundation stone was laid by Prince Albert in 1861, shortly before his death. The imposing building next door was built as an hotel by Sir William Hamilton Beattie in 1902 for the North British Railway Company. Beside this now is the Waverley Market, a multi-purpose shopping centre with a City of Edinburgh tourist information office. Past Waverley Station, around the corner in Market Street is the City Art Centre, run by the district council, and the Fruitmarket Gallery run by the Scottish Arts Council. At the foot of the Mound,

Inside the National Gallery of Scotland

opposite the Royal Scottish Academy, is the world's oldest floral clock, laid out with over 20,000 plants and with electrically driven hands.

Along the south side of the street, inserted into the gardens, are various memorials. West of Waverley Bridge, before the Scott Monument, is a statue by Mrs D. O. Hill of David Livingstone, the missionary and explorer. Beyond this is the figure of Adam Black, twice Lord Provost of Edinburgh, at one time the city's Member of Parliament, and founder of A. & C. Black, the publishing house. Nearby is Steell's statue of the distinguished Professor John Wilson (pen-name Christopher North). Close to the Floral Clock stands a marble image of the poet Allan Ramsay, again by Steell. Next is Sir Frank Mears' memorial to the Royal Scots, the Edinburgh-based regiment which is the oldest of the line of the British Army and served, according to legend, as 'Pontius Pilate's Bodyguard'.

Further along is Birnie Rhind's equestrian statue playing tribute to another famous Scottish regiment – the Royal Scots Greys. It commemorates officers and men who fell in the Boer War and subsequent conflicts. The most recent memorial to be erected is in tribute to Robert Louis Stevenson who, exiled for health reasons in the South Seas, yearned for the 'precipitous city' of his childhood. Designed by Ian Hamilton Finlay and raised by public subscription, it charmingly depicts a garden within a garden.

On the north side of Princes Street, at the east end, is Register House, designed by Robert and James Adam and the first major work to be started in the New Town in 1774. Financed by a £12,000 grant from the profits gained from forfeited Jacobite estates, it is one of the first buildings ever to have been built for the purpose of storing public records and incorporates one hundred vaulted rooms within thick stone walls to combat fire risk. It houses such important documents as King David I's 1140 charter to MELROSE Abbey (property of the Duke of Roxburghe) and the Declaration of Arbroath (1320). In front of the building is an heroic statue of the 1st Duke of Wellington on horseback; next door, set back from the roadway, is the Court of the Lord Lyon King of Arms.

At the far east end of Princes Street is Waterloo Place where it was intended that a triumphal arch should be built to celebrate British deliverance from the French. Two side arches were constructed but, through lack of funds, the main one never materialized. On

The main lower gallery of the National Gallery

Waterloo Place there is the Old Calton Burying Ground which incorporates some unusual tombs and a memorial to Scottish soldiers killed during the American Civil War. It features a statue of Abraham Lincoln with a freed slave kneeling in gratitude at his feet. Further on towards Regent Road is St Andrew's House which, with New St Andrew's House located in the St James Centre complex behind Register House, compromises the administrative headquarters of the Secretary of State for Scotland. Still on the right-hand side of the road, opposite Regent Terrace, there is a grandiloquent memorial to Robert Burns.

On the left of Regent Road is the Crown Office, formerly the Royal High School and a proposed home for a Scottish Assembly. Behind is Calton Hill, approached from a lane at the side of the Crown Office. From the summit can be seen a detailed panorama of the city, and there is a tower commemorating Admiral Lord Nelson and the British victory at Trafalgar. From the top of this, even finer views of the surrounding landscape can be enjoyed. There is an Observatory here and Edinburgh's Folly, the unfinished remains of a replica of the Parthenon erected to commemorate the fallen of the Peninsular War. Alas, once again funds ran out. A monument in the shape of a small temple commemorates Dugald Stewart, Professor of Philosophy at Edinburgh University in the early 19th century.

From the east end of Princes Street, main roads run north towards the port of Leith, east towards Portobello, MUSSELBURGH and the coast, and south towards DALKEITH and PENICUIK. Much restoration and landscaping work has been carried out and the benefits can clearly be seen around the University areas of Newington and to the south and in Leith Walk where extensive tree planting has taken place. On St James Square, where tenements were extensively cleared away, is St Mary's Catholic Cathedral in front of the bulk of the St James Centre. Sir Arthur Conan Doyle, of Sherlock Holmes fame, was born in 1859 in a house in Picardy Square.

Behind Princes Street, the New Town drops down the hill to the north in regulated squares, rows and terraces. At the west end of George Street is Charlotte Square where the imposing former St George's Church has been adapted as West Register House. Next door is the headquarters of the Scottish Arts Council, and on the north side is the headquarters of the National Trust for Scotland, which has refurbished a former home of the Marquises of Bute as an example of a New Town Georgian house. Charlotte Square, St Andrew Square and the streets that run between them – notably George Street, where the Assembly Rooms provide facilities for the city's great social occasions – house the financial and banking institutions for which Edinburgh is famous. In the centre of St Andrew Square is a tall, 150-ft monument carrying a statue of Henry Dundas, 1st Viscount Melville, the 'uncrowned king of Scotland' who managed the country for Prime Minister William Pitt. The Royal Bank of Scotland building behind the statue has one of the finest banking halls in existence; it was once the home of Sir Lawrence Dundas, indeed built for him in 1772, but lost in a game of poker.

Parallel to George Street runs Queen Street on which stands the Royal College of Physicians with its wonderful Adam interiors. Sir James Young Simpson first experimented with chloroform in a house at Number 52, and further along towards the east is a 'Venetian Gothic Palace' containing the Royal Museum of Scotland. Exhibits include prehistoric arrowheads, decorated Celtic stones, Prince Charles Edward Stuart's silver canteen, jewellery which once belonged to Mary Queen of Scots, clocks and early bagpipes and tartans. In the Scottish National Portrait Gallery here are likenesses of famous Scots from the 16th century to the present – Mary Queen of Scots, the Stuarts, Flora MacDonald, David Hume, Ramsay MacDonald and Hugh MacDiarmid. Artists whose work is exhibited include Epstein, Gainsborough, Kokoschka, Lely, Raeburn, Ramsay and Reynolds. The gallery also holds a fascinating collection of early Scottish photography.

Heriot Row also runs parallel with George Street. Although he was born in Howard Place at Canonmills further north, Robert Louis Stevenson's childhood years were spent at Number 17, and in the gardens opposite this house is a small pond with an island, said to have inspired *Treasure Island*.

The roads to the north-west lead to Inverleith, a pleasant residential area with schools and playing fields and the Royal Botanic Garden. Founded in the 17th century, the plant collection here is of unique botanic importance. Among the items of interest are the plant exhibition hall, a demonstration garden including Scottish plants and culinary herbs, a woodland garden and an arboretum. The rock garden is

Pavement artist in Princes Street

world-famous, as are the magnificent rhododendrons and the peat and heath gardens. In the glass exhibition houses can be seen displays of exotic plants ranging from rare orchids to succulents. Inverleith House, in the centre of the gardens, is now an exhibition centre and shows video introductions to the gardens. From the lawn behind the house can be seen one of the best landscape views of the central Edinburgh skyline.

Travelling back towards the west end via Stockbridge, you come upon Edinburgh's river, the Water of Leith, which in fact flows from the Pentland Hills into the Firth of Forth at Leith Docks. Long neglected, for some time silted up with effluent from various mills along its course, this sparkling stream is coming to life again with the building of a pedestrian footpath along its length. The Water of Leith Walkway Trust and Edinburgh District Council using Job Creation labour have succeeded in making Edinburgh people aware of the river in their midst. And as it flows from Stockbridge towards the Dean Village and under the lofty Dean Bridge, built by Thomas Telford in 1832, the walker comes on St Bernard's Well, a small waterside temple complete with statue. Close by is Ann Street, designated Britain's most attractive street by the poet Sir John Betjeman. Ann was the wife of Sir Henry Raeburn who had a financial interest in the building of the street.

Sunken out of sight of the high town is the Dean Village where a great deal of renovation and new building has taken place. The painter Aleksander Zyw has a studio here and Well Court is a surprising square of red Teutonic-style buildings, a Victorian experiment in community dwelling. In this picturesque haven, tucked away beside the Water of Leith, it is sometimes hard to remember that the bustle and traffic of the town is less than half a mile away. Follow the Water of Leith Walkway a short distance to Belford Road and the Scottish National Gallery of Modern Art, housed in a former school building of dramatic proportions. Scotland's national collection of 20th-century paintings, sculpture and graphic arts was founded in 1960. There are works by major British, European and American artists such as Arp, Balthus, Bonnard, Dufy, Ernst, Giacometti, Kirchner, Léger, Lichtenstein, Matisse, Miro, Picasso and Vuillard. Scottish art is strongly represented. The 12 acres of grounds include pieces of sculpture by Henry Moore, Barbara Hepworth and Jacob Epstein.

Edinburgh to the east

The east end of the New Town, having fallen into disrepair early this century, is being steadily cleaned and restored, the spacious Georgian and early Victorian buildings taking on a new life; and the streets and squares here are equally as magnificent as those in the central areas. There is, for example, Drummond Place, where the author Sir Compton Mackenzie lived until his death in 1972; and Gayfield House, an astonishingly beautiful mansion next to a garage in East

Ann Street, 'Britain's most attractive street'

London Street, was once the town house of the Earls of Haddington. On the left of the main road to the coast is the Meadowbank Sports Centre built for the Commonwealth Games in 1970. Further on is Portobello, which acquired its name from a house by the sea belonging to a Scottish sailor who had been involved in the capturing of the Spanish fortress of Puerto Bello in the early 18th century. Sir Harry Lauder, the music-hall legend, was born here in 1870.

Skirting Holyrood Park, on the way to Portobello, there is a fine drive around Arthur's Seat, and a car park for those wishing to walk to the summit, 822 ft high. The exposed rocks on the west side are known as Samson's Ribs, and below this point is a road which runs to Duddingston, a pretty dormitory village on a loch in the shadow of Arthur's Seat, much restored by local conservationists. Prehistoric and Roman earthworks have been discovered

Well Court, Dean Village (see p. 74)

here. Duddingston's Norman church was greatly altered in the 17th century and the minister here in the 19th century was the Revd John Thomson (1778–1840), an accomplished painter who built an octagonal tower near the loch and called his studio 'Edinburgh' so that when an unexpected caller arrived to see him, his servant could in all honesty tell them that the minister was 'in Edinburgh, and would not be back before nightfall'. The Sheep's Heid Inn claims to be the oldest licensed premises in Scotland. Duddingston Loch is a bird sanctuary and on the far side lies Prestonfield House, designed by Sir William Bruce for the Dick family in 1687 and now a prestigious hotel.

Edinburgh to the north

Leith Walk is being reinstated as a grand boulevard leading to Edinburgh's port; to this end this wide street has been landscaped and

many of its buildings restored. Half-way down is a public house at the point where Edinburgh joins Pilrig. Different licensing laws once meant that when closing time came in Edinburgh, customers could cross over to the other half of the pub and continue drinking in Pilrig. Leith Walk was once 10 ft lower, proof of which can be seen in the lower half of Haddington Place where only the top floor of a house is level with the present road, the bottom floor being sunk into a basement. Pilrig House has been restored by the architect Michael Laird and Wimpey Homes Ltd.

Leith was incorporated with Edinburgh as late as 1929 and still maintains a fierce individuality. Many Leithers still do not think of themselves as citizens of Edinburgh, but the massive restoration programme initiated by the Scottish Development Agency, the City of Edinburgh, Lothian Regional Council and Leith Enterprise Trust in recent years has drastically altered the character of the place, bringing fashionable restaurants, art galleries and up-market housing and promoting the image of 'Leith-sur-Mer'. Many fine buildings survive: the Assembly Rooms in Constitution Street date from 1788. Lamb's House in Water Street was where Mary Queen of Scots rested upon her return to Scottish soil and, being the most ancient dwelling house in Leith, it was restored by the National Trust for Scotland and is now a day centre for Edinburgh and Leith Old People's Welfare Council. To the west the coastal road runs past Leith Harbour to Newhaven and Granton, passing various small industrial estates. At Granton is the Royal Forth Yacht Club and HMS Claverhouse, a Royal Naval Reserve establishment on shore.

Edinburgh to the south

Across North Bridge, past the *Scotsman* newspaper offices, the Old College of the University of Edinburgh stands to the right beyond Chambers Street where the magnificent Victorian Royal Museum of Scotland is situated. Further on in Nicolson Street is the Royal College of Surgeons of Edinburgh, which houses a collection of rather disturbing anatomical items kept in jars. Behind Nicolson Street to the west are the University buildings of George Square and the McEwan Hall which accommodates the Student Union. Part of the original Georgian George Square survives. The Queen's Hall in Newington is a popular venue for conferences and concerts, and on Dalkeith Road is the Royal Commonwealth Pool (built for the Commonwealth Games in 1970) with swimming, sauna and weight-training facilities. Next door are the University of Edinburgh's Pollock Halls of Residence. On Blackford Hill is the Royal Observatory. This area, known as the South Side, is heavily residential, providing spacious neo-Georgian houses, many now divided into flats. To the south-east is Liberton, a village on a hill with a fine parish church. The University of Edinburgh has its school of agriculture and

Ramsay Garden (see p. 68)

departments of engineering, applied mathematics, genetics and the Edinburgh Regional Computing Centre at Kings Buildings on West Mains Road. At ruined Craigmillar Castle, now in the middle of a housing estate, Mary Queen of Scots often stayed, and it was here that Darnley's murder was planned.

It has long been an Edinburgh tradition to make jokes about the refinement of the Morningside accent. Morningside has been a prosperous suburb since the mid-19th century, approached through Bruntsfield with its spacious links (open grassland). Along Colinton Road, Napier College of Commerce and Technology is on the right; it seems unprepossessing from the road, but in the courtyard, perfectly preserved, is 16th-century Napier Castle where John Napier (1550–1617) invented logarithms.

Colinton has very much the appearance of a village and is another fashionable suburb. Nearby are Redford Infantry and Cavalry Barracks, and Merchiston Castle School set in spacious playing fields. The 19th-century judge and antiquary Lord Cockburn lived at Bonaly Tower, now converted into flats. Through Colinton Dell, Gillespie Road joins with the Lanark Road which runs from Slateford and Craiglockhart through Juniper Green and Currie into the Pentlands and the source of the Water of Leith. Balerno is the last dormitory suburb in this direction, with the beautiful 17th-century gardens of Malleny House open to the public.

To the south-west, on the northern slopes of the Pentlands, is the Hillend Ski Centre with an artificial ski slope which is lit up at night and which, from the centre of Edinburgh, has been jokingly pointed out as 'a stairway to God'. Nearby Swanston village is associated with Robert Louis Stevenson whose family rented Swanston Cottage, a charming, privately owned house here, for holidays.

Edinburgh to the west

At the west end of Princes Street stands St John's Episcopal Church, which has a fine ceiling, and next door, below Lothian Road, is St Cuthbert's Parish Church. Further up Lothian Road is the Usher Hall, given to the city by the brewing family of that name, and Festival Square with its fountain and statue. Along Queensferry Road, which follows the coastline of the Firth of Forth towards the Forth Road and Rail Bridges at SOUTH QUEENSFERRY, there are residential districts to the left and right. Between Davidson's Mains and Barnton is Lauriston Castle, now held in trust by Edinburgh District Council but once in the possession of the Napier family and incorporating a 16th-century tower. Barnton is a well-off residential area with large mansions, and from here the road runs down to the pretty village of Cramond, situated where the River Almond flows into the Firth of Forth. The 17th-century church is famous, as is the village, from Muriel Spark's novel, *The Prime of Miss Jean Brodie*. Cramond Inn was once a haunt for smugglers, and the cottage-style houses here are reminiscent of those found along the coast of Fife. This is a popular place for yachtsmen, and a tiny ferry-boat will transport passengers over to the Dalmeny Estate on the opposite side of the River Almond. Offshore Cramond Island can be reached on foot at low tide. The Romans obviously liked Cramond for they had an extensive camp here which has been excavated and has yielded some interesting treasures.

On the GLASGOW Road on the other side of Corstorphine Hill is the Scottish National Zoological Park in 70 acres of landscaped hillside. Attractions include Scotland's only gorilla, tiger and lion cubs, chimps and a rhino calf. The Antarctic penguins here are the largest self-sustaining colony in a zoo anywhere in the world.

Back towards town is Murrayfield, another fashionable residential district and best known for the Scottish Rugby Union's international football ground. The adjoining ice rink is popular with curling clubs. Towards GLASGOW is the village of Corstorphine which has a 15th-century church with pre-Reformation tombs. There is a 17th-century circular dovecot and, close by, the Dovecot Studios, a tapestry workshop.

From the Maybury Roundabout, the road runs towards Edinburgh Airport and past the Royal Highland Showground at Ingliston, site of Scotland's largest agricultural show which is held annually in June.

Finally, visitors to Edinburgh may be interested to note that, in keeping with its international status as a capital city, Edinburgh is twinned with Xian in China, San Diego in the USA, Nice in the South of France, Munich in West Germany, Vancouver in Canada, Florence in Italy and Dunedin in New Zealand.

The Edinburgh International Festival

JOHN DRUMMOND,
Artistic Director 1978–83

Edinburgh, for all its beauty and distinction, is a surprising place in which to find one of the world's greatest arts festivals. Although traditionally Scotland has a strong sense of language and a high standard of literacy, it has never demonstrated a comparable interest in the performing arts. This may in part be due to the continuing legacy of Calvinism with its deep suspicion of enjoyment and its equation of pleasure with sin. Yet at least since the 18th century, Edinburgh can make claims to have been a cultured capital where the arts were appreciated and even encouraged, provided of course that they knew their place.

The 19th century built galleries and museums in the city; the turn of the century brought theatres and an excellent room for concerts, the Usher Hall. Though provided by a whisky magnate, it had as a condition of the gift an embargo on the sale of alcohol on the premises, one of those Edinburgh ironies that seem not to surprise the native. If in the past forty years much has changed, some responsibility for that can be attributed to the Edinburgh International Festival. Its double achievement has been to give the city an international reverberation unparalleled in its history and at the same time, through its example, to have transformed the cultural scene throughout Scotland. Nothing in the history of the arts since the Enlightenment has had such influence.

The Festival was born of adversity. In the closing months of the Second World War the then Lord Provost, Sir John Falconer, conceived the idea that the city could play a role in healing those divisions that had torn Europe apart in the previous decade. Not for nothing had Edinburgh been called 'the Athens of the North'. Almost by chance, Falconer met the then Administrator of Glyndebourne Festival Opera, Rudolph Bing, himself a refugee from the Nazi-controlled area of Europe. Bing was ambitious to spread Glyndebourne's influence beyond its tiny Sussex theatre. Together they won support from the fledgling Arts Council, from a more nervous City Council and from one or two local arbiters of taste whose encouragement was crucial. It has often been said that no one in Edinburgh applauds until they look around to see who else is applauding. The Countess of Rosebery, a good musician, and Mrs Sybil Maitland, who had a fine art collection, were as important to the establishment of the Festival as Bing.

Right from the start, Bing's background guaranteed an international outlook. In the first Festival in August 1947 Edinburgh witnessed moments of poignant reconciliation, most notably that of the great Jewish conductor, Bruno Walter, with the Vienna Philharmonic Orchestra. Despite austerity, civic anxiety and lack of creature comforts – Edinburgh's only licensed restaurant closed at 9pm – the idea caught on. The first Festival even made a profit, something those resolutely hostile to its existence have never let successive Directors forget. But the Edinburgh Festival of Music and Drama, as it was then called, was launched, quickly imposed a pattern largely unchanged today and within a few years came to seem inevitable. Edinburgh, it had become apparent, was an ideal festival city.

All good festivals take place in towns which you would happily visit even if there were no festival. Salzburg, Bath, Aix-en-Provence, Dubrovnik, Adelaide – all are highly attractive places and of a human dimension. You can walk in them; indeed, you want to walk in them, for they are visually stimulating and satisfying. One of the greatest achievements of the Scottish Enlightenment was the creation of a superb architectural context in Edinburgh's New Town, balancing the fascinating, if grimmer, streets of the older city, stretching from the Castle down to Holyrood on the opposite hill. The long light evenings of summer and the unself-conscious charm of so many of the inhabitants drew an enthusiastic response from visitors from all over the world. For a time at least the attractions of the city disguised the lack of facilities for the Festival, but it very soon became clear that the provision of theatres was hardly adequate for the demands of an international festival and the great Opera House controversy was born.

It must be remembered that in a northern Protestant country with no tradition, the word 'opera' has dangerous connotations – lavish, lascivious, no doubt, and probably not 'our kind of thing' at all. The necessary expenditure for a new building became a political football and the argument was focused on finding a site, the famous hole in the ground, next to the Usher Hall. And there, despite all attempts, it has remained. Edinburgh now boasts some of the best restaurants in the United Kingdom, the pubs are open for almost longer than anyone needs, there are good new hotels and even Waverley Station has been unbelievably prettied up, but there is still no opera house. Nor do I believe there ever will be: the moment has passed. The cultural leadership of Scotland was won by Glasgow, an altogether more energetic place. But this is no disaster. The cities are, after all, quite close and Edinburgh's role with its Festival may even have been reinforced, since in those three weeks of the summer it becomes such a different place from the Edinburgh of the rest of the year.

The irony of the Opera House debate is that the King's Theatre, where opera has usually been presented, is – at least, from the auditorium – a most attractive space, one of the best designs of its architect, Frank Matcham. But the stage is small and until 1985 there was no orchestra pit. Rows of expensive seats had to be removed to accommodate the even more expensive musicians, hardly an economic solution. Transferring productions from Glyndebourne, the mainstay of the opera programme for the first thirteen years, was relatively unproblematic. But the situation became more difficult as other European cities rebuilt their theatres with modern stage machinery and designers became more ambitious. By the 1970s it was hard to find good productions that could be fitted adequately on to the King's Theatre stage. Yet such was the reputation and attraction of the Festival that major companies continued to visit. Each year the miracle happened and international opera seasons were presented that involved great stars like Callas, Nilsson, Sutherland, Schwarzkopf and Gobbi. Under the direction of Lord Harewood (1960–5) a whole new repertory was discovered, most notably in the first visit of the Prague Opera in 1964 and its revelation of the genius of Janaček, now such a staple of our opera stages, but then almost totally unknown. The influence of the Festival hastened the creation of Scottish Opera, who soon took a significant and deserved place in the programme.

In the face of the wider problems, Peter Diamand, the longest-serving Director (1966–78), decided to mount his own Festival productions, culminating in 1977 with an amazing staging of *Carmen* by Piero Faggioni, with Claudio Abbado conducting and Teresa Berganza and Placido Domingo leading the cast. For sheer dramatic intensity the production has never been bettered in our time. But the price was high. Too large a proportion of the Festival's budget was going on this one area and when I took over in 1978 I felt the need to redress the balance. However, it was a very hard decision.

Until my appointment, all the Festival's Directors had spent their lives primarily involved with music and inevitably it tended to predominate. The Usher Hall concerts provide the largest box-office income. Every year ten or more orchestras with great conductors had trooped in and out of the city, which took this luxury very much for granted. Yet few other festivals could match the quality in so concentrated a period of time. Although in 1951 the New York Philharmonic, under Mitropoulos and Walter, had been almost an orchestra in residence, the normal pattern was of a rapid change-over; there would be perhaps two or three concerts per orchestra, interspersed with a few starry recitals. Among the many conductors who occupy a special place in the Festival's history, none had a greater following than Carlo Maria Giulini whose annual visits were always great occasions. The Edinburgh Festival Chorus, founded in 1966, became an additional reinforcement to the concert programme and Arthur Oldham trained it to become one of Europe's best amateur choirs.

Chamber music was initially performed in the Freemasons Hall, whose bathroom acoustics and creaking chairs failed to damp the quality of great music played by the finest ensembles. Since 1979 the elegant Queen's Hall has largely supplanted it for the Morning Concert series, one of the special delights of Edinburgh – 'the best possible way to wake up', as J. W. Lambert described it. The Festival has played a role in the encouragement of young performers and of new music, though the local audience, who now outnumber the visitors, are not surprisingly conservative in their taste and even major new works can draw disappointing houses. One of the least helpful myths of the Festival is that everything is sold out: would that it were so. It is sadly all too easy to get tickets for anything away from the mainstream. Of course, it is a question of balance and there are always full houses for those distinguished soloists whom, over the years, Edinburgh has taken to heart. The regular appearances of Kathleen Ferrier, Jessye Norman, Daniel Barenboim, Dietrich Fischer-Dieskau, or the Amadeus Quartet, gave them a special relationship with audiences and the warmth of their reception could be sensed even over the radio. But for sheer inventiveness Edinburgh never exceeded the daring of the first year when a Festival quartet was assembled, consisting of Artur Schnabel, Josef Szigeti, William Primrose and Pierre Fournier, to mark the triple anniversaries of Schubert, Mendelssohn and Brahms. However much conditions change, music still has a special status and no artists ever omit from their biographical details the fact that they have appeared at the Edinburgh Festival.

It was always said that the theatre was a poor relation and the present Director, Frank Dunlop,

Festival fireworks (Sean Hudson)

who took over in 1984, is the first to come from a theatrical background. Yet when I look back over forty years of festivals, quite as much theatre comes to mind as opera or concerts. The Edinburgh Festival even has a place in the history of 20th-century drama through Tyrone Guthrie's use of the Assembly Hall of the Church of Scotland, in which seemingly unpromising space the thrust-stage was re-invented – later to be exported to Stratford Ontario, the Guthrie Theatre in Minneapolis and elsewhere. Guthrie's discovery of the Assembly Hall and the Church of Scotland's surprising agreement to its use in 1948 for that splendid monument of Scottish literary history, Sir David Lindsay's *Ane Satyre of the Thrie Estaits*, is one of the Edinburgh legends. The statue of John Knox still stands in the forecourt of the Assembly Hall with a minatory finger pointing heavenwards, the benches are still the hardest in the world, but the place has a marvellous atmosphere, whether for Roger Planchon's *Three Musketeers*, Ian McKellen's famous alternation of *Richard II* and *Edward II* or Bill Bryden's reworking of the medieval Mystery Plays performed by the National Theatre of Great Britain.

The pretty little Lyceum Theatre saw the premiere of T. S. Eliot's *The Cocktail Party* and has hosted visits from foreign companies as wide-ranging as Strehler's Piccolo Teatro of Milan, the Rumanian Bulandra, the Georgian Rustaveli, Japan's Bunraku, Pina Bausch and even cabaret by Marlene Dietrich, or the revue *Beyond the Fringe*, one of the biggest successes of the third Director, Robert Ponsonby (1956–60). Once again, the backstage conditions defy description – hemp lines are still in use, a real piece of 19th-century history. But as with the King's, the results triumph over the conditions. Temporary theatres have been created in other places, memorably in the Haymarket ice-rink for Ronconi's *Orlando Furioso*, in Murrayfield ice rink for Maurice Béjart's *Sons of Aymon* and in Moray House gymnasium for the *Britannicus* of the Théâtre de la Salamandre. No building, however small or however grand, is safe from possible conversion, adaptation, or use during the Festival, especially since the growth of the Fringe whose contribution to drama has been out of all proportion to its simple beginnings.

The Fringe started as a protest by a number of Scottish artists at being excluded from the Festival programme. There has always been keen debate about how much Scotland's own art and artists should be reflected. The only criterion, I believe, should be quality, but nationalism is a potent force, especially in the tall tenements of the Old Town. Here was born in an upper room the splendid Traverse Theatre, the most consistently innovative small theatre of its time. On the Fringe also Richard Demarco insisted, to the despair of funding authorities, on using his art gallery to break down barriers between the visual and performing arts, putting a Polish theatre group like Kantor alongside the newest in painting and sculpture.

At its worst, the Fringe can be disorganized, self-regarding and immature. At its best it has competed with the main Festival on equal terms. Above all, it has vitality, something sometimes in short supply in the grander venues of the main programme. Rivalry was anyhow productive and, whatever was said in public, Festival Directors and Fringe Administrators have always got on together. The Fringe was lucky that developments in contemporary theatre favoured small spaces rather than the 19th-century proscenium arch. In recent years Frank Dunlop has done much to

Fringe Sunday crowds (Roddy Martine)

create a real World Theatre season in Edinburgh and stolen the theatrical attention back from the Fringe. But both sides continue to have their importance and the jollity of Edinburgh on Fringe Sunday is something no one can ignore.

There are many things the Fringe can never do and some that the main Festival has found increasingly difficult. In this troubled area fall art exhibitions. The second Edinburgh Director, Ian Hunter (1950–5), was particularly successful in this field, largely through working with the art historian David Talbot-Rice. It was also easier in those days to obtain paintings on loan for temporary exhibitions and every year in the fifties great names like Rembrandt, Renoir, Cézanne and Gauguin were featured. As recently as 1979 I found it still possible to put on at very short notice a major Degas show in the National Gallery's new extension. But it took real co-operation, and, as everyone knows, gallery and museum directors prefer their own ideas to anyone else's.

The Arts Council did a certain amount with their small gallery in Charlotte Square and later in the Fruit Market. However, the main festival shows have tended to be installed in the Royal Scottish Academy, a touchy institution whose members often gave the impression that they would prefer their own work to be seen. Nevertheless, its great portico on Princes Street regularly led to outstanding visual experiences, even if some of the most memorable were improvised elsewhere. Richard Buckle's Diaghilev exhibition in 1954, mounted in the Edinburgh College of Art, inspired a renewal of interest in that whole period, while his later exhibition about Jacob Epstein in Waverley Market re-established a forgotten reputation. Demarco sought links with the new in other countries, most memorably in 1970 with Strategy Get Arts (a palindrome) which revealed to the UK for the first time the vitality of the new German school in Düsseldorf.

Edinburgh has always been able to present unique and unexpected events. It has the advantage of being not just a music festival but dedicated to all the arts. It can even, as in the last Festival for which I was responsible in 1983, carry a theme. Under the heading 'Vienna 1900', all the various areas of Festival activities played their part. The spoken word, whether in poetry, readings or lectures, has always had an honourable place. But of all the arts, dance has had the most difficult role, through the absence of any adequate stage, though for many years the Empire Theatre, now a bingo hall, attracted companies of the grandeur of the New York City Ballet and the Royal Ballet. In recent years the cavernous Playhouse Theatre has been rehabilitated and has challenged companies with its limited stage and its total absence of wing space.

If I seem to stress the problems connected with presenting performances, it is perhaps because this became a key pre-occupation of all the Festival Directors. The tremendous achievement of early Festivals meant that there has never been a shortage of companies wishing to be seen in Edinburgh. Showing them at their best has been the difficult part. Much has been written over the years on the parsimony of the city towards an event that is a huge source of income for the whole community. Bernard Levin christened the annual financial debate 'the Grudging of the Money'. Adequate funding is difficult in any major arts enterprise, but I believe that some of the criticism over the years has been unfounded and even exaggerated. Edinburgh is a small city of less than a million people, saddled in recent years by a confusing form of two-tier local government. The District Council – the old city council – funds the Festival, but it is the Regional Council which collects the rates. Of course, there will always be, as in any city, a substantial number who cannot see the point of channelling cash into the Festival and would rather any available money were spent in other ways. But there is a core of real enthusiasm and support which has perhaps been most clearly demonstrated in recent years by the huge growth in funding from the private sector through sponsorship. Nevertheless, gratifyingly the largest income still comes from the box office – a sure test that the Festival is in touch with its audience.

It has become fashionable in recent years to claim that the Festival is too big. The excellent Edinburgh Film Festival, the Television Festival, the Jazz Festival and the Book Fair have all clambered aboard, adding to the variety and daunting the visitor with a plethora of choice. Yet the essence of festivals is that they go beyond the conditions of normal life and I have always found the multiplicity of activity, from the Military Tattoo to the smallest one-man show, stimulating and rewarding. Despite all the difficulties, to be asked to run the Edinburgh Festival is one of the greatest privileges in the arts world today. All those of us who have done it have found our lives changed by the experience. Circumstances may alter, Directors and their different policies come and go, public attitudes vary, but the essence remains. In this northern city an event takes place every year which has fed the imagination and enriched the experience of millions. As Lord Harewood put it in his tribute on the Festival's twenty-fifth anniversary, it is impossible to see the city again without 'that lifting of the spirit which is commonly associated with love'.

Ednam (4/A6) *see* Kelso

Eildon Hills, The, *Borders* (3/D5)
Border legend has it that King Arthur and his knights sleep beneath the Eildons and that one day they will awake to ride again. There is also a tradition that these three hills were once one and were split in three by the Borders wizard Michael Scott who sought employment for the devil. Dominating the local landscape, their magical quality cannot be denied. The Eildon Tree Stone marks the spot where Thomas the Rhymer is said to have met the Queen of the Faeries and entered through the hill with her into Faeryland where he remained for seven years.

The Eildon Hill Walk is signposted from the centre of Melrose; the walk has much of interest to the tourist. A view indicator has been situated on the central summit at the highest point of 1,385 ft. Sir Walter Scott had a particular affection for this view and observed, 'I can stand on the Eildon Hills and point out forty-two places famous in war and verse.'

Eskdalemuir, *Dumfries and Galloway* (6/F2)
There was a Roman camp here at Raeburnfoot, and in 1905 an observatory was built at 800 ft on the moors. This is a small village surrounded by rolling hills of great beauty. Ettrick Pen stands 2,270 ft high to the north-west and Eskdale to the south. In 1967, the Kagyu Samye Ling Tibetan Centre was established here. It is now a thriving international community and has pottery, wood-carving and carpet-weaving workshops. There is a painting studio and a printing press. Meditation, healing and Buddhism are taught.

Four miles south, Castleo'er Hill Fort can be seen on a ridge just before the spot where the White Esk River joins with the Black Esk River.

Ettrick, *Borders* (3/A7)
The village of **Ettrick** lies on the Ettrick Water, north of Eskdalemuir. James Hogg, the 'Ettrick Shepherd', 19th-century poet and author, lived here and a monument stands on the site of the cottage in which he was born in 1770. He died in 1835 and his grave is in the churchyard. A woman known as Tibbie Shiel was proprietress of the inn of the same name standing beside St Mary's Loch, where Hogg and his cronies would regularly meet. She died in 1878 and her grave is also in Ettrick churchyard.

The Loch of the Lowes joins St Mary's Loch

St Mary's Loch

Statue of James Hogg, the 'Ettrick Shepherd'

and the Meggat Water flows into the north-west of St Mary's Loch at Cappercleuch. The Meggat Valley was recently flooded to create a great reservoir and a spectacular scenic road leads over to Talla Reservoir and Tweedsmuir. Thomas Telford, the bridge builder, was born here. At the north end of St Mary's Loch is the old churchyard of St Mary's Kirk and the ruins of Dryhope Tower, rebuilt in the 17th century and said to have been the birthplace of Mary Scott, the 'Flower of Yarrow', who married 'Auld Wat of Harden' from whom Sir Walter Scott proudly claimed descent. To the north-east lies the Vale of Yarrow and Ettrick Forest, once part of the Caledonian Forest and a royal hunting ground. Here may be seen some of the most gloriously beautiful scenery in the Scottish Border country.

The attractive village of Ettrick Bridge lies downstream in the heart of Ettrick Forest. There is a story that the bridge was built by Walter Harden after an incident which took place when he was crossing the river on horseback after a raid and carrying a small baby. The horse stumbled and the baby was drowned. There is a commemorative stone which survived when the bridge was washed away in 1707.

Sir Walter Scott's grandfather lived in Oakwood Tower, built in 1602, which stands near the river. Kirkhope Tower, which dates from the 16th century, was built by Walter Harden. Nearby are the remains of a Roman fort. The former Liberal leader, David Steel, has his home in the village.

Eyemouth, *Borders* (4/C3)
Made a free burgh of barony by King James VI in 1597, this picturesque fishing town retains cobbled streets and an old-world charm. Situated between Hare Point and Nestends, Eyemouth has a breakwater which dates from 1770. The harbour is shielded by the 'Hurkars' rocks and overlooking these is a Georgian mansion, Gunsgreen House, where smugglers would gather in the 18th century. There are safe bathing beaches nearby. Oliver Cromwell is reputed to have erected the tower which is presently used as a golf clubhouse.

The area is rich in smuggling legend and there are caves and passages in the coastal cliffs to north and south. In a great storm in 1881, Eyemouth endured an appalling disaster when half of the fishing fleet was sunk and over a hundred men drowned. A tapestry depicting this event can be seen in the Eyemouth Museum which deals with all aspects of the local fishing industry. A scenic cliff-top walk from Eyemouth leads to St Abbs via Coldingham. There are public facilities for diving which has become a popular sport here.

Sir Samuel Brown, the engineer responsible for the 1820 Union Suspension Bridge over the River Tweed, the first of its kind in Britain, lived at Netherbyres. Coldingham Priory, 3 miles to the north-west, was founded *c.*1147, but was partly destroyed by Oliver Cromwell in 1648. The choir has been restored and now forms the parish church, one of the oldest still in use.

Fairlie (1/B3) *see* Largs

Fala, *Lothian* (3/C2)
This village on the Lammermuir Hills in the heart of rich sheep-farming land is also known as Blackshiels after an inn there which was once used as a shieling for the Black Friars of Soutra. Cakemuir Castle, parts of which date from the 16th century, stands by the burn of the same name. It is said that Mary Queen of Scots stopped off at Cakemuir to change out of the page's disguise in which she had escaped from the siege of BORTHWICK Castle in 1567.

Fenwick, *Strathclyde* (1/D4)
Five hundred feet above sea level and surrounded by rich dairy farming, this village comprises High Fenwick and Laigh Fenwick. The church dates from 1643 and was restored this century after a fire. Some 17th-century jougs have survived, reminders of a time when individuals could be clapped in irons for trouble making and even breaking the Sabbath. John Fulton (1800–54), designer of the orrery in the Glasgow's People's Palace, lived and worked in Fenwick and, completely self-taught, became a mathematician. In 1769 the first co-operative society in the world is said to have been established here. There are many historical links with the Covenanting cause and the village claims to have more martyrs' graves than anywhere else in Scotland.

Galashiels, *Borders* (3/C5)
A busy manufacturing town famous for woollens and textiles; the Scottish College of Textiles was established here in 1909. It may interest the visitor to know that the word 'tweed', so strongly associated with Galashiels, does not derive from the great river of that name but came about from a slip of the pen by an English clerk misreading the Scots word *tweel* (meaning a fabric in which weft-threads alternately pass over one warp-thread and then under two or more to produce diagonal lines). As Galashiels is so very much a centre for the industry, there is a Woollen Museum at Waverley Mills, and the Border Wool Centre can be visited at North Wheatlands Mill. At Peter Anderson in Waverley Mills, there are guided mill tours which show the process of tartan weaving.

In 1337 a troop of English soldiers was surprised after picking wild plums and all were killed. From this event comes the town slogan: 'Sour plums'. Each June this is one of the events celebrated in the Braw Lads' Gathering, which re-enacts the history of Galashiels. Although the town featured in the dowry agreements of King Henry IV and Princess Margaret Tudor, it did not become a municipal burgh until 1864.

The mercat cross dates from 1695 and the war memorial clock tower was designed by Sir Robert Lorimer. In front of this is an imposing bronze statue depicting a Border mosstrooper by Thomas Clapperton. Old Gala House, a 15th-century mansion which was once the home of the Scots of Gala, is now a museum and interpretation centre for the district.

Galloway Forest Park, *Dumfries and Galloway* (5/F2)
Two hundred and fifty square miles of spectacular scenery make up this impressive park which incorporates Merrick (2,765 ft), the highest hill in southern Scotland. The land is owned by the Forestry Commission and includes several areas of forest and numerous lochs.

The Galloway Deer Museum is established in a converted farm steading by Clatteringshaws Loch, 6 miles west of NEW GALLOWAY. There are features on deer and other Galloway wildlife, and historic and geological information.

The Battle of Glentrool took place in 1307. Robert the Bruce, who was a fugitive at the time, won a decisive victory when he and a small band of followers surprised a much larger English force by rolling boulders down on top of them. A granite boulder erected in 1929 commemorates this event.

Galloway Forest Park offers a wide range of leisure diversions centred on Glen Trool – forest trails, fishing, a red deer range, a wild goat park

The fishing fleet, Eyemouth

and forest drives. On a hill near the A712 is Murray's Monument, erected to commemorate a shepherd's son who became a Professor of Oriental Languages at Edinburgh University. In 1915 Bronze Age treasures dating from 1000 BC were discovered in Glen Trool and can now be seen at the National Museum of Scotland in EDINBURGH.

Galston, *Strathclyde* (1/D5)

In the Upper Irvine Valley, Galston's industries encompassed mining, lace making and cotton weaving, but today the pits are closed. Burn Anne runs through the town and to the north is Loudoun Castle.

Lace manufacturing was already being carried out in the Irvine Valley from before the 19th century, but expanded fast in the three burghs of Galston, Newmilns and Darvel when Alexander Merton introduced power to the looms in 1876. Newmilns and Darvel lie 1 mile apart; the former has an 18th-century tolbooth, while the latter's main claim to fame is that Sir Alexander Fleming, discoverer of penicillin, was born here in 1881.

Left: St Abbs harbour (see p. 86)
Below: Wild goats in Galloway Forest Park (see p. 87)

Cardoness Castle, a former stronghold of the McCullochs of Galloway

Garlieston (5/F6) *see* Wigtown

Garvald (3/D1) *see* Gifford

Gatehouse of Fleet, *Dumfries and Galloway* (5/H5)
On the Water of Fleet, close to where it flows into Fleet Bay, an inlet of Wigtown Bay, this town was planned in the late 18th century as a centre for cotton manufacturing and other industries. Laid out by James Murray, for whom gracious Cally House, now a hotel, was built in 1763 to designs by Robert Milne, Gatehouse of Fleet once boasted six cotton mills, a tannery and a brewery. Its industries had declined by the mid-19th century, and today it is a sleepy, unspoiled place with residential and tourist appeal. One building, which had continued in use until 1930 as a mill for manufacturing wooden bobbins, has now been restored as a visitor centre.

At the Murray Arms, a typical main-street Scottish coaching inn, Robert Burns is said to have written down the words of 'Scots Wha Hae'. Cardoness Castle, which dates from the 15th century, was once a stronghold of the McCullochs of Galloway. Nearby is Trusty's Hill where there is a monument to Samuel Rutherford, the 18th-century religious scholar. On the same hilltop are the traces of an Iron Age fort and a rock carved with Pictish symbols. At Cairnholy there are two small chambered cairns dating from the Neolithic period (2000 BC), the survivors of a large group.

Gifford, *Lothian* (3/D2)
A tidy village which grew up in front of the entrance gates of the great house of Yester, home of the Marquises of Tweeddale. Yester Castle, which stands on the original estate, was erected in 1268 by Hugo de Gifford, said to have been a 'prince of darkness'. The castle is now ruined, but the underground 'Goblin Ha' ', a magnificent vaulted hall said to have been built by goblins, remains in remarkable condition. The lands of Yester were acquired through marriage by the Hay family and, in 1646, John, 8th Baron of Yester, was created 1st Earl of Tweeddale. The 2nd Earl became lord chancellor of Scotland in 1694. Yester House, the work of William and Robert Adam and Robert Brown, was sold by the widow of the 11th Marquis for tax reasons and the present owner is the inter-

nationally known impresario Gian Carlo Menotti, who has plans to create a Scottish Glyndebourne there one day.

The village church dates from the early 18th century; a plaque on the wall commemorates the birth in 1723 of the Revd John Witherspoon who emigrated to America and was a signatory of the American Declaration of Independence. He was first president of New Jersey College, which later became Princeton University.

At the end of the long avenue which leads from the gates of Yester stands a mercat cross, and alongside this avenue flows Gifford Water. Four miles north in the Lammermuir Hills is **Garvald**, where the church dates from the 12th century and, like most of the surrounding buildings, is constructed of red East Lothian sandstone. Those in search of tranquillity find their way to Nunraw Abbey, which was built by Cistercian monks in the 1950s. Nunraw was originally a grange belonging to a convent in HADDINGTON and was founded in the 12th century. In the 16th, the property fell into the hands of the Hepburn family after having had three prioresses of that name. The Scottish parliament met here in 1548 to decide the best course of action for the five-year-old Mary Queen of Scots.

Girvan, *Strathclyde* (1/A9)

A popular seaside resort with plenty of diversion for young and old. There is fishing on the Girvan Water and easy access to the GALLOWAY FOREST PARK. The herring fleet was once the main industry, but today tourism, although seasonal, provides the major employment. There are 1½ miles of safe, sandy beach and, in addition, a modern heated indoor swimming pool. Bowling is a favourite pastime and there are tennis courts within Morton Recreation Grounds. The main shopping centre is Dalrymple Street and there are several delightful parks and gardens – Victoria Park with its roses; Orchard Gardens; McCreath Park; and Knockcushan Gardens. On Sunday afternoons in the summer visitors can enjoy silver- and brass-band concerts, and on Thursday evenings displays of Highland dancing.

To the north of Girvan in the Girvan Valley is Kilkerran House, the seat of the Fergusson chiefs, where there are still occasional gatherings of Clan Fergusson. It was built around an old tower in the 17th century on lands owned by the

Chambered cairn at Cairnholy (see p. 89)

Gifford church

family since the 15th century and enlarged in 1815. Four and a half miles north-east of Girvan are the gardens of **Bargany**, surrounding the beautiful house which was once the home of the Dalrymple Hamilton family; these are open to the public. There is a wooded garden centred on a lily pond encircled by azaleas and rhododendrons. An extensive walled garden and rock garden are other attractions for horticultural enthusiasts and there is public access from March until October.

Nearby is Killochan Castle, a substantial fortified house still a private residence and home of the Cathcart family until 1954. South of here, at **Old Dailly**, is Penkill Castle, built in the 15th century with later additions. Dante Gabriel Rossetti and his sister Christina, with other pre-Raphaelites, came here for inspiration. There are 17th- and 18th-century items of furniture, paintings and tapestries, and the Penkill Room has a famous curse on it. The castle is open to the public by appointment only.

Two miles south of Girvan are the ruins of 16th-century Ardmillan House, where Mary Queen of Scots stayed in 1563. Six miles south is Carleton Castle, now a ruin, but the seat of a

Kennedy baron who is reputed to have disposed of seven of his wives by pushing them over the cliffs into the sea. His eighth wife, however, obviously had some premonition of her impending fate and managed to get rid of him first.

Travel down the coast with fine views of AILSA CRAIG out to sea and turn inland towards **Colmonnel** past Knockdolian Castle, a 16th-century tower house owned first by the Grahames, then the Kennedys, the McCubbins family and now by the Duchess of Wellington. The village of Colmonnel, situated in the glen of the River Stinchar, takes its name from St Colmonella who died in AD 611. Sir Robert Lorimer's work can be seen in the church and at Bardrochat, a hilltop mansion which belongs to the McEwen family.

The 16th-century Kennedy stronghold, Kirkhill Castle, ½ mile north-west of Colmonnel, is now in ruins. The ruins of Craigneil, ½ mile south-east, which was a hiding place for King Robert Bruce, can still be seen.

Gladsmuir, *Lothian* (3/C1)
West of HADDINGTON, this small village, where coal mining was the main industry, was also a meeting place for witches, thirteen of whom were burned here in 1661. The family of George 'Jingling Geordie' Heriot, silversmith and financier to King James VI (who was also King James I of England), came from Gladsmuir and in the 18th century Dr William Robertson, the historian, was minister of the church before he became principal of Edinburgh University.

Glasgow, *Strathclyde* (1/E2)
Glasgow is full of energy and a determination to discard an unfortunate image of inner-city deprivation acquired since the turn of this century. It is extraordinary how a metropolis so rich in life and character could have been allowed to become so derelict, but the fault lies with the planners who tore out Glasgow's tenement heart in the 1950s, removing whole communities to out-of-town housing estates and new towns, to 'green belts, trees and flowers', to use the words of a popular folk song. Now the tide has turned, however. Not for nothing was Glasgow chosen to host the 1988 Garden Festival and nominated European City of Culture 1990. The largest city in Scotland is shrugging off the early 20th century's legacy of industrial decline.

As long ago as AD 543, St Kentigern, otherwise called St Mungo, is recorded in Welsh documentation as bishop of Gartnwl, ruler of the region around Glasgow. It was about this time that he built the church, in which he was later buried, and in 1136 a cathedral was erected on the site, overlooking the Molendinar Burn. This fine medieval place of worship is, curiously, entered from the side. Part of the 1197 crypt remains, and the Laigh Kirk, which serves as Glasgow's parish church, is impressive, as is the vaulted crypt known as Blackadder's Aisle.

Set out on the wooded area above the cathedral is the Necropolis (Cemetery), opened in 1832. This was the eccentric inspiration of Provost James Ewing who had the backing of the Merchant's House of Glasgow; it was conceived

The Necropolis, Glasgow

as an ornamental garden for the dead, where virtually every kind of architecture in the world is represented. Each Glasgow 'worthy' had a tomb styled in the manner of the place where his money had been made; and dominant over all is the statue of John Knox, the work of Robert Forrest. Emphasising the protean nature of Glasgow, a Jews' enclosure lies not far from Egyptian Vaults and Catacombs.

West of the cathedral is Provand's Lordship, built in the 15th century for the priest in charge of old St Nicholas Hospital; it is credited with being the oldest house in Glasgow. It is now a museum containing exhibits of stained glass, portraits and furniture relating to the city.

Glasgow was made a royal burgh in 1454 and prospered as a Lowland city, unaffected by the dynastic turbulence which, for the most part, took place in the north and east of Scotland. When Cromwell subjugated the country and came through Glasgow in the mid-17th century, the city remained unscathed despite the fact that certain citizens pronounced their opinions of the Protector in very certain terms. Almost one hundred years later, Prince Charles Edward Stuart retreated through Glasgow from England

GLASGOW

and levied a toll, which was greatly resented but later reimbursed by the Whig government in London. By then, prospering from the tobacco trade with the Virginias, Glasgow was something of a republican stronghold and remained unimpressed by the Young Pretender, even when he was proclaimed regent at Glasgow Cross. The present cross replaced the original in 1929.

Geographical location was all-important, and Glasgow, two thirds of the way up the coast of Britain with a sea estuary on the western seaboard, was ideally situated to service Britain's international trade routes. By the end of the 17th century the city had become a major gateway to the New World. Glaswegian businessmen became the middlemen for the European tobacco trade with the American colonies and there dawned a period of prosperity which looked as if it might end with the 1775 American War of Independence. Not so, however, for with the River Clyde widened and deepened, big ships could offload their cargoes as far upstream as the city centre. The cotton trade followed on tobacco, preceding the railway, as Glasgow evolved as the ship-building centre of the world.

The prospect of employment at this time brought immigrants from the Highlands, Lowlands and Northern Ireland to this great, booming, industrial city. This was a golden age which was to last right up until the end of the Victorian era. The subsequent racial mix brought about by this influx of labour is the key to the present-day Glasgow personality – quick-witted, open and friendly, but balanced by an undercurrent of aggressive sarcasm.

The power of steam played a crucial role in Glasgow's prosperity, and it was at Glasgow University that this was first harnessed by James Watt. In 1812 the *Comet*, the world's first

Above: Glasgow City Chambers *(see p. 97)*

Below: Detail of the Templeton building *(see p. 99)*

Above: The Winter Gardens, the People's Palace *(see p. 99)*
Opposite: Marble staircase, Glasgow City Chambers

paddle steamer, was launched, and from then on it was big business. 'Clyde-built' became a world-renowned catchphrase; Glasgow 'the second city in the Empire'.

On the back of all the wealth generated, Glasgow developed as the ultimate Victorian city, much of which has survived. Although its north side has been modernized, George Square is a good example. The statues here are of Queen Victoria, Prince Albert, Robert Burns, Sir Walter Scott, Lord Clyde, Sir John Moore, Thomas Campbell, Dr Thomas Graham, James Oswald, James Watt, William Ewart Gladstone and Sir Robert Peel. The magnificent City Chambers building is a lasting reminder of Glasgow's Victorian greatness. Designed by William Young, a native of PAISLEY, who received his early professional training in Glasgow, it is in the Italian Renaissance style, its walls faced with Polonaise and Dunmore stone. It covers an area of 6000 square yd and ten million bricks were used in the construction. The Tower stands 216 ft high. The foundation stone was laid in 1883, and Queen Victoria inaugurated the building in 1888. The total cost of the chambers (including furnishings) was £578,232, and the first meeting of the council took place on the 10 October 1889.

The marble interiors are unquestionably grand – the entrance hall built after the plan of a Roman church, almost unique in its proportions and blending of stone, marble and mosaic. The marble staircase forms a vista of marble halls and arches 180 ft in length; the council hall has a stained-glass dome and walls of Spanish mahogany, the upper part treated in Tynecastle tapestry. The Banqueting Hall carries on its walls murals relating to the city's history. Throughout the building there are stunningly beautiful decorated ceilings. It is indeed a palace fit for men of achievement and stature. In 1923 an extension was opened by the Princess Royal on the east side of John Street. Designed by John Watson in pure Roman style, its cost (including furnishings and fittings) was £555,082. Inflation, it would appear, was with us even then.

At this juncture it is probably appropriate to refer to Glasgow's coat of arms, granted to the city in 1866. A half-length figure of Glasgow's patron saint, St Mungo, is shown on a helmet above a shield. The emblems – the fish and ring, the bird, the tree, the bell – which were used in ancient seals, are all incorporated. In 1975, under local government reorganization, Glasgow became a district within Strathclyde Region. A new patent was granted, the only alteration being that the helmet was replaced by a crown of thistles, an appropriate symbol of a statutory district. The promotional slogan 'Glasgow's miles better', created in the 1980s to improve the city's image abroad and to inspire local civic pride, has happily not quite obliterated the ancient motto: 'Let Glasgow flourish'.

For those wishing to make a logical tour around the centre of the city, an appropriate start from the cathedral is the High Street, at the foot of which is Glasgow Cross, the Tolbooth Steeple built in 1626 and the Tron Steeple of 1637, a part of St Mary's Church which was not burnt down in 1793 by the local branch of the Hellfire Club. The Tolbooth is all that remains of the prison described in Sir Walter Scott's *Rob Roy*; its high steeple carries a crown, as does St Giles' Kirk in EDINBURGH and King's College in Aberdeen. The Tron Theatre in Parnie Street is the home of the Glasgow Theatre Club and specializes in contemporary drama and musical events.

Gallowgate, along which condemned prisoners were taken to meet their doom, is now best known for the 'Barras', a weekend open-air market where, even nowadays, bargains can be found. To the south is the Saltmarket in which stands St Andrew's Parish Church, built in the mid-18th century, and St Andrew's-by-the-Green, the oldest Episcopal church in Glasgow, now transformed into office accommodation for the West of Scotland Housing Association. Glasgow Green is the oldest public park in Britain. Should you receive the Freedom of the City of Glasgow, this entitles you to graze your flock of sheep on Glasgow Green, and also to hang out your washing in front of the City Chambers. The extraordinary replica of the Doge's Palace in Venice, built for the carpet manufacturers Templetons in 1889 by William Leiper, is now a business centre. The first monument erected in honour of Lord Nelson was placed on Glasgow Green in 1806. Close by is one of Glasgow's remarkable museums, the People's Palace, which contains items relating to trades and industry, labour movements, women's suffrage, entertainment and sport. Paintings by the artist John Knox and the writer Alasdair Gray are on display, and there are portraits

of St Mungo and Billy Connolly, the comedian.

Massive shopping developments have taken place in Glasgow in recent years, notably the St Enoch complex off Argyle Street which involved an investment of £62 million. Part of Argyle Street was pedestrianized, paving the way (if you will excuse the pun) for Buchanan Street and Sauchiehall Street which have also benefited from improvements. In Queen Street is Stirlings Library, housed in one of the few Georgian buildings left in the city, once the home of a tobacco lord, William Cunninghame. It features a 30-ft-high barrel-vaulted roof, monolithic pillars and magnificent coffered ceiling. The

Templeton's grand building of 1889, modelled on the Doge's Palace in Venice

library places special emphasis on the pictorial arts and music.

Off Buchanan Street is the £20 million Princes Square shopping precinct, and off Ingram Street is the Old Sheriff Court, a Grecian Doric justiciary building designed by William Stark and erected in 1814, and which served as the City Chambers until 1844. Jocelyn Square, formerly 'Jail Square', was the site of public hangings, the last of which was in 1865. Hutchesons' Hall on Ingram Street is a Visitor Centre. Buchanan Street has been attractively landscaped and pedestrianized and, with Sauchiehall Street, carries some of Glasgow's more upmarket shops. At the northern end is the politically renamed Nelson Mandela Square, formerly St George's Place, where there is the Stock Exchange, entirely rebuilt in 1971 within the existing walls which are an exceptional example of Venetian Gothic architecture dating from 1877. St George's Tron Church on Buchanan Street, dating from 1807, was designed by William Stark and has a Wren-inspired tower.

The University of Strathclyde buildings are

Above: Glasgow School of Art
Right: The Library, Glasgow School of Art

situated on George Street. This modern, technological university evolved from an institute founded in 1796. At the corner of Buchanan Street and Sauchiehall Street is the site of the £24 million concert hall built as a base for the Scottish National Orchestra. Scottish Opera, also Glasgow-based, already has a home at the Theatre Royal in Hope Street. The SNO, Scottish Opera and Scottish Ballet, which has its headquarters in West Princes Street, have all won adulatory acclaim with national and international tours.

The name of Charles Rennie Mackintosh, architect and designer extraordinary, is intimately linked with Glasgow, but sadly, although he had a few impressive patrons, he was not taken entirely seriously by his own generation when he set out to create a Scottish architectural style encompassing all aspects of design. Born in 1868, he joined the firm of Honeyman and Keppie as a draughtsman. In 1890 he won the 'Greek' Thomson scholarship which took him to France and Italy. During the 1890s he also became associated with Herbert McNair and the sisters Frances and Margaret Macdonald, the latter becoming his wife. As 'the Four' they exhibited graphic and craft work in the then innovative Art Nouveau style. At the age of twenty-eight, no doubt through the influence of Fra Newberry, director of the Glasgow School of Art, Mackintosh won the limited competition to design their new premises. This building, in Renfrew Street, is undoubtedly his master-

piece and was built in two sections – the east half in 1897, the west half in 1907. Each facade of this exceptional building reflects a totally different facet of the architect's imagination.

Another Mackintosh gem is Miss Cranston's Willow Tea Room in Sauchiehall Street. Stuart and Kate Cranston, members of a family who owned a hotel in George Square, commissioned Mackintosh and his wife to design chairs, interior decor, cutlery and, in the case of the Willow Tea Room, inspired by Sauchiehaugh, the 'willow meadow' upon which Sauchiehall Street was built, the entire building. The upper floor still operates as an eating house, but the remainder of the building is a furniture and jewellery shop.

Disenchanted with his lack of recognition, Mackintosh retired to live in France where he took up painting in watercolours. He died in 1928.

Also in Renfrew Street is the Royal Scottish Academy of Music and Drama, housed in new premises opened by the Queen Mother in 1988.

The M8 motorway skirts the city centre, closing it off from outer Glasgow to the north and sweeping on to the Kingston Bridge over the Clyde. From Renfrew Street and Cowcaddens, streets drop down towards the River Clyde in parallels, almost American in style, although they were here long before America planned her major cities. And Glasgow has its own underground railway system, in appearance almost toy-town, running on a 2-circle system and servicing central points. Scottish Television has its headquarters at Cowcaddens, and in nearby Buccleuch Street the National Trust for Scotland has refurbished a tenement house, a classic reminder of the old Glasgow way of life.

On hot sunny days there is a holiday atmosphere about Sauchiehall Street where shoppers, office workers and idlers come to promenade, to see and be seen. Glasgow's citizens take a great deal of trouble over their appearance and the latest fashions and hairstyles are always on parade. Sauchiehall Street is lined with interesting shops, restaurants and stores. The McLellan Gallery is an important centre for art exhibitions, displays of sculpture and furniture, and for craft fairs. The Regimental Museum of the Royal Highland Fusiliers has uniforms, pictures, medals and mementos relating to the regiment's three hundred years of history. Here too is the Third Eye Centre, a multi-purpose arts centre with a packed programme of events including drama, dance, music, readings, talks, films and festivals. There is a spacious gallery, a studio theatre and an excellent bookshop.

Each May, Glasgow hosts MayFest, an international celebration of music and the arts. Traditionally, July is the month when Glasgow folk take their holidays and go 'doon the Watter' to Clyde coastal resorts.

Down on the north bank of the Clyde there is an attractive walkway beside the Broomielaw. The old clipper ship moored at Victoria Bridge is the SV *Carrick*, formerly the *City of Adelaide*, built in Sunderland in 1864. She now serves as the headquarters of the RNVR Club. On Clyde Street is St Andrew's Roman Catholic Cathedral, an example of Gothic architecture with a 'college chapel' front of 1816 and plaster-vaulted interior. At Bridgegate four square towers of decreasing dimensions are all that remains of the Merchants House of 1659. A ship in full sail is mirrored on top of the present Merchants House in West George Street.

From Clyde Street, go along the Broomielaw, under the Kingston Bridge to the west, and you will find the modern Scottish Exhibition and Conference Centre which was opened by HM the Queen in 1984.

Glasgow to the west

Much rebuilding has taken place around Charing Cross, where the motorway splits Sauchiehall Street. Residential rather than commercial accommodation has been encouraged in a bid to attract home owners back into the city centre. The Mitchell Library in North Street is the headquarters of Glasgow's forty-three libraries. Founded in 1874, it contains more than one million volumes with particular emphasis on Robert Burns, Scottish poetry and music. The Glasgow collection details the history of the city and includes the works of Glasgow authors. Recently extended, this is now the largest public reference library in Europe. Behind, entered from Granville Street, is the Mitchell Theatre, venue for meetings, lectures and amateur drama productions.

The western half of Sauchiehall Street leads to Kelvingrove Park, on the banks of the River Kelvin. The Art Gallery and Museum here boasts of having the finest civic collection of British and European paintings, including some superb impressionist paintings. There are also displays of natural history, archaeology, history and ethnography; and collections of silver, pottery, porcelain and arms and armour. The building, designed by Sir J. W. Simpson and Milner Allen, was opened in 1902; the back door curiously opens on to the main road, the entrance being behind the building and facing up to Glasgow University across the park. Glasgow comedians such as Stanley Baxter and Jimmy Logan have fond memories of the entertainers who performed here in the open air off Kelvin Way every Saturday in the summer months. In the park is a fine statue of Thomas Carlyle, and it was here that Glasgow held the first of its International Exhibitions in the summer of 1888. At the top of the park is an equestrian statue featuring Field-Marshal Earl Roberts.

Opposite the Art Gallery and Museum is Kelvin Hall, formerly Glasgow's exhibition centre, transformed in 1988 into an international sports arena and a Museum of Transport. Facilities in the sports arena include tennis, badminton, five-a-side football, weightlifting, athletics, table tennis, archery and hockey. The Museum of Transport includes a reproduction

of a typical Glasgow street in 1938. Other features are a display of ship models and a walk-in motor car showroom with cars from the 1930s up to modern times. There are Glasgow trams and buses, Scottish-built motor cars, fire engines, horse-drawn vehicles, commercial vehicles, cycles and motor cycles, railway locomotives and a Glasgow subway station.

The University of Glasgow, which appropriately stands on University Avenue, was founded in 1451 when Bishop Turnbull obtained papal authority. The University stood in the High Street for four hundred years until it was moved to its present imposing site on Gilmorehill in 1870; the main building here was designed by Sir George Gilbert Scott. Bute Hall was added in 1882, and the University continued to grow.

A former student, William Hunter, who died in 1783, bequeathed fine collections of early printed books, manuscripts, coins, archaeological specimens and paintings to the University. They are housed in the Hunterian Art Gallery along with important paintings by James McNeill Whistler and Scottish paintings of the 19th and 20th centuries. Changing displays from the collection of 15,000 prints, the largest holding in Scotland, are mounted in the print

Museum of Transport, Kelvin Hall

gallery. A great attraction is the Mackintosh House, a replica of the demolished home of Charles Rennie Mackintosh with the four principal interiors reconstructed. This forms part of the gallery, and changing displays from the extensive Mackintosh drawings collection are shown in the additional Mackintosh House Gallery.

Roads to the west lead to Dumbarton, with the Erskine Bridge crossing the River Clyde, PAISLEY, Barrhead and CLYDEBANK, severely bombed during the war and where, in the great John Brown's shipyard, the *Queen Mary*, *Lusitania*, *Queen Elizabeth* and *QE2* were built. The Great Western Road travels from St George's Cross past fine terraces and crescents, over the sturdy Kelvin Bridge. At Queen Margaret's Drive, BBC Scotland has its headquarters. Opposite are the Botanic Gardens, 42 acres of floral displays with pleasant walkways. The Kibble Palace, originally erected by the engineer John Kibble at his Clyde Coast home, was given by him to Glasgow and re-erected in the Botanic Gardens in 1873. It contains tropical vegetation interspersed with white marble statues by Gascombe John, Hamo Thornycroft and others.

Opposite: The Kibble Palace (see p. 103)

Further along Great Western Road is Kelvin Court, erected in 1936. It was to a flat in this building belonging to Lord Bilsland that the fugitive Rudolf Hess, Hitler's deputy, was taken after his aircraft had crash-landed at Eaglesham. South off Great Western Road are the districts of Hillhead, Dowanhill, Hyndland, Partick, Broomhill and Jordanhill. The comedian Billy Connolly was born and grew up in Hyndland Street in Partick, and the legendary Jack Buchanan had a house towards the top of the hill. The Scottish Film Archive, the repository for Scottish Film Records, and the Scottish Central Film and Video Library are based at Victoria Crescent in Dowanhill. At Victoria Park is the Fossil Grove discovered in 1887, stumps of extinct trees that grew 330 million years ago.

Over the river – Glasgow to the south

The Clyde Tunnel, passing under the River Clyde between Whiteinch and Linthouse, was a great feat of engineering. Opened by the Queen in 1963, it consists of twin tunnels and lies 3 miles downstream from Glasgow Bridge. The most significant recent development was the landscaping of the 120-acre site of Prince's Docks for the Garden Festival in 1988. The Bell's Bridge is the first new footbridge to span the river for a hundred years or so, and pivots to allow the passage of shipping. One third of the Garden Festival site has been retained as open space and for development as a riverside science park.

Over Victoria Bridge is the area which probably suffered most from the inner-city clearances of the 1950s, the Gorbals. Curiously, one spectacular survivor remains in Gorbals Street – the Citizen's Theatre, Glasgow's innovative repertory theatre which presents some of the finest and most intriguing drama productions in the country. Formerly the Royal Princess's Theatre, it was built by Campbell Douglas in 1878. The repertoire ranges from obsessive German drama to Noël Coward; although the area is still run-down and derelict, the seats are rarely empty.

In Florence Street a plaque commemorates Benny Lynch, the Gorbals boy who became a world, European and flyweight boxing champion. Gorbals Street runs into Victoria Road which leads to Queen's Park, named after Mary Queen of Scots and famed for fine floral displays. Parallel is Pollokshaws Road which splits at Shawlands into Kilmarnock Road running off to the south-west towards Newlands, crossing the Macquisten Bridge built by the engineer Peter Macquisten in 1832 over the White Cart Water. Pollok Country Park covers 361 acres of parkland and gardens, formerly the grounds of Pollok House, the family home of the Maxwells which was presented to Glasgow by Mrs Anne Maxwell Macdonald in 1966. Pollok House contains a fine collection of Spanish paintings and other European masters, furniture from 1750 to 1820 and displays of silver, ceramics and glass. It was built by William Adam in the 18th century and is a particularly graceful example of Georgian architecture. In the grounds are the St Mungo herd of Highland cattle, the Old Stables Courtyard and Sawmill, the Demonstration Garden. There is also a Countryside Ranger Service.

On his death in 1944 a Clyde shipowner, Sir William Burrell, who in fact had lived at Hutton Castle, west of Berwick-upon-Tweed, presented

Stained glass in the Burrell Collection

to the city of Glasgow his magnificent collection of 8000 items ranging from treasures of the ancient world and oriental art to paintings. He made certain specifications as to how they should be housed, and the award-winning gallery, designed by a group of architects, but notably Barry Gasson, is to be seen in Pollok Country Park. It was opened by the Queen in October 1983 and attracts visitors from all corners of the world.

Seventeenth-century Haggs Castle on St Andrew's drive is a museum designed for children. It features a reconstructed kitchen, a Victorian nursery and an 18th-century cottage. Further south lie BARRHEAD, Nitshill, Thornliebank, Cathcart and Giffnock; the park at Rouken Glen is considered by many to be Glasgow's finest, in a city with over seventy parks.

Glasgow to the east

On the eastern edge of Glasgow at Calderpark is the zoo. Here is a city safari of lions, polar bears, leopards, monkeys, camels, deer, elephants, wallabies and porcupines.

Districts to the east encompass Dennistoun, Springboig, Cambuslang and Uddingston. Cambuslang was formerly a cluster of 18th-century villages with a colony of handloom weavers. In 1742 the 'Cambuslang Wark', a great outdoor religious festival, took place here. There is a wooded public park and a viewpoint over Cathkin Braes. Rutherglen was given a charter in the 12th century by King David I, and Rutherglen Castle was burnt by the Regent Murray for supporting Mary Queen of Scots after the Battle of Langside in 1568. Nowadays, Rutherglen is noted for manufacturing chemicals and for its paper mills. The mercat cross is modern, but the Kirk Port dates from the 17th century, and the early 16th-century steeple contains a Dutch bell of 1635. In King Street is the Rutherglen Museum of Local History which has continually changing displays of material related to the town. Castle Milk, lying 1½ miles south, incorporates a 16th-century tower. It is said that Mary Queen of Scots spent the night here before the Battle of Langside, but it is more likely that she stayed at Cathcart Castle, the ruins of which can be seen 2 miles north of Clarkston, on the White Cart River.

Glasgow to the north

Springburn, Maryhill, Bearsden and Bishopbriggs lie to the north of the city. In Ayr Street

at Springburn is a museum showing the social history of the place – it was once the largest locomotive-manufacturing centre in Europe. In Garscube Road, which runs into Maryhill, the Queen's Cross Church, built in 1897 in Art Nouveau Gothic style, has been transformed by enthusiasts into the headquarters of the Charles Rennie Mackintosh Society. It houses an information centre, reference library and book stall.

The Portland Vase, superbly displayed in the Burrell Collection

Bearsden, pleasantly situated at the foot of the Campsie Fells, is one of Glasgow's most fashionable and consequently most affluent suburbs. Bishopbriggs, situated near the Forth and Clyde Canal, lies on the Roman Antonine Wall. Huntershill House in Crowhill Road, once the home of the Muir family, now contains the Thomas Muir Museum. It serves as a recreational centre and has a room devoted to the life and work of Thomas Muir, the radical reformer.

Cruises for the disabled on the Forth and Clyde Canal are run by the Seagull Trust.

Glasgow has always embraced the spirit of international friendship; it is twinned with Rostov-on-Don in the USSR, Nuremberg in West Germany, Turin in Italy and Dalian in China.

Museums and Galleries in Glasgow

JOHN JULIUS NORWICH

Let us make no bones about it: Glasgow has always been unfortunate in its public image. Outside Scotland, and particularly among ignorant Sassenachs like myself, Edinburgh tends to steal the thunder. It is the romantic old Scottish capital; it is undeniably beautiful; it annually explodes into a glorious and increasingly multi-faceted Festival, about which John Drummond writes with his usual eloquence elsewhere in this book; it boasts, in Princes Street, one of the grandest thoroughfares in all Britain – and, half-way down that thoroughfare, the National Gallery of Scotland, perhaps the most satisfying gallery of its size in the world. Glasgow, by contrast – the second city in the British Empire, as it always used to be called – is primarily associated in the southern mind with business and industry, grime and smoke, and with a raucous, raffish spirit more accurately reflected by Sir Harry Lauder than Sir Walter Scott.

Not for the first time the southern mind has got it wrong. Glasgow is indeed a thriving industrial city, but that is only the beginning. It is also far older and more venerable than most people realize. Its University was founded by Pope Nicholas V in 1451, which makes it the fourth oldest in Britain, after Oxford, Cambridge and St Andrews; and where culture is concerned – particularly in the visual arts – it can hold its own with Edinburgh (which had no university till 1583) any day of the week. It possesses, first of all, no fewer than three superb public collections, of which there will be more to say in a moment. But the cultural awareness of a community cannot be measured exclusively by the number and quality of the works of art that it contains; if it could, a handful of generous benefactors could turn any city overnight into an ancient Athens. What gives Glasgow its unique *cachet* is its own artistic record. If, towards the end of the last century, you wanted to buy Impressionist paintings without crossing the Channel, it was here, rather than to London or Edinburgh, that you had to come, to seek out not one but several distinguished and highly knowledgeable dealers. The greatest of them all was Alexander Reid; a personal friend of many of the Impressionists, he had actually shared a Paris apartment with Van Gogh, whose haunting portrait of him hangs in Glasgow Art Gallery and Museum in Kelvingrove Park. And that is another thing we English tend to forget: that since the days of Mary Queen of Scots, and perhaps even before, it has been the French rather than we ourselves who have exerted the dominant influence in Scottish cultural life.

The turn of the century also saw the heyday of what was known as the Glasgow Style; and the Glasgow Style was very important indeed. Its leading spirit was the astonishing Charles Rennie Mackintosh; but Mackintosh was by no means an isolated phenomenon. His wife Margaret Macdonald, their colleagues and followers – Margaret's sister Frances, George Walton, E. A. Taylor, Jessie King and perhaps a dozen others, many of them from the Glasgow School of Art, whose building was designed by Mackintosh and is still flourishing today – all made their contribution, and together earned for their city a place in the world of Art Nouveau comparable with Paris and Brussels, Barcelona and Prague.

A whole group of Glasgow Style interiors –

Chinese Tea Room (Glasgow Art Gallery and Museum)

including the almost alarmingly blue 'Chinese Tea Room' from the Ingram Street branch of Miss Cranston's chain of tea rooms that was once a feature of the city – can also be seen at Kelvingrove, rubbing shoulders with 'Archaeology' and 'Arms and Armour' (in which, incidentally, do not miss the Gothic Milanese field armour). Indeed, one of the attractions of this gargantuan building (opened by Princess Louise as part of the Great Exhibition of 1901) is the extraordinary variety, as well as the quality, of its contents. There are, as might be expected, splendid sections devoted to geology and natural history (including a fascinating group of items made from endangered species and confiscated by the Customs and Excise); more surprising are the specialized collections, reminders of the incorrigible Scottish *penchant* for far-flung travel, such as the Eskimo and Red Indian artefacts donated by Mrs Wilkie, sister-in-law of the Bishop of Alaska, or the three hundred-odd Cypriot antiquities amassed by Sir Robert Hamilton Lang, sometime HM consul and manager of the Imperial Ottoman Bank in Nicosia. Of the magnificent Ancient Egyptian Collection, a large part came to Glasgow through the agency of Sir Flinders Petrie, the leading British Egyptologist for well over thirty years before the First World War – though the most massive donation of all, a huge sarcophagus of reddish granite, was a gift of the Trustees of Hamilton Estates. The 10th Duke of Hamilton had originally acquired two; the other he decided to be buried in himself.

So much for the ground floor; upstairs, the gallery is devoted to the decorative arts and to its dazzling collection of paintings. Among the former, the most irresistible item is the Seton Murray Thomson Collection of carved and sculptured horses – 449 of them in over thirty different materials, including rock crystal and malachite, *papier-mâché*, mother-of-pearl and even celluloid, coming from every corner of the globe and dating from the 15th century BC to relatively modern times. Mr Thomson had a single criterion: that each piece should be a good representation of a horse. No other museum in the kingdom boasts anything comparable – which makes it all the sadder that the collection is not always on show.

And so to the paintings. Thanks, perhaps, to those same old Scottish links with France, the real pride of Glasgow is its French Collection. Apart from one wondrous Renaissance picture of a saint with a donor attributed to the Master of Moulins, and three or four landscapes by Gaspard Dughet or his followers, nearly all are of the 19th and 20th centuries: Courbet and Corot (his distinctly unsettling portrait of Mlle de Foudras); Renoir and Matisse and Monet (a radiant view of Ventimiglia); Seurat and Signac and Sisley; Gauguin and Vuillard; Braque, Derain (a painting of the Thames at Blackfriars) and Picasso. Among the Italians, one remembers especially a Bellini Madonna and Child, a Botticelli Annunciation and, of course, the two famous attributions to Giorgione, the *Portrait of a Man* and *The Adulteress Brought before Christ* which once belonged to Queen Christina of Sweden. The Dutch are majestically represented by Rembrandt's *Man in Armour* and *Carcass of an Ox*, stalwart support being given by a distinguished if predictable collection of landscapes, still-lifes and interiors.

Among the British pictures, the unquestioned *pièces de résistance* are Turner's *Modern Italy* and Whistler's celebrated portrait of Carlyle, looking almost unbearably sad and vulnerable; apart from these – particularly if time is short – the greatest interest is inevitably provided by the Scottish painters: Raeburn's strangely moving double portrait of Mr and Mrs Robert Campbell of Kailzie, landscapes by Norie and Nasmyth and an enchanting picture by John Knox celebrating *The First Steamboat on the Clyde, c. 1820*. Among

Raeburn's portrait of Mr and Mrs Robert Campbell of Kailzie (Glasgow Art Gallery and Museum)

Sandstone portal dating from 16th century which gives access from the Courtyard into the North Gallery of the Burrell Collection. It comes from Hornby Castle in Yorkshire and the name 'Conyers' on the arch refers to William Lord Conyers (1468–1524) who refurbished the 14th-century castle at great cost. The elaborate heraldic display is typical of many such sumptuous entrances of the Early Tudor period.

the High Victorians, it is impossible not to stop before David Wilkie's *The Cottar's Saturday Night* or Robert Herdman's dramatic *Execution of Mary, Queen of Scots*; while *The Last of the Clan* by Thomas Faed – a poignant reminder of the enforced emigration after the Highland Clearances – also compels attention.

Towards the end of the century came Scotland's answer to the Barbizon School: 'the Glasgow Boys', led by James Guthrie, John Lavery, George Henry and James Paterson. These were followed by the Colourists – Samuel Peploe, Francis Cadell, John Fergusson and Leslie Hunter – all four of them, like the Boys, French-inspired and so good that one is astonished that they are not better known outside Scotland. Occasionally, to be sure, the flavour of *outre-Manche* becomes a little overpowering: Hunter's *Old Mill, Fifeshire* has perhaps a little too much of Cézanne, while among the painters of the present century there is a William Gillies that could easily be a Braque and a still-life by Anne Redpath barely distinguishable from a Matisse. But in nearly all of them we find an energy and exuberance that lifts the spirit and reminds us, again and again, what an exciting place for an artist Glasgow must have been – and, I suspect, still is today.

More works of these specifically Scottish schools of painting can be seen in the Hunterian Museum of Glasgow University. It takes its name from William Hunter, the famous surgeon and anatomist whose bequest of 1783 still forms the nucleus of its collection of Old Masters: they include a Rembrandt sketch for the *Entombment of Christ* and a magnificent landscape by Philips Koninck, a pair of fine animal pictures by Stubbs and three exquisite Chardins. The dominant presence in the Hunterian galleries, however, is a surprising one: that of James McNeill Whistler. Largely ignored in England, he had always been revered north of the border, especially by the Glasgow Boys, who had been instrumental in getting him an honorary degree in 1903, just a few months before he died; and between 1935 and her own death in 1958 his sister-in-law and heir, Miss Rosalind Birnie Philip, gradually made over to the University an enormous collection of paintings and pastels, drawings and prints, to say nothing of furniture and oriental ceramics from Whistler's house and studio.

Elsewhere in the Hunterian, the style changes; and once again, but far more dramatically than at Kelvingrove, we enter the strange, austere world of Charles Rennie Mackintosh. Indeed, the experience this time is one of total immersion, for we have only to ascend a short flight of stairs to find ourselves in Mackintosh's own house, 78 Southpark Avenue, transported and reconstructed in its present setting – this part of the new Hunterian building having been given the same system of fenestration, and even a similar south and east orientation, as the original dwelling. The University points out that, although the Mackintoshes sold the house and its contents as early as 1919, the earliest surviving photographs date only from 1933 and that the reconstruction cannot therefore be guaranteed as accurate in every detail; one can only say that the work could not conceivably have been done with more sensitivity and skill. Whether we should ever choose such decorative schemes for ourselves is, to say the least, open to question; what is certain is the visionary genius of Mackintosh, and the sheer power of his creative imagination.

Most of the furnishings and contents of this extraordinary house were presented to the University by the sons of William Davidson, who had bought it from the Mackintoshes after the First World War; the Hunterian has been fortunate indeed in its benefactors. If, however, there is one man to whom the citizens of Glasgow should be grateful above all others, that man is the late Sir William Burrell, for it is doubtful whether any other municipality, in all history, has ever received so munificent a gift as that which, in 1944, he and his wife conferred upon his native city. He was a born collector. His first picture was bought in 1877 when he was sixteen – his father, we are told, was furious that he had not spent the money on a cricket bat – while his last major purchase was made at the age of ninety-six: eighty years' continuous collecting, during which time he amassed a collection of some eight thousand objects, an average of two acquisitions a week. His range was breathtaking: it embraced Sumerian and Assyrian statues, reliefs from Ancient Egypt, Greek amphorae, Chinese jades and bronzes, Japanese prints, Persian tiles, Turkish carpets, French and German tapestries, arms and armour, works in gold, silver and glass, early furniture, and pictures ranging from those by Memling, Bellini and Cranach to the French Impressionists and his beloved compatriot Joseph Crawhall.

Never did he pay more than £14,500 for a single item – and that only once, for his Frans Hals portrait; and only very, very rarely was he sold a pup.

His greatest passion of all was for the church art of medieval Europe; in this field in particular, the Burrell Collection is of world class. Perhaps the most spectacular items are the several monumental portals and arches, bought from the William Randolph Hearst collection in 1953–4 (when Burrell was well into his nineties) and forming an integral part of the museum's structure. Every bit as beautiful, however, are the various representations of the Madonna and Child, carved in wood or limestone, ivory or alabaster, the chalices, reliquaries and *châsses*, and the radiantly beautiful stained glass – more than six hundred panels of it, dating from the 12th to the 17th centuries.

But stained glass, even more than most other works of art, demands perfect presentation if it is to make its proper impact, and not the least of the strengths of the Burrell Collection is the superb building in which it is housed. It was opened as recently as 1983, nearly forty years after the original gift, which included £450,000 for its construction; but there were several difficulties along the way, the principal one being Sir William's insistence that it should be sited within 4 miles of Killearn in Stirlingshire and – since he was rightly concerned at the appalling levels of air pollution then prevailing – not less than 16 from the Royal Exchange in Glasgow. This problem was not solved until 1967, when Mrs Anne Maxwell Macdonald presented Pollok House and its surrounding park to the City Corporation. The new site thus offered was only some 4 miles from the centre of Glasgow and thus well within the forbidden zone; but in the intervening quarter-century the air had grown incomparably cleaner and the Burrell Trustees were easily persuaded to waive Sir William's former conditions. The result was the *tour de force* by Barry Gasson that we see today: a building set not in the middle of the surrounding meadow but at its edge, allowing the neighbouring trees to dapple and diffuse the light, and somehow contriving – with the occasional vista through a long enfilade of rooms – to link the real woodland with the fabulous forests of the tapestries and even with the stained glass beyond. Our one regret must be that Sir William Burrell never saw his collection in its permanent home; but we can at least be grateful that, at long last, it has been given a building worthy of it.

When you arrive in Pollok Park, you should visit the Burrell Collection first; you will enjoy it far more if you are feeling fresh and ready for anything – and besides, it may take you longer than you think. But then, on leaving, it is well worth making the short journey up to Pollok House, a fine, well-furnished stone mansion of the mid-18th century with good interior plasterwork, in which the Stirling Maxwell family amassed, over the years, a remarkable collection of paintings. Of these a surprising number are Spanish; among them are two portraits by El Greco, two Murillos and two Goyas. The English school includes Hogarth and Blake; the latter's exuberant portrayal of all the Canterbury Pilgrims (Chaucer included) setting out from the Tabard Inn proves, in a curious way, to be the most memorable of the lot.

Among the city's other attractions, you may visit a venerable stone building just opposite the Cathedral known enigmatically as Provand's Lordship, which dates from 1471 and claims to be the oldest house in Glasgow. If you have young offspring with you, you may also like to take them to Haggs Castle, a museum of history designed especially for children. Neither of these, however, is essential. What you should not miss is the People's Palace, a museum exclusively devoted to the history of Glasgow and its inhabitants from its foundation in 1175 to the present day. It includes, among many other delights, a splendid recreation of an 18th-century printing press and some fascinating material concerning the tobacco trade, on which much of the city's early prosperity was based. More recent times are represented by trades union banners, various items relating to the suffragette movement, examples of local metal casting, tiles and stained glass, and some glorious memorabilia of the Victorian and Edwardian music hall.

The People's Palace makes the perfect culmination of any cultural tour of Glasgow. Alone among the museums and galleries of the city, it is Glaswegian through and through, and proud of it. Besides, after we have feasted our eyes and refreshed our spirit with the international beauties of Kelvingrove, the Hunterian and the Burrell, it is no bad thing to steep ourselves in the atmosphere of the place itself – to try to understand its character, its attitude, what makes it tick. Inevitably, we shall fail: it takes more than a casual visit of a day or two to get to the heart of this most individual – even idiosyncratic – of cities. But we shall learn more about Glasgow from the People's Palace than from most places; and if, when its doors close, we decide to continue our education in the nearby pub, we shall quite probably learn a good deal more. In any case, we shall have richly deserved it.

Glenluce, *Dumfries and Galloway* (5/C5)
Around 4000 BC, the first inhabitants of Scotland settled on the shores of Luce Bay. At the head of the bay and close to where the Water of Luce flows into the sea, the present village is set on the eastern slope of the glen. There is a motor museum on the edge of the town. The ruins of the Cistercian Glenluce Abbey, founded in 1190 by Roland, Lord of Galloway, can be seen on the wooded eastern banks of the river north of the village. King James IV and Mary Queen of Scots both called in here on pilgrimages to WHITHORN. In 1590, stones from the abbey were used by Thomas Hay, son of the last abbot, to build nearby Castle of the Park. To the north-east are the ruins of Carscreugh Castle, once owned by the Dalrymples of Stair, whose daughter Janet was the inspiration for Sir Walter Scott's Lucy Ashton in *The Bride of Lammermoor*.

Five miles up the Water of Luce is **New Luce** where, in the 17th century, the minister Alexander 'Prophet' Peden, a leading figure in Covenanting times, terminated his ministry by closing his pulpit and setting off on to the moors, never to return.

The cloisters, Glenluce Abbey

Gordon (3/E4) *see* Kelso

Gorebridge, *Lothian* (3/B2)
Two local pits provided work for this mining community until they were closed in 1962. For many years gunpowder was manufactured at Stobs Mill and it is said that gunpowder from here helped to sink the French fleet at Trafalgar. A school existed in Gorebridge as early as 1618 and a subscription library was founded in 1818 with some six hundred volumes. In 1980 a leisure centre was opened and there is a traditional open-air market held in the town every Friday.

Three miles east of Gorebridge stands Crichton Castle, a late 14th-century tower with wings added in the 15th century. It was once the home of Sir William Crichton, Chancellor to King James II. In 1581 it was owned by the Earl of Bothwell, who built on an Italianate wing. A mile north of here is the 15th-century Collegiate Church which in 1641 was decreed by Act of Parliament to be the church of the parish.

Situated to the south-east of Gorebridge is Borthwick, a 15th-century tower house, best known as the castle to which Mary Queen of Scots and the Earl of Bothwell fled after their wedding. When the castle was surrounded by the rebel Scottish nobles, the Queen escaped disguised as a page boy. Cromwell attacked Borthwick Castle with cannon in 1650 and the public records of Scotland were brought here for safe keeping during the Second World War. The property is still owned by the Borthwick family and, having been restored at the turn of the century, is leased out for small conferences and special occasions.

Temple, 2½ miles to the south-west of Gorebridge, takes its name from the land which once belonged to the Knights Templar of Jerusalem, whose presence in the area can be traced back to the 12th century. Near Pathhead is Vogrie Estate Country Park, which belongs to the district council and attracts thousands of visitors. There is a children's adventure playground and a walled garden. Residential accommodation is available for organized groups in the stables; ranger-guided walks take place regularly throughout the year.

Two miles west of Gorebridge is the attractive hamlet of **Carrington**, judged the best-kept village in Britain in 1978. Cottages retain their original pantiled roofs, and the parish church, which was built in 1711, features pointed latticed windows and sundials on the corners. A

Above: The courtyard, Crichton Castle
Preceding pages: Crichton Castle from below

previous 14th-century structure belonged to the Abbey of Scone.

Gourock, *Strathclyde* (1/B1)
Situated on the Firth of Clyde looking over to Kilcreggan and Loch Long, Gourock is a holiday resort and yachting centre. Clyde pleasure steamers sail from the pier through the Kyles of Bute. The town has been famous for herring curing since the 17th century.

King James IV sailed from Gourock to the Hebrides in 1494, but there are no remains left of Gourock Castle where he stayed, or the castle which replaced it in the 18th century. Near to where it stood on Tower Hill, however, is Granny Kempock's Stone, 6 ft high and believed to be of mystical prehistoric origin. In 1622 a group of witches were burnt at Gourock including one Mary Lamont, a teenage girl, who confessed

to having wanted to throw Granny Kempock's Stone into the sea to cause shipwrecks.

Greenlaw, *Borders* (4/A5)
On the edge of the Lammermuirs and situated on the Blackadder Water, the town dates from the 17th century and for over one hundred and fifty years was the market town of Berwickshire until DUNS took over. In 1696 Sir Patrick Hume of Polwarth erected a mercat cross, but when the County Buildings, now swimming baths, were built, this was discarded only to be rediscovered in 1881 and re-erected. Ruined Hume Castle, which dates from the 13th century, was the original seat of the Home family. It was stormed by Somerset in 1547, by Sussex in 1596 and by Cromwell in 1650, so it certainly can be said to have served its country.

Three miles from Greenlaw is the village of **Polwarth** with its attractive green. Marchmont House was built in the mid-18th century by John and Robert Adam from designs drawn up by their father, William. The mansion was owned this century by the McEwen brewing family, but it is now the property of the Sue Ryder Foundation.

Greenock, *Strathclyde* (1/B1)
On the south side of the Clyde Estuary, Greenock became an important ship-building and industrial town in the 18th and 19th centuries. A charter allowing it to trade overseas was granted in 1681 and a prosperous herring trade developed, hence the town motto: 'Let herring swim that trade maintain'. Sadly, the herring trade went into decline. In 1760 the first square-rigger was launched and by 1900 the harbour area covered almost 200 acres.

James Watt, the inventor of the steam engine, was born in Greenock in 1736. The McLean Museum and Art Gallery run by Inverclyde District Council houses items relating to his career, as well as an art collection and natural history and shipping exhibits. The tombstone of Robert Burns' 'Highland Mary', who died in 1789, can be seen in the local churchyard. The world's first Burns Club was instituted in Greenock in 1802. The imposing 1818 Customs House on the sea front is of particular architectural interest.

Greenock experienced both the peaks and troughs of the industrial revolution. In the Second World War it was badly damaged by German bombs. Much of the area has that run-down look only too apparent in places where old skills have been surpassed by more modern, streamlined techniques elsewhere. Nevertheless, Inverclyde is a buoyant area and there is much to see. Apart from the many parks in the district, there is the Cornalees Centre where visitors can explore the nature trail and the historic aqueduct which once supplied Greenock with water. On Lyle Hill stands the Free French Memorial in memory of French sailors who lost their lives in the Battle of the Atlantic. As with all Clyde locations, yachting is a major pre-occupation.

Port Glasgow, once called Newark, was founded in 1668 to be a harbour for Glasgow before the Clyde was deepened towards the end of the 18th century. It became a ship-building centre, and on display is a fine replica of the *Comet*, the first commercial steamship in Europe, built here by James Wood in 1812. Newark Castle, built by the Maxwell family in the 15th and 16th centuries, was given to the nation by Sir Hugh Shaw Stewart in 1909.

Near Langbank is Finlaystone House, home of the chief of Clan Macmillan. Robert Burns was a visitor here, and a tree here is said to have been planted by John Knox. Mrs Macmillan has amassed a splendid collection of dolls from many countries and has arranged exhibitions of Celtic art and Victoriana. The country estate provides woodland walks, nursery and formal gardens, adventure playgrounds and pony trekking.

Gretna Green, *Dumfries and Galloway* (6/G5)

Until 1940, runaway couples could be married here under Scottish law by a single declaration before witnesses. Elopers can still, however, take advantage of Scots law allowing marriage at the age of sixteen without parental consent. Two of the original blacksmiths' shops can be visited and 'fun' weddings are held in their anvil marriage rooms.

Beside Gretna Green Kirk is 'Prince Charlie's Cottage' where the Young Pretender is said to have passed a night on his return from England in 1745. Nearby the Battle of Solway Moss took place in 1542 on English soil. On hearing the news of his army's defeat, King James V, staying at LOCHMABEN Castle, experienced a complete nervous and physical collapse and died shortly afterwards. Moments before his end, he heard of the birth of his daughter, Mary Queen of Scots.

Gullane, *Lothian* (4/C1)

A famous golfing village with three of its own eighteen-hole courses adjoining the Luffness Course to the south; to the east is the championship course of Muirfield, regularly home to the British Open. A Heritage of Golf Exhibition can be visited on West Links Road; it tells the story of golf from its arrival in Scotland from Holland in the 15th century. Gullane Hill rises 200 ft and the beaches here are very popular with bathers in the summer, especially since the local authority has taken steps to control the sand spread and has restored the grassy dunes. There are many fine mansions at Gullane, which continues to serve as a commuter town for EDINBURGH.

Haddington, *Lothian* (3/D1)

A magnificently restored town which was created a royal burgh in the 12th century by King David I. Haddington was the birthplace of King Alexander II and in the centuries to follow lay directly on the path taken by invading English armies, the consequence being that it was destroyed several times. The reformer John Knox was educated at the local school in Haddington, and the great Victorian exponent of 'self-help', Samuel Smiles, was born here in 1812.

Haddington was one of the first towns to take the overspill from GLASGOW in the 1950s and the local community has played an important role in protecting the town from the ravages wrought by planners in that decade. Haddington is therefore rich in houses of historic and architectural interest, superbly restored. In the 1970s a remarkable initiative was taken by the Lamp of the Lothian Collegiate Trust, led by Elizabeth, Duchess of Hamilton. The ancient red sandstone Parish Church of St Mary has been beautifully restored. This 'Lamp of the Lothians' lay half in ruins after the Siege of Haddington in 1547 when King Henry VIII of England's army came forth to force marriage upon the infant Mary Queen of Scots. A great dividing wall was then built to cut off the ruined half from the nave which thereafter provided the Church of Scotland with its parish church for the next four centuries or so. In the 17th century a side chapel was built to the north of the choir to house the Renaissance tombs of the Maitland Duke and Earls of Lauderdale.

In late medieval times, pilgrims used to come to the Shrine of Our Lady of Haddington at **Whitekirk**, about 8 miles to the north-east. In 1425 Piccolomini, a papal legate who later became Pope Pius II, walked there from DUNBAR in search of the shrine only to discover that it had disappeared. He made his way to Haddington and discovered that the burghers were rebuilding St Mary's Church once again and had rebuilt the shrine in this new church as an 'alterage of the Blessed Virgin and the Three Kings'. A wall niche probably marks the spot where the shrine stood, and close by was built the Lauderdale Aisle, thus prompting the Episcopalian 17th Earl of Lauderdale to promote the idea of annual

Church of St Mary, Haddington

Haddington House

interdenominational pilgrimages. In recent years over 1200 pilgrims from all the mainstream churches have been drawn here for a grand jubilee of unity and worship.

Haddington House, which dates from the 17th century, has been restored and serves as a headquarters for the Collegiate Trust with regular concerts and art exhibitions. The lovely rose and herb gardens (St Mary's Pleasance) bank on to the River Tyne. Nearby is Poldrate Mill, a three-storey corn mill with undershot waterwheel, restored to house an arts and community centre.

The Town House of Haddington dates from 1748, and the birthplace of Jane Welsh (1801–66), the doctor's daughter who married Thomas Carlyle, is open to the public. Carlyle came to Haddington to court her, and the Lamp of the Lothian Collegiate Trust has recreated a contemporary interior, with furniture and pictures recalling literary associations of her lifetime.

Three miles south of Haddington is **Bolton**, a small and picturesque East Lothian village in the heart of rich farmland. Unexpectedly, you find that Robert Burns' mother, his sister and brother are buried in the churchyard. The reason for this is simply that his brother, Gilbert, was factor to a nearby farm. The church itself was built in 1809 with stone from Lord Blantyre's quarry at Abbeymains.

Lennoxlove, formerly called Lethington and the home of Mary Queen of Scots' secretary, William Maitland, is 2 miles away. It incorporates a 15th-century tower. The name Lennoxlove commemorates 'la Belle Stuart', the doctor's daughter who became a mistress of King Charles II and in 1667 eloped with Charles Stuart, Duke of Richmond and Lennox. The house was bought by Lord Blantyre in the 18th century and is now the home of the Duke of Hamilton, housing many of the treasures from the demolished Hamilton Palace, and is seasonally open to the public.

Hamilton, *Strathclyde* (2/B4)

A pleasant town set in industrial surroundings, Hamilton was made a royal burgh in 1548. Mary Queen of Scots came here after her escape from Loch Leven Castle and before the Battle of Langside. Oliver Cromwell made his headquarters here in 1651. Hamilton Palace, the great house built for the Dukes of Hamilton between 1822 and 1829, was demolished in 1927 when underground mineworks caused the foundations to start sinking. Many of the treasures were taken to Lennoxlove, near Bolton in East Lothian.

Hamilton District Museum is housed in a 17th-century coaching inn complete with stable block and 18th-century assembly room. Displays include costume, archaeology, art and a reconstructed Victorian kitchen. The Cameronians (Scottish Rifle) Regimental Museum is at Mote Hill, off Muir Street. It displays uniforms, medals, banners and documents relating to the regiment and to Covenanting times. The Old Parish Church of Hamilton is the only such building designed by William Adam. Erected in 1734, it contains the pre-Norman Netherton Cross and the Covenanters' 'Heads' Memorial.

The Strathclyde Country Park, with man-made loch, nature reserve, sandy beach and various sporting facilities, lies on both sides of the M74 between Hamilton and BOTHWELL. It also contains the Hamilton Mausoleum, built in the mid-19th century by the 10th Duke of Hamilton. This has huge bronze doors and is famous for its echo.

Chatelherault Country Park on the southern outskirts of the town incorporates 360 acres of woodlands and pleasant country walks as well as the magnificently restored hunting-lodge of the Dukes of Hamilton, designed by William Adam and built in 1732 – the most extravagant 'kennels' ever conceived, and now a major visitor attraction.

Hawick, *Borders* (3/D7)

Pottery and coins from the 12th century were found here in the Hawick Mote, but the town that we see today was partly rebuilt after the English destruction of 1570, the main section over the past century. Hawick now has an established reputation for the manufacture of quality knitwear and an impressive rugby team. It is also the centre of a thriving farming community. Each year the town celebrates an event which took place after the tragic disaster of Flodden, when a group of local youths routed an English raiding party and captured the Hexham Pennant. There is a statue paying tribute to these heroes in the main square. Hawick Common Riding, which is held in June and lasts for two days, is probably the best-known of Border riding festivals. The modern Teviotdale Leisure Centre offers a number of facilities, including a swimming pool.

Sunset near Hawick

Hermitage Castle

On the western outskirts of the town is Wilton Lodge Park, set in 107 acres and ancestral home of the Langlands family. It now houses the Hawick Museum and Art Gallery, displaying a splendid collection of Scottish Border relics and natural history items. A separate section deals with the history of the woollen trade.

Six miles north-east of Hawick, beneath the Minto Hills, lies **Minto**, a neat little village which grew up around Minto House, designed by Archibald Elliot for the 1st Earl of Minto. The church here was designed by William Playfair in 1831 and to the east of the village stands Fatlips Castle, once another stronghold of the Turnbull family.

South of Minto is **Denholm**, where an obelisk commemorates John Leyden (1776–1811), poet and friend of Sir Walter Scott. Sir James Murray, editor of *The Oxford Dictionary of Quotations*, was born here. Nearby is **Bedrule**, where the 'fighting Turnbulls' once had their stronghold. Bedrule church, which sits high above the Rule Water, has fine stained glass and armorial bearings. William Turnbull, born in 1400, became Bishop of Glasgow and in 1451 founded Glasgow University.

Four miles to the south of Hawick is Stobs Castle, once the seat of the Elliot family, who later moved to their other estate at Redheugh, near Newcastleton. Further south is Hermitage Castle, rising defiantly from flat, marshy land. Restored in the 19th century, Hermitage has known many conflicts and was occupied by the Comyns, de Soulises, Grahams, Douglases, Dacres, Hepburn Earls of Bothwell and the Scotts of Buccleuch. In 1566 Mary Queen of Scots made an exhausting trip here from JEDBURGH to visit her wounded lover, the 4th Earl of Bothwell. The building's four towers and four walls are in excellent condition.

Newcastleton, on the Liddel Water and 3 miles from the Border, was created as a handloom-weaving village in 1793 by the 3rd Duke of Buccleuch; most of the Liddesdale land round about is still owned by Buccleuch Estates.

Hestan Island (6/B6) *see* Auchencairn

Houston, *Strathclyde* (1/D2)

An attractive dormitory town for GLASGOW with a mercat cross restored in 1713. Houston House dates from the 19th century. North of the town is St Peter's Well. Beyond this is the Barochan Cross, a Celtic structure dating from the 12th century.

Howgate (3/A3) *see* Penicuik

Humbie (3/C2) *see* Pathhead

Inchcolm Island (2/F1) *see* South Queensferry

Innerleithen, *Borders* (3/B5)

The Rivers Tweed and Leithen meet at this Peeblesshire mill town which, in the 19th century, was renowned as a watering place: St Ronan's Well, a mineral spring, tumbles from the slopes of Lee Pen above the town. The church here was granted to the monks of KELSO by King Malcolm II in 1159 and held the right of sanctuary. In the High Street, Robert Smails Printing Works have been taken over by the National Trust for Scotland.

The lands of Traquair were once part of a royal hunting forest. Traquair House, known originally as Traquair Castle, has played host to twenty-seven kings, and the lands were originally presented by King James III to his half-brother, the Earl of Buchan, who in turn gave them to his son, James Stuart, ancestor of the present owner. Enlargements to the old keep had already begun when James Stuart fell with his king at the Battle of Flodden in 1513. About 1640, the first Laird of Traquair re-modelled the front of the house as we see it today, extending the existing buildings southwards and adding the steep slated roof and dormer windows. He also re-routed the River Tweed, then encroaching on the foundations, to its present course which is referred to as the 'New Water'.

The story goes that the 'Steekit Yetts' (or Bear Gates) were permanently closed after the departure of Prince Charles Edward Stuart, who had called on his cousins to solicit help on his march south into England in 1745. They are not to be opened until a Stuart once again sits on the throne of Scotland. Traquair House is a popular visitor attraction and the Laird sells worldwide the ale made in his own brewhouse.

Another notable mansion in the area is Glen House, a Victorian country house belonging to the Tennant family. It is now leased out for conferences and house parties, but until quite recently HRH Princess Margaret, Countess of Snowdon, spent her holidays here as the guest of Lord and Lady Glenconner. Further along the River Tweed at **Walkerburn** is the Scottish

Museum of Woollen Textiles which features an exhibition showing the growth of the Scottish textile trade.

Innerwick, *Lothian* (4/A2)
The English army razed the Hamilton stronghold of Innerwick (or Ennerwick) Castle to the ground in 1547, but some ruins remain. In the 12th century, the Baronies of Thornton and Innerwick were conferred on Walter Stewart by King David I and confirmed by King Malcolm IV in 1157. In the reign of King David II, the lands passed to Sir Walter Hambleton of that Ilk ('Ilk' being the senior member of that family), ancestor of the Earls of Haddington. The remains of Innerwick Castle can still be seen.

Innerwick church dates from the late 18th century. A minister of Innerwick in 1822 was celebrated for having had discussions with a ghost, a Mr Maxwell, Laird of Cool. A small book entitled *The Laird of Cool's Ghost*, featuring conferences and meetings between the Revd Ogilvie and the ghost of the Laird of Cool, became something of a best-seller in the early 19th century.

South of DUNBAR a large limestone works seems to cover the entire surrounding landscape with white dust. At **Skateraw** a harbour was once erected for the shipping of limestone and the import of coal. Nearby once stood a chapel dedicated to St Denis, but this was washed away by the sea over a hundred years ago.

There is an attractive country road inland from Innerwick to **Oldhamstocks** which runs through undulating scenery and rich farmland made up of deep, fertile red soil and little valleys. The village of Oldhamstocks occupies a terrace on the top of the north bank of the Oldhamstocks Burn, which is formed by a confluence of rivulets rising from the Monynut Water. Oliver Cromwell passed a night at the inn here and claimed that he had slept 'as sweetly as though I had lain in Abraham's bosom'. In former times country fairs took place on the village green. There is a curious sundial in the parish church which dates from the 16th century.

Inveresk (3/B1) *see* Musselburgh

Inverkip, *Strathclyde* (1/B1)
At the mouth of the River Kip on the Firth of Clyde, this village was known as Auldkirk in former days when the inhabitants of GREENOCK came here to worship. Inverkip church was once owned by PAISLEY Abbey and was held by the monks until the Reformation. Dr James Young, the discoverer of paraffin, is buried in the churchyard.

There are many ancient tales of witchcraft and smuggling in these parts, but the skyline today dispels such thoughts, being dominated by the South of Scotland Electricity Board power station chimney which serves as a landmark for miles around. Inverkip Castle, a late 15th-century tower, stands in the grounds of the Ardgowan estate, owned by the Shaw Stewart family who descend from a natural son of King Robert III. Ardgowan House, built in 1798, has a beautiful, ruined chapel. The coast road travels south towards AYR with spectacular views across the estuary to the hills of Cowal, Bute and Arran.

Irvine, *Strathclyde* (1/C5)
A royal burgh and manufacturing town and port which became the last of Scotland's new towns. The old town dates from the 13th century; standing at the confluence of the River Irvine, the Annick Water and the River Garnock, it proved an ideal site for a variety of manufacturing industries.

Mary Queen of Scots came to Seagate Castle in 1563, but this is now a ruin. The lands were once owned by the Montgomerie family who became Earls of Eglinton and built the racecourse which they owned until 1924. The 300-acre estate of Stane (sometimes called Stonarig) that once surrounded Stanecastle had a chapel, churchyard and small village. The castle is reputed to have been a nunnery in medieval times, but now all that remains is a solitary square tower, once part of the old manor house.

In 1781 Robert Burns came to live in Irvine to learn the flax-dressing trade. He stayed for two years. The restored buildings where he lived and worked now provide a home for the Ayrshire Writers' and Artists' Society. Visitors can see his refurbished attic bedroom. His statue stands on the Town Moor. A handsome, two-storey, red sandstone building was donated to the local Burns Club by the Paterson brothers in memory of their father, a former provost of Irvine. Irvine Burns Club, founded in 1826, is the oldest continuous Burns Club in the world. Among the several treasures in the museum is a collection of original manuscripts prepared for the KILMARNOCK edition of Burns' poems published in 1786. Irvine parish church and graveyard contain the grave of the poet's friend David Sillar ('Dainty Davie') and a stone in memory of Helen

Tugboat, Scottish Maritime Museum

Miller, one of the 'Mauchline Belles' whom Burns honoured in his verses.

The Scottish novelist John Galt was born in Irvine in 1779 and educated at the local Academy, which was founded in 1572.

Irvine is a contrast between the old and the new. The Glasgow Vennel, for instance, which has been fully restored, recalls the days when Irvine was GLASGOW's main seaport and goods were transported to the city by cart. In fact, the Vennel was the main exit eastwards from Irvine. At the Scottish Maritime Museum, visitors can go aboard historic ships moored in the harbour. These include a Scottish puffer and the former Irvine Harbour tug. A restored Edwardian shipyard worker's flat, a wooden boat workshop and historic machinery can also be seen.

What is described as 'an unforgettable "underwater" experience' may be encountered at Sea World, where marine life can be observed at close hand. Specially designed caverns display everything from delicate sea anemones and starfish to lobsters and conger eels.

Irvine's Magnum Leisure Centre is Scotland's top and the UK's sixth major tourist destination, offering a wealth of recreational and sporting facilities which include twin flumes, a swimming pool, a sauna and solarium, a sports hall, squash courts, an ice rink, bowls and table tennis and a fitness salon in addition to a theatre and cinema. In the 250-acre beach park there is a summer funfair, a boating lake, pitch-and-put and trim-track. On the outskirts of Irvine is Eglinton Park which occupies the former Eglinton Montgomerie estate. Displays in the visitor centre explain the natural history of the area, the formal past and the origins of the Eglinton Tournament of 1839. Every August a popular local diversion is the Marymass Fair which involves a Riding of the Marches. The Irvine Harbour Festival is held annually in July.

At Ardeer, to the north-west, is the chemical and explosives factory, situated on a spot chosen by the Swedish dynamite pioneer and founder of the Nobel Prize, Alfred Nobel.

Isle of Whithorn (5/H6) *see* Whithorn

Jedburgh, *Borders* (3/E6)

Situated 10 miles from the Border with England, this former county town lies in the valley of the Jed Water. It is on the main road from Carlisle to EDINBURGH and consequently lay in the path

Restored arch, Jedburgh Abbey

of any invading English army. A church was built here as early as the 9th century and an abbey was founded by King David I in 1118 for Augustinian canons from Beauvais in France. The abbey is mostly in the Norman and Transitional styles, and remains of the domestic buildings have been uncovered.

Jedburgh Castle, which was attacked many times, was one of the five fortresses ceded to the English by the 1174 Treaty of Falaise, providing security for the ransom of King William the Lion. King Malcolm IV died there in 1195, and it was at the wedding of King Alexander III to Jolande of Dreux that a ghost appeared to warn of the King's approaching demise, which took place when he fell from his horse at Kinghorn in Fife. The castle was demolished in the 15th century and in 1825 a reform jail was built on the site. Rooms have been reconstructed to recreate the 'reformed' system of the 19th century. The jail is part of the Jedburgh Town Trail.

In 1566 Mary Queen of Scots came to Jedburgh to dispense justice at the County Court. A 16th-century bastel (or fortified) house was put at her disposal; now known as 'Queen Mary's House', it serves as a museum containing relics associated with the Queen. This also forms part of the Jedburgh Town Trail.

Like other Border towns, Jedburgh is famous for its textiles and rugby team, seven-a-side matches having been invented locally at MELROSE. The Jedburgh Border Games, said to have taken place for over one hundred years, are held at Riverside Park in July.

Two miles south, on the Jed Water, is Ferniehurst Castle, owned by the Marquis of Lothian. The Kerr family have held these lands for seven hundred years and the first castle was built in the late 15th century. Ferniehurst has recently been restored and the Marchioness of Lothian has personally supervised the interior decoration, maintaining the character and style of the original fortress. There is a Kerr Family Museum and flats are available for rent by members of the Kerr Clan Society. The castle was known as Scotland's frontier stronghold and the Kerrs of Ferniehurst were in the front line of every invasion; not for nothing did the Earl of Surrey write to King Henry VIII of England about the valour of the Jedburgh fighters.

Kailzie Gardens (3/A5) *see* Peebles

Keir (6/B2) *see* Thornhill

Kelso, *Borders* (4/A6)

A market town with an elegant square, Kelso is situated on the Rivers Tweed and Teviot in the heart of rich agricultural and fox-hunting country. A bridge was built over the River Tweed here in 1754, but in 1797 it was washed away in a flood and replaced three years later by a five-arched bridge. This bridge was modelled on old Waterloo Bridge over the River Thames

Street in Kelso

by the same engineer, John Rennie. Two lamp posts here were retrieved from Waterloo Bridge when it was demolished.

Polish troops were stationed in Kelso during the Second World War and presented a plaque to the town hall in gratitude for local hospitality. Buildings in the town are fine and elegant and there is a sense of space and thoughtful planning. Kelso Abbey was founded in 1128 on the instructions of King David I, and Vatican records show that it was the largest of the Border abbeys. In 1545, however, it was used as a stronghold against the Earl of Hertford's English invasion and the hundred defendants, including the monks, were ruthlessly slaughtered and the abbey destroyed.

Detail of column head, Kelso Abbey

Floors Castle, to the north-west, is a magnificent mansion begun in 1721 to the design of William Adam; in the 1840s, however, it was dramatized by William Playfair. It is the home of the 10th Duke and Duchess of Roxburghe and was used as the setting for Tarzan's ancestral home in the film *Greystoke*. The castle is open to the public from May to September and has many fine paintings, tapestries and items of furniture and china on display. Some 400 yd from the castle stands a holly tree marked with a white post. This is the spot where, in 1460, King James II of Scotland was accidentally blown up and killed by an exploding cannon while laying siege to Roxburgh Castle. The earthworks of Roxburgh Castle can be seen to the south-west. This 13th-century royal residence was destroyed by the Scots after the tragic death of their king.

Six miles to the north-west of Kelso is **Smailholm**, which has a parish church dating back to the 13th century, although it has been rebuilt several times. Smailholm Tower is a

The drawing room, Floors Castle

16th-century Border peel tower, 57 ft high. It houses an exhibition of dolls and tapestries based on Sir Walter Scott's *Minstrelsy of the Scottish Borders*. Scott spent some of his childhood staying at nearby Sandyknow Farm which belonged to his grandfather.

Mellerstain House, home of the Earls of Haddington, lies 8 miles to the north-west of Kelso. Begun in the early 18th century by William Adam, it was completed between 1770 and 1778 by his son, Robert. The library is widely considered to be the finest Adam room in Scotland and contains one of the best decorated ceilings in the original colours. The heroine of Mellerstain is Grisell Hume, daughter of Sir Patrick Hume, later Earl of Marchmont. It was she who, aged twelve, carried her father's message to his friend George Baillie, imprisoned in the EDINBURGH Tolbooth on a charge of treason. In exile in Holland, Grisell was courted by George's son, another George, penniless and also exiled after his father's execution in 1684. When Prince William of Orange acquired the British throne from his father-in-law, King James VII and II, however, the estates were restored and Grisell and George were married. Their youngest daughter, Rachel, married Charles, Lord Binning, in 1717 and the estate and title eventually passed to George's great-great grandson, by which time the family name had been changed to Baillie. The spectacular terrace and loggia on the south side of Mellerstain were added by Sir Reginald Blomfield in 1909, and the house is open to the public from May until September.

One mile away at **Gordon** is Greenknowe Tower, dating from 1581 and once a stronghold of the Pringle family. **Sprouston** is 2 miles north-east of Kelso and at Hadden Rigg near here 3000 English horsemen were routed by the Scots in 1549. **Ednam**, standing only 2½ miles north-east on Eden Water, is notable for its manse where the poet James Thomson, author of 'Rule, Britannia!' was born in 1700. Henry Francis Lyte, author of the hymn 'Abide With Me', was also born in Ednam.

To the south-east, on the Bowmont Water, are **Town Yetholm** and **Kirk Yetholm**. Once the inhabitants here were busily involved in smuggling whisky, and this was the home of the Faa family, the royal house of the gypsies which died out in the 19th century. Sir Walter Scott modelled his famous character Meg Merrilies on Jean Gordon, wife of Patrick Faa. Patrick, in fact, was transported for fire raising, three of

their sons were hanged for sheep stealing and the fourth was murdered by another gypsy. Jean herself met a waterlogged end when she was flung into the River Eden for expressing Jacobite sympathies.

Kilbarchan (1/D2) *see* Paisley

Kilbirnie, *Strathclyde* (1/C3)
This town prospered from its large steelworks. The Barony Church, however, is one of the oldest in Scotland still being used for worship. It is the old church of St Brendane, dating back to 1275, although the present church is mostly 17th century. Notable features are the beautiful carvings in oak of the Craufurd Gallery, and the

tomb of Captain Craufurd built in 1594. Coats of arms were added in the 18th century when a grandson of Crawford of Kilbirnie was created 1st Viscount Garnock.

The ruins of Kilbirnie Place, Ladyland and Glengarnock Castle can still be seen. Although most of the remains of Kilbirnie Place date from 1627, it probably existed at a much earlier time. The Earl of Craufurd and his family narrowly escaped when the castle caught fire in 1756, and legend has it that there is a secret underground tunnel running from the castle to the Barony Church almost 1 mile away, but it has not been found. Glengarnock Castle is considered the oldest surviving castle in the west of Scotland; it was the home of Hugo de Morville briefly in the 12th century when he ruled the lands of Cunninghame on behalf of King David I.

Smailholm Tower (see p. 127)

Kilmacolm, *Strathclyde* (1/C2)
A well-off residential area since the 19th century and also considered to be a holiday resort. The local church has tombs of the Earls of Glencairn from an earlier church, and 2 miles to the south-east, on a road leading to HOUSTON, is the ruined Church of St Fillan and a rock where it is said that the saint would sit when baptising children. The nearby Holy Well was said to have healing powers for children with rickets. Two miles south-west are the remains of Duchall

Castle, a stronghold of the Lords Lyle, and believed to be haunted. Duchal House is the home of Lord Maclay.

Kilmarnock, *Strathclyde* (1/D5)
The Kilmarnock edition of the poetry of Robert Burns was printed here by John Wilson, and there is a statue of the bard in Kay Park, the work of the sculptor W. G. Stevenson.

The 14th-century fortified keep and 15th-century palace, Dean Castle, was the ancient home of the Boyd family. It houses a collection of armour, medieval arms, musical instruments and tapestries. The surrounding Country Park comprises over 200 acres of farmland and there is a riding centre. Off London Road is the Dick Institute which has a collection of geological specimens and a mass of local archaeological items, as well as weaponry and natural history exhibits. The Art Gallery here is always lively with varied exhibitions throughout the year.

Kilmarnock is primarily an industrial manufacturing town producing a wide range of goods ranging from light engineering to whisky. An interesting diversion is to take a guided tour of the Johnny Walker blending and bottling plant. The first Scottish lord mayor of London, Sir James Shaw Bt, was born in Kilmarnock, as was the painter Robert Colquhoun (1914–62).

Kilmaurs (1/D4) *see* Stewarton

Kilsyth, *Strathclyde* (2/B2)
A mining town at the foot of the Kilsyth Hills, Kilsyth was largely rebuilt after the First World War. In 1645 the Marquis of Montrose defeated the Covenanters here and relics of this confrontation are on display at Colzium House which is open to the public all the year round. Colzium Castle was destroyed by Oliver Cromwell, but the ruins can be seen in the park which boasts a large collection of trees and shrubs, a walled garden, a museum, pet's corner, tearoom and arboretum. Colzium House was built in the 19th century and, in addition to featuring items of local interest, has a fine picture collection.

Kilwinning, *Strathclyde* (1/C4)
An abbey was built here in the 12th century by King David I for Tironensian/Benedictine monks, but only ruins remain. The abbey was attacked in 1559 and by 1560 any worship contrary to the new Protestant Confession of Faith was forbidden. The Ancient Society of Kilwinning Archers hold an annual shoot at the abbey where they re-enact the ancient tradition of 'shooting the papingo', which is, in fact, a decorative item of church masonry.

The Mother Lodge of Kilwinning, which was founded about the time that the monastery was being built, is the oldest freemasonry lodge in Scotland. King James I patronized it and presided for a time as Grand Master. The Mother Lodge was the highest authority in granting charters until 1736 when the Grand Lodge of Scotland was constituted.

On the road to DALRY is Dalgarven Mill which dates from 1620. This restoration of one of Ayrshire's most outstanding vernacular buildings has enabled the story of the families who lived and worked in the countryside in the last century to be told, and the museum is of particular interest to local antiquarians.

Kippford, *Dumfries and Galloway* (6/B6)
A great centre for yachting enthusiasts on the estuary of the River Urr on the Solway Firth. Little has changed in this picturesque village of whitewashed cottages, locally called the Scaur. In common with most settlements on the Solway, it was once a haunt of smugglers. There is a rocky beach, but bathing is not recommended as the currents can be treacherous.

Kirkcudbright, *Dumfries and Galloway* (5/H5)
The capital of the old Stewartry (a term applied to Crown property and administered by a steward instead of a sheriff) and an old royal burgh, this pretty town attracted an art colony in the late 19th century and has consequent associations with many fine painters and craftsmen. Broughton House in the High Street was the home of E. A. Hornel (1864–1933) and now contains a display of his paintings and furniture and a library. The garden, in summer, is most attractive. Down a nearby lane is the house which was occupied by the artist Jessie M. King (1875–1949). Examples of her work and that of other local artists can be seen at the Stewartry Museum in St Mary Street. Prehistoric articles, relics of domestic life and crafts associated with the history of the area are also on display. The Kirkcudbright Summer Festival takes place annually from mid July until the end of August.

Overlooking the harbour of Kirkcudbright is 16th-century McLellan's Castle, built by a provost of the town, but unfortunately a ruin since the 18th century. Other features of note are the well-preserved 17th-century tolbooth

The harbour, Kirkcudbright

and the mercat cross which dates from 1610.

Six and a half miles south-east is **Dundrennan**, where Mary Queen of Scots spent her last night on Scottish soil in the abbey, of which only ruins remain. Founded in the late 12th century at the time of transition from Romanesque to Gothic architecture, this Cistercian abbey was annexed to the Chapel Royal at Stirling. To the south, at Port Mary, the Queen boarded the ship which was to take her to England and the mercy of her cousin, Queen Elizabeth.

To the north of Kirkcudbright once stood Tongland Abbey. Its most famous abbot was John Damian, who fell to his death from the battlements of Stirling Castle while attempting to prove to King James IV that it was possible to fly.

Kirkintilloch, *Strathclyde* (1/F1)
Once a station on the Antonine Wall, Kirkintilloch became a royal burgh in the 12th century. A town trail involves a walk taking in the wall and the medieval peel. The Barony Chambers at the Cross provides an absorbing museum of the social and industrial history of the town and the surrounding area, and the Auld Kirk Museum in the Cowgate is used for temporary exhibitions, including the work of local clubs and societies. Woodhead Park is the largest of its kind in Strathkelvin. At Merkland Road the outdoor recreation centre provides an all-weather athletics track and facilities for putting, bowling and other sporting activities.

Kirkliston, *Lothian* (2/F2)
Parts of the parish church here date from the 12th century and it features a carved Romanesque doorway. Buried in the Newliston Aisle are the 1st Earl and Countess of Stair, the latter associated with Sir Walter Scott's *The Bride of Lammermuir*.

To the south-west stands Newliston House. The 2nd Earl of Stair commissioned William Adam to design a new mansion but he died in 1747, and when the property was acquired by the Hog family, Robert Adam was approached to build the existing house. West of the town are the ruins of Niddry Castle which stand on the Hopetoun estate. Mary Queen of Scots was brought here by Lord Seton after her escape from Loch Leven Castle in 1568.

Kirkton Manor, *Borders* (3/A5)
Four miles from PEEBLES, this village (also

known simply as Manor) lies on the Manor Water, surrounded by rolling Border hills. It has a small church and there are a number of ruined tower houses in the area. It was at Hallyards Manor that Sir Walter Scott came to stay in 1797 and here that he was inspired to write *The Black Dwarf*, the main character of which he based on David Ritchie, known as 'Bowed Davie'. Ritchie's cottage with its dwarf door lies nearby and he is buried in the local church.

Kirk Yetholm (4/B7) *see* Kelso

Kirkoswald, *Strathclyde* (1/B8)
Built in the late 18th and the early 19th centuries, Kirkoswald lies south-west of Maybole, and it was to a school here run by Hugh Rodger that the young Robert Burns came to study surveying. It was here that his head was turned by a 'charming filette who lived next door to the school', and he possibly imbibed at the inn with Douglas Graham of Shanter Farm, later immortalized with John Davidson, the village cobbler, in 'Tam O'Shanter'. The National Trust for Scotland opens Souter Johnnie's Cottage, the thatched home of John Davidson, as a museum of Burnsiana and contemporary tools of the cobbler's craft. Davidson, Hugh Rodger and Douglas Graham are buried here in the old churchyard.

The Old Kirk, Kirkoswald

Lamington, *Strathclyde* (2/D6)
An attractive village facing Tinto Hill near the banks of the River Clyde in east Lanarkshire. People used to climb Tinto Hill carrying stones as a penance. The Parish Church of St Ninian was rebuilt in 1828, but retains a Norman arch and a bell dating from 1647.

North of the village are the ruins of Lamington Tower, dating from the 16th century, which was once part of a fortress known as the Bower of Wandell. The lands here were said to have belonged to the Bradefoot (or Bradefute) family whose daughter, Marian, was reputedly the murdered wife of Scotland's hero, Sir William Wallace. Some historians dispute that Wallace ever married, but there was some connection and local people used to refer to the ruin as 'Wallace's Tower'.

Lanark, *Strathclyde* (2/C5)
A castle was built here in the 12th century by King David I and the town grew up around it, although nothing remains of the original fortification. Lanark was prominently involved in the Wars of Independence and there is a tradition that Sir William Wallace's alleged wife, Marian Bradefoot, came from Lanark. An imposing statue of Wallace was erected in 1882, and once there was a famous racecourse on the outskirts of the town.

In the 18th century the entrepreneur David Dale, in partnership with Richard Arkwright, created **New Lanark**, a village of sandstone houses and mill buildings some seven storeys in height, situated on a magnificent stretch of the River Clyde. It was to be an experiment in community living and a cotton-spinning centre encompassing factory management, housing and education organized on socialist principles. Dale and Arkwright parted, but Dale was joined by his son-in-law, Robert Owen (1771–1858), who made his home at Braxfield House, formerly the home of the hanging judge, Lord Braxfield.

Owen left Scotland in 1827 for America where he set up a similar project, New Harmony. The mills finally closed in the 1960s and the New Lanark Association was formed to maintain and

The Counting House, New Lanark

adapt the buildings and encourage new enterprise. A major conservation initiative has been under way for some time now, incorporating craft industries and tourist attractions such as the Heritage Trail. The Falls of Clyde Centre, located in the old dyeworks building, attracts visitors who want to see the nearby waterfalls such as Corra Linn, which has a 90-ft fall. Corehouse Nature Reserve lies not far distant and Corehouse, the home of the Cranstoun family, is open to the public on written request.

Three miles north-west of Lanark is Lee Castle, once the seat of the Lockharts. The story goes that King Robert I's friend, Sir Simon Lockhart, returned from the Crusades with the Lee Penny, said to have miraculous powers of healing. It is the original of Sir Walter Scott's *The Talisman*.

Six miles to the north-west is Craignethan Castle, a well-preserved 16th-century ruin, once a stronghold of the Hamilton family. It overlooks the River Nethan; the oldest part, a tower defended by an outer wall pierced with gun ports and a wide stone ditch, was built by Sir James Hamilton of Finnart.

On the A73 to the north-west is the Cartland Bridge, built by Telford in 1822 over the gorge of the Mouse Water. It is one of the highest and most imposing-looking bridges in Scotland.

Langholm, *Dumfries and Galloway* (6/G3)
A town on the River Esk within 10 miles of England. In the 18th century this was a market town and a cotton mill was opened, founding an important cloth-making industry. It is still a centre for the production of high-quality woollen cloth and woollen goods, and there is also a ceramics factory. The Scottish nationalist poet Hugh MacDiarmid (Dr C. M. Grieve) was born at Langholm, and a steel and bronze sculpture at Whita Hill Yett by Jake Harvey commemorates his literary achievements. On the same hill is an obelisk in memory of Sir John Malcolm, one of a family of brothers from Burnfoot who all received knighthoods. Another of them was Governor of St Helena at the time of Napoleon's imprisonment.

Two miles north-west of Langholm a baronial mansion houses the Craigcleuch Scottish Explorers' Museum. Here there is an exhibition of carvings in jade, coral, ivory and wood, and prehistoric tribal sculptures. Six miles north-west of the town there is a memorial to the engineer Thomas Telford who was born nearby.

Kelburn Castle, near Fairlie

He was involved in building Langholm Bridge and some houses in the New Town of Langholm. The annual Common Riding is a dramatic and exciting event.

Largs, *Strathclyde* (1/B3)
A popular Clyde coast resort with good amenities for young and old. The long promenade offers splendid views out to sea and of the offshore islands, notably Great Cumbrae (one of the ISLES OF CUMBRAE), Bute and Arran.

In 1263 King Alexander III fought off the invading army of King Haakon of Norway, driving the Vikings into the Hebrides; through this victory Scotland was subsequently to acquire the Hebrides and the Isle of Man. At the south end of the esplanade, a local landmark known as 'the Pencil', erected in 1912, commemorates this event. The Largs and District Historical Society has a museum at Kirkgate House, Manse Court. This includes a library of books and photography, local records, items of Ayrshire embroidery and Mauchline ware.

Situated in the Old Burial Ground is the Skelmorlie Aisle, all that remains of the old parish church. This jewel-like monument was erected in 1636 by Sir Robert Montgomery of Skelmorlie Castle as a memorial to his wife. Part of the aisle is of unusual Italianate design; the ceiling has been painted with decorative local views and some abstract scenes.

Largs is the home of the Inverclyde National Sports Training Centre. The modern marina is enormously busy during the summer months, and the Largs and Millport Regatta takes place each July. Another popular event in recent years has been the annual Viking Festival in September.

Kelburn Castle, near **Fairlie**, has been in the possession of the Boyle family since the latter part of the 12th century, but the extension to the old keep dates from 1581. In 1703 David, Lord Boyle of Kelburn, was created 1st Earl of Glasgow in recognition of the part he played in drawing up the Act of Union between England and Scotland which came into effect in 1707. Times change, and the 10th Earl of Glasgow has gone into the tourism business, opening the Kelburn Country Centre in 1977 – helped, it must be said, by generous grants from the Countryside Commission for Scotland. There are recreational activities such as nature walks, pony trekking, an adventure course, children's stockade and a pets' corner. The 18th-century farm buildings form a small village square. At Kelburn there is also an excellent eighteen-hole golf course; the seventh tee is only 300 yards from the front door of the castle. The Earl and Countess regularly welcome members of the Boyle family from all over the world.

Lasswade (3/B2) *see* Bonnyrigg

Lauder, *Borders* (3/D4)

A charter making Lauder a royal burgh dates from 1502, but the imposing town hall is 18th-century. The Church of St Mary, built by Sir William Bruce in 1673 and intermittently repaired, is cruciform in design. Sir John Cope spent a night here after his defeat at the Battle of Prestonpans in 1745. The location of the old Lauder Bridge is not certain, but it was here that Archibald, Earl of Angus, known as 'Bell-the-Cat', hanged the favourites of King James III.

The dominant family in the area were the Maitlands, who held lands at Thirlestane for centuries. William Maitland was secretary to Mary Queen of Scots and his brother became lord chancellor of Scotland and 1st Baron Thirlestane. His son was created 1st Earl of Lauderdale in 1642, and the 2nd Earl became

Thirlestane Castle

the 1st and only Duke of Lauderdale. It was the Duke who instructed Sir William Bruce to build on to the old family castle, creating the imposing mass which now reflects the magniloquent Baroque taste of the time. The castle, which has been magnificently restored, is open to the public from May until October.

Within Thirlestane Castle are exhibits illustrating various aspects of Border country life from prehistoric times to the present day, and reflecting traditions, folklore and land use. The owner has amassed a collection of toys for display in period-designed rooms.

Leadhills, *Strathclyde* (2/C8)
On a windy ridge of the Lowther foothills, Leadhills is the second highest village in the Lowlands of Scotland; gold and lead were mined here as early as Roman times. Gold from this area is incorporated in the crown of Scotland which can be seen in the Crown Room at EDINBURGH Castle. The lead mines here, however, were closed early this century.

The poet Allan Ramsay (1686–1758) was born at Leadhills where his father was superintendent of mines. In 1741 he presented the village with a miners' subscription library; today detailed 18th-century mining documents and local records can be inspected here. An obelisk celebrates the memory of another famous son, William Symington (1764–1831), who built an experimental steamboat.

Lennoxtown, *Strathclyde* (1/F1)
Originally part of the Clachan of Campsie, lying below the Campsie Fells, Newtown of Campsie, otherwise known as Lennoxtown, was founded in the 18th century as a result of the growth in the calico-printing industry.

Two miles north-west is Lennox Castle, erected in the mid-19th century for the Lennox of Woodhead family and designed by David Hamilton.

Lesmahagow, *Strathclyde* (2/C6)
This village stands on the River Nethan which joins the River Clyde at Crossford. Benedictine monks from KELSO established a priory here in the 12th century on lands granted to them by King David I. Once there were rich orchards, and it is believed that these monks pioneered the Clydesdale fruit-growing tradition. The area has strong Covenanting traditions and a monument at Skellyhill commemorates one of their number, a farmer called David Steel, shot in 1686.

Leswalt, *Dumfries and Galloway* (5/B4)
Two miles south-west of this village is Lochnaw. There are traces of a dismantled 13th-century castle situated on an island, and the early 16th-century keep still stands on the shores of the loch. The Agnews of Lochnaw became hereditary sheriffs of WIGTOWN in 1451, but earlier, in 1426, Andrew Agnew had been appointed constable of Lochnaw Castle. The present Lochnaw Castle is in excellent condition and was bought by an Australian, Miss Del Agnew, in the 1950s; it is run as a guesthouse. Her forebear, Sir James Wilson Agnew, went to Tasmania in about 1840 and later became President.

Lilliesleaf (3/D6) *see* Selkirk

Linlithgow, *Lothian* (2/E6)
There was a royal residence here as early as the 12th century, but the present fine palace was initiated by King James I, enlarged by his successors, burned down in 1424 and rebuilt. The Chapel and Great Hall are 15th-century and in the quadrangle is a richly carved fountain dating from the 16th century. King James V was born at Linlithgow Palace in 1512; his daughter, Mary Queen of Scots, was also born here as her father lay dying at Falkland Palace after the battle against his brother-in-law, King Henry VIII of England, at Solway Moss in 1542. The last Scottish parliament met in Linlithgow Palace in 1646 and Prince Charles Edward Stuart stayed here in 1745. In 1746 the palace was occupied by troops under General Hawley when fire broke out, leaving the existing remains.

St Michael's Parish Church nearby is considered one of the finest examples of a medieval parish church in Scotland. It was rebuilt after the disastrous 1424 fire, and the fine medieval crown steeple collapsed in 1820. An appeal fund was launched this century, leading to Geoffrey Clarke's controversial replacement steeple in 1964.

At the Manse Road basin is the Canal Museum which shows records, photographs, audio-visual displays and relics of the history and wildlife of the Union Canal in former canal stables built when the canal was opened last century. Rowing boats and canoes can be hired and the passenger boat *Victoria*, a replica of a Victorian steam packet, carries passengers on pleasure cruises. The Union Canal, which was opened in 1822, originally ran from Edinburgh to lock 16 on the Forth and Clyde Canal and was

31 miles long. A tow-path provides an enjoyable walkway.

Two nearby country parks are a great attraction. Muiravonside Country Park offers woodland walks, a campsite and barbecue area; 657-acre Beecraigs includes a trout farm, target and field archery courses, water sports, angling, orienteering, rock climbing and picnic areas. There is a ranger service and information area.

Five miles south-west of Linlithgow is Torphichen Preceptory, once the principal Scottish seat of the Knights Hospitallers of St John. An exhibition here tells their story. Four miles north-east is Blackness Castle, a 15th-century stronghold and one of the four Scottish castles which the articles of the Act of Union (1707) required to remain fortified. It has been used as a prison, a powder magazine and a youth hostel. Four miles to the east is the House of the Binns which has been occupied for over 350 years. It was the home of General Tam Dalyell (1615–85) who founded the Royal Scots Greys in 1681 and it is lived in today by his descendant of the same name, the controversial Labour member of parliament, although it is now owned and maintained by the National Trust for Scotland. There are fine plaster ceilings and, in the grounds, a visitor trail.

Linlithgow Palace (Scottish Tourist Board)

Livingston, *Lothian* (2/E3)
In the reign of King David I, about 1120, a merchant called Leving from Flanders bought land near the River Almond, built a home and set up a business. Leving's Town grew over the following centuries until, in 1962, it was designated Scotland's fourth new town. Covering an area of 10 square miles, Livingston is now the largest town in Lothian Region after the city of EDINBURGH, 15 miles to the east. The target population for the designated area is 70,000 which, through natural growth, is expected to reach 100,000 during the 21st century. Today over three hundred companies, including some internationally known names, 'make it in Livingston' (as the advertising slogan says) – forming a wide and diverse business community. At the centre is Howden House, the 18th-century home of Sir Henry Raeburn, Scotland's great painter, which is now a community centre. There are four main industrial estates and Kirkton Campus Science Park is reserved for high-technology industry with a research and development centre.

Diversions can be found at Deer Park Golf and Country Club, and there are facilities in the town for indoor and outdoor bowling, a private snooker club, swimming, curling, ice skating and basketball. At the Craigwood and Forum Centre enthusiasts can enjoy badminton, gymnastics, volleyball and indoor football. For those with even more appetite for action, there is an outdoor trim course, a skatepark and a BMX bike track. From all this, you get the impression that Livingston is rather an energetic and healthy place to live.

A new attraction for visitors is Livingston Mill Farm, a restored 18th-century working farm complete with animals, water mill, picnic sites, visitor centre and nature walks.

Loanhead, *Lothian* (3/A2)
The Romans had a camp here at Mavisbank on the edge of the town. But it was not until the 16th century that Loanhead came into its own when an Edinburgh burgess was given the rights to extract coal from the properties of Dryden and Loanhead. A charter of 1669 to Sir John Nicolson allowed the holding of a weekly market and an annual three-day fair to take place in October.

Although coal has been a way of life for Loanhead, the only surviving pit in the neighbourhood is Bilston Glen, considered 'Scotland's show-piece pit'. Two industrial estates have been established featuring stationery manufacture, whisky bottling and blending, and food-essence production. Mavisbank House was designed jointly by William Adam and his patron, Sir John Clerk of PENICUIK. This lovely Georgian mansion was badly damaged by fire in 1973.

Lochmaben, *Dumfries and Galloway* (6/D3)
An ancient royal burgh on an inland loch 9 miles north-east of DUMFRIES, Lochmaben dates from the 13th century when the de Brus family acquired these lands. A stone castle put up in the early 14th century was held by the English, but the present castle was probably built in the reign of King James IV. Mary Queen of Scots visited Lochmaben Castle in 1565, and it was held against the Scots by Lord Maxwell in 1588 when it was taken by King James VI and the facing stones quarried away. William Jardine, a ship's surgeon with the East India Company, who formed the Hong Kong-based trading partnership of Jardine Matheson in the 1830s, was born in Lochmaben.

Two and a half miles to the south-south-west is Rammerscales, a Georgian manor house begun in 1760 for Dr James Mounsey, physician to the Tsarina Elizabeth of Russia. It has some interesting Jacobite relics and is open to the public during the summer.

Lochwinnoch, *Strathclyde* (1/C3)
A small manufacturing town at the south-west end of Castle Semple Loch. The Lochwinnoch Community Museum features a series of exhibitions on the historic background of local agriculture, village life and industry. A purpose-built Nature Centre with an observation tower overlooks the marsh of the Nature Reserve, which is reached by walking through the woods. The country park based on Castle Semple Loch covers 200 acres, and visitors can enjoy angling and boating. The 18th-century mansion house, which stood close to the original Castle Semple, was burnt down in 1924. There is a monument to the 1st Lord Semple, who founded the Collegiate Church here in 1504 and fell at Flodden.

Lockerbie, *Dumfries and Galloway* (6/E3)
This pretty town grew up around the 16th-century Johnstone Tower and, being in the heart of wealthy farming country, was a centre for lamb and horse sales as far back as the 17th century. A long-enduring feud existed between the Johnstones and the neighbouring Maxwell family, which culminated in 1593 with a particularly bloody rout when Lord Maxwell and seven hundred of his men were killed. Lockerbie Tower has subsequently served as the town jail. Now bypassed by the Carlisle road, Lockerbie successfully retains its 17th/18th-century character. There are Roman and prehistoric sites to be seen in the area.

Lockerbie was the tragic scene, in December 1988, of Britain's worst air disaster when 270 people were killed, eleven of them on the ground when part of the Pan-Am Boeing 747 crashed onto a quiet residential street.

Lyne, *Borders* (2/F5)
Standing on a tributary of the River Tweed, ruins of a Roman camp dating from the 1st century lie near the small church which dates from the 17th century. The surrounding countryside is very lovely: to the north can be seen the Meldon Hills. Across the River Tweed to the south is Barns Tower, dating from 1488 and mentioned by John Buchan in one of his

Crossraguel Abbey *(see p. 140)*

novels. Three miles away are the rather sinister ruins of Drochil Castle, built in the late 16th century by the Regent Morton. It has palatial proportions and Morton certainly intended to retire here. He began building in 1578, but was executed for complicity in the murder of Lord Darnley. He met his end in 1581 on the Maiden, a guillotine he himself had brought to Scotland, and building work on Drochil Castle was discontinued. Three miles up the valley to the north is Romanno Bridge, near which is 16th-century Halmyre House, once the property of the Gordon family.

Mauchline, *Strathclyde* (1/D6)
A village which was immortalized by Robert Burns. In Castle Street is the Burns House Museum which contains memorabilia of the poet and a collection of folk objects. On the upper floor is the room which he took for Jean Armour in 1788; it has been furnished with period items. In the main house there is a collection of Mauchline boxware and an exhibition devoted to curling and curling stones, made in the village. Mauchline churchyard is the scene of 'The Holy Fair', and four of the bard's daughters are buried here. Poosie Nansie's ale house, which inspired 'The Jolly Beggars', is still in use today.

Three miles west of Mauchline a monument commemorates the place where it is said that Burns took his leave of 'Highland Mary', otherwise Mary Campbell from Dunoon. They exchanged vows, but she died the following autumn.

Maxwelltown (6/C4) *see* Dumfries

Maybole, *Strathclyde* (1/C8)
Facing the southern uplands on rolling hillsides over 200 feet above sea level, this has long been known as the capital of Carrick and is now the fifth largest town in Ayrshire. Maybole Castle was the stronghold of the Kennedys, Earls of Cassillis who built CULZEAN Castle. They were a stormy dynasty who became Marquises of Ailsa and they still occupy Cassillis House which is based on a 14th-century mansion situated 4 miles north-east of Maybole.

The first church in Maybole was built in 1193 and dedicated to St Cuthbert. The ruins of a Collegiate Church, built by the Kennedys of Dunure in 1371, can still be seen. Two miles from the town centre are the ruins of **Crossraguel Abbey**, founded in the 13th century and one of the few Cluniac settlements in Scotland. It was rebuilt several times and the extensive remains of the church, chapter house, cloister and domestic buildings are exceptionally fine; they are also well preserved compared with those of religious establishments nearer the border.

Seven miles south-east of Maybole, the village of **Straiton** stands on the edge of picturesque hill country but immediately surrounded by rich farmland. St Cuthbert's Church dates from 1750 and contains a pre-Reformation chantry chapel. There is a wooden ceiling and a carved frieze as well as a stained-glass window depicting the four evangelists. The window was installed in 1900 to commemorate a member of the Hunter Blair family who live at the nearby mansion of Blairquhan. Built for Sir David Hunter Blair,

3rd baronet, Blairquhan is considered William Burn's most successful commission. This Tudor-style masterpiece was completed in 1824 and today paying guests can stay in the house which is also open to the public during August. It is worth a visit if only to see the fine collection of Scottish colourists accumulated by the present owner's father. The stone obelisk which can be seen on a far hill commemorates a member of the Hunter Blair family killed in the Crimean War. The Hunter Blairs also had a town house at Maybole which, incorporating an ancient clock tower, became the Maybole Tolbooth.

From Straiton, the B741 leads to **Dalmellington** and Loch Doon. Dalmellington prospered as an iron-works town on the River Doon which flows into Bogton Loch to the west near Calcairnie Linn waterfall. Loch Doon Castle, dating from the early 14th century, was devised to fit the island upon which it was originally built. It was dismantled because of a hydro-electric scheme on the loch and re-erected on the shore. The walls are 7 to 9 ft thick and about 26 ft high.

Loch Doon Castle

Melrose, *Borders* (3/D5)

The great abbey at Melrose was founded by King David I in 1136 for Cistercian monks. Owing to its location it was badly knocked about during the Wars of Independence, but parts of

Melrose Abbey *(see p. 141)*

the nave and choir dating from a rebuilding of 1385 include some of the best and most intricate work of that time to survive in Scotland. On the roof, for example, there is the figure of a pig playing the bagpipes.

The Earl of Hertford finally destroyed the abbey in 1544, but the remains are impressive. A major restoration was undertaken in 1822 at the instigation of Sir Walter Scott and at the expense of the Duke of Buccleuch, who then gave the abbey to the Scottish people. It is said that when the Scottish army returned from fighting the Moors in Spain, they brought with them the heart of King Robert I which, in accordance with his wishes, they had carried with them since his death in 1329. The story goes that the heart was buried in Melrose Abbey, although there is no exact indication as to where.

With its close proximity to ABBOTSFORD, the home of Sir Walter Scott, Melrose has become a busy tourist centre. At Melrose Station, recently restored and converted by the architect Dennis Rodwell, there is a craft shop, a model railway, exhibitions and a restaurant. On Annay Road is the Melrose Motor Museum which houses vintage cars ranging from Bentleys to an Austin Seven, motor cycles, cycles and an automobilia display.

Priorwood Gardens beside the abbey specialize in flowers suitable for drying. There is a small formal garden and a National Trust for Scotland visitor centre.

Mid Calder, *Lothian* (2/E3)

The three towns of **East Calder**, Mid Calder and **West Calder** lie close to one another west of EDINBURGH. At East Calder is the Scottish Wildlife Trust's Almondell Country Park, which has nature trails leading up into the Pentland Hills. Once all three towns prospered from the shale oil industry and the area is littered with shale bings (or heaps) which have been substantially landscaped to blend in with the surrounding countryside.

Mid Calder, on the River Almond, was once a coaching stop on the EDINBURGH–GLASGOW road here. Part of the church dates back to 1541 and before, but it is mostly modern. At Calder House in 1556 John Knox first administered communion under Protestant rites. Frédéric Chopin stayed at this same mansion in 1848 during his visit to Scotland.

Millport (1/A3) *see* Cumbrae, Isles of

Minto (3/D6) *see* Hawick

Moffat, *Dumfries and Galloway* (2/E9)
Chartered as a burgh in 1648, Moffat became a popular spa town with its famous hydropathic hotel, built in Victorian times but destroyed by fire. The sulphur spring no longer attracts many visitors, but anglers come for the fishing on Moffat Water and the River Annan. This has always been an important sheep-farming area and a massive bronze ram stands on the Colvin fountain, erected in 1875 in the town centre in tribute to this industry. Situated in the old bakehouse in the oldest part of the town is the Moffat Museum. The Scotch oven, a traditional furnace for baking bread, is a feature of the ground floor. The town is a popular centre with visitors since it offers an excellent range of shops and is a splendid base for touring the eastern part of Dumfries and Galloway, Borders Region and central Scotland.

A famous son of Moffat was Air Chief Marshal Lord Dowding, head of Fighter Command in the Second World War and leader of 'the Few'. The bronze plaque in his memory was designed by D. Bruce Walker. There is also an annual service held in his memory.

Moniaive, *Dumfries and Galloway* (6/A2)
An appealing village set in land between the Craigdarroch and Dalwhat Waters. Moniaive was created a burgh of barony under King Charles I, but today it seems to have discarded this status for a more pastoral image. There is a monument to James Renwick, a Covenanter executed in 1688.

To the south-west is Maxwelton House, once the home of the Laurie family and, therefore, until she married, the home of Annie, immortalized in the popular song written by William Douglas of Fingland. The house dates back to the 14th/15th centuries and was originally a stronghold of the Earls of Glencairn. In the 1960s it was purchased by the Stenhouse family who pulled down the Victorian additions and restored the older house. There is now a museum of early kitchen, dairy and small farming implements, and the gardens and parts of the house are open to the public at various times.

Annie Laurie married Alexander Ferguson in 1710 and went to live at Craigdarroch, 2½ miles away to the west. The present house was built in 1729 by William Adam, and the Fergusons are buried in the nearby Glencairn churchyard.

Bronze ram on the Colvin fountain, Moffat

Motherwell, *Strathclyde* (2/B4)
Situated on an old Roman road, the town takes its name from an old healing well; a plaque on Ladywell Road marks its position. Until the 19th century Motherwell was an agricultural village, but coal and an ironworks brought massive changes to the area. The Dalzell Iron Works, founded by David Colville, changed over to steel and became the largest steelworks in the country. The population grew accordingly and, in 1920, Motherwell amalgamated with neighbouring **Wishaw**. The town is, incidentally, twinned with Schweinfurt in Bavaria.

To the south is Dalzell House, which has a 15th-century peel tower. The building was enlarged by the Hamilton family and has recently been converted into luxury dwellings.

On the high moors to the north-east is **Shotts**, once a busy centre dependent on iron and coal. Kirk o' Shotts parish church sits 900 ft above sea level overlooking the village of Salsburgh; it was built in 1821 on the site of a 15th-century chapel. The Duke of Monmouth's army camped nearby on the way to the Battle of Bothwell Bridge in 1679 and Shotts has strong Covenanting traditions. The Shotts Highland Games takes place in July; one of the main attractions is the world-famous Shotts and Dykehead Pipe Band.

Musselburgh, *Lothian* (3/B1)
Known as 'the honest toun', Musselburgh, situated on the River Esk, is a dormitory for EDINBURGH and maintains a staunch individuality as a burgh created in 1632. A bridge over the river joining Fisherrow with Musselburgh was built in 1807 by John Rennie.

Part of the town was burnt in 1544 by the Earl of Hertford and his English army; three years later the Scots were defeated at the Battle of Pinkie nearby. Pinkie House is an early 17th-century mansion, built for the Seton family but with subsequent additions. It has a splendid painted gallery and lovely plaster ceilings and is now incorporated as part of Loretto School. The Chapel of Loretto was founded in the 16th century with a hermitage. Repeatedly destroyed, its stones were finally used to build the Tolbooth which dates from 1590.

The White House, Inveresk

King James IV is said to have played golf on the course in Musselburgh in 1504 and the racecourse is a popular diversion. The Brunton Halls and Theatre is a successful local amenity financed by a bequest from the son of the founder of the local wireworks. It was designed by architects Rowand Anderson Kininmonth & Paul and officially opened by the Queen Mother in 1971. Musselburgh is twinned with Champigny-sur-Marne in France and Resignano Marittimo in Italy.

On the outskirts of the town is Newhailes, once the home of the antiquary and historian Lord Hailes of the Scottish Court of Session. He was visited here by Dr Samuel Johnson who declared that Newhailes had one of the finest libraries in the land. The house was restyled by William Adam in 1720 and added to in 1757.

To the south-east is the elegant village of **Inveresk** where there was once a Roman military camp. An Inveresk Preservation Society has been set up to protect the large number of 17th- and 18th- century houses and the character of the village. Inveresk Lodge is owned by the National Trust for Scotland; the garden (which is open to the public) has a good shrub border and a selection of climbing roses.

In 1567 Mary Queen of Scots' army was

defeated at Carberry Hill by the Scottish nobles. Carberry Tower dates from the 16th century and was converted into a mansion in 1819. It is currently used as a leadership training and conference centre.

New Abbey (6/C5) *see* Dumfries

Newbattle, *Lothian* (3/B2)
Newbattle kirk dates from 1727 and the manse from the 17th century. The abbey here was founded in 1140 for the Cistercian order of monks. Successive raids by the English, notably that of King Richard II in 1385, virtually destroyed Newbattle Abbey by the time of the Reformation when it passed into the hands of Mark Ker, who was appointed abbot. The present building dates from 1580, but the crypt is much earlier. Mark Ker's descendants became the Earls (later Marquises) of Lothian. The abbey and 125 acres were given to the nation by Philip, 11th Marquis of Lothian, in the 1930s after being in his family for nearly 400 years; it is now an adult residential college. Newbattle Bridge, over the River South Esk, dates from the 18th century and is faced with ashlar.

Newcastleton (6/H3) *see* Hawick

The Galloway Hills near Carsphairn

New Galloway, *Dumfries and Galloway* (5/H3)
Credited with being the smallest royal burgh in Scotland, New Galloway was granted its charter in 1633. Standing on the River Ken, it is a popular base for anglers. Just north of the town is Kells churchyard where there are interesting Adam and Eve stones; the gravestone of a Covenanter shot in 1685 is also worthy of attention. To the south are Loch Ken and the ruins of Kenmure Castle, a Gordon stronghold previously held by the Lords of Galloway.

Also on the River Ken is the village of **St John's Town of Dalry**, so called since there is an ancient stone in the village street upon which the saint is supposed to have rested – a reminder of the fact that the lands were owned by the Knights Hospitallers whose patron saint was St John the Baptist. King James IV visited Dalry in the early 16th century and there are two local ruins of interest – Earlston Castle, built by the Gordons in 1665, can still be seen, but the former site of Lochinvar Castle (reputed home of 'Young Lochinvar') is now covered by the water level of the modern reservoir.

This is splendid country, comprising forests,

lochs and hills of incomparable beauty. To the south-west lies the Glen Trool Forest, part of the magnificent GALLOWAY FOREST PARK.

New Lanark (2/C5) *see* Lanark

New Luce (5/C4) *see* Glenluce

Newtongrange, *Lothian* (3/B2)
South of DALKEITH, this was the largest mining village in Scotland, owing its status to the Lady Victoria Colliery which closed in 1981. The village has its own tavern, run by a trust representing the villagers, with all profits being used for the good of the community. Newtongrange is designated a Conservation Area with projects to rehabilitate the village and to provide new employment. In 1984 a Mining Museum was opened, based on the former colliery and linked by the Coal Heritage Trail with PRESTONGRANGE in East Lothian.

Newton Stewart, *Dumfries and Galloway* (5/F4)
A bustling market town on the River Cree. The name derives from a third son of the Stewart Earls of Galloway, who obtained a charter in the 17th century for a burgh of barony. Across the river is Minnigaff, an ancient suburb. Newton Stewart is today a holiday retreat offering excellent fishing on the River Cree and at Loch Trool, set in the heart of the surrounding GALLOWAY FOREST PARK. John Buchan wrote about Bargaly Glen, 3 miles to the east, in his novel *The Thirty-Nine Steps*.

Newton St Boswells (3/D5) *see* Boswells

North Berwick, *Lothian* (4/D1)
This seaside town sprang up on a promontory between two sandy bays. It was incorporated as a royal burgh by King Robert III and this was confirmed in 1568 by King James VI, who in 1591 thoroughly approved of the trial and burning which followed a night when ninety-four witches and six wizards were accused of dancing with the devil. North Berwick was formerly a busy fishing port, and a paddle steamer travelled here weekly from Leith. Today it is a popular yachting resort and relies on tourism, although it is within commuting distance of EDINBURGH. The North Berwick Museum in School Road has galleries devoted to natural history, archaeology and the life of the town. It is housed on the upper floor of a former school.

Offshore is the **Bass Rock**, which rises 312 ft above the sea. Half-way up the rock was once a garden and the ruins of St Baldred's chapel, named after an 8th-century hermit who founded the monastry at TYNINGHAME. In the 14th century the Bass Rock was owned by the Lauder family, but was eventually sold to the government in 1651 for the incredibly high sum, in those days, of £4000. It then became a state

Seashore at North Berwick

prison for Covenanters. In 1691 four young Jacobite prisoners succeeded in shutting out the entire garrison of fifty while they were unloading coal. Reinforcing themselves with twelve further conspirators, they held out for three years before surrendering on 'honourable terms'.

The Bass Rock is now a bird sanctuary, providing one of the few nesting colonies for the gannet. Guillemots, razorbills, shags and kittiwakes also make their nests on the jagged ledges. Gulls and puffins nest in large numbers on the grassy slopes, and the rock has been designated a Site of Special Scientific Interest by the Nature Conservancy Council. Boat trips from North Berwick harbour can be made by arrangement.

East of the town is Tantallon Castle, formidable fortress of the Black Douglas. The walls are 14 ft thick, the well which supplied the defenders with fresh water dropping 100 ft into rock. It was once considered the most impregnable castle

Bass Rock (see p. 146)

in Scotland; but at the beginning of the 18th century the president of the Court of Session bought the castle from the Douglas family and dismantled it, leaving it to decay. It is now under the care of the Historic Buildings and Monuments Directorate of Scotland and is open to the public. The other great landmark of this attractive resort is North Berwick Law, rising to 613 ft above sea level. It can be seen from as far away as EDINBURGH and Fife, and the view from the top is spectacular. On the summit of this ancient volcanic core have been placed the jaws of a whale.

Old Dailly (1/B9) *see* Girvan

Oldhamstocks (4/A2) *see* Innerwick

Ormiston (3/C2) *see* Tranent

Paisley, *Strathclyde* (1/D2)
An abbey for Cluniac monks was founded here in 1163 by Walter Fitz Alan, steward of Scotland and ancestor of the royal house of Stuart. In 1307 it was almost completely destroyed by order of King Edward I of England, but was rebuilt after the Battle of Bannockburn in 1315. In 1553 the tower collapsed, wrecking the north transept, crossing and choir. For three hundred and fifty years the nave served as the parish church, but in this century the great abbey has been restored by Sir Robert Lorimer. The choir contains stained glass and the tombs of Princess Marjory Bruce and King Robert III. The Barochan Cross, a weathered Celtic cross attributed to the 10th century and standing 11ft high, can be seen in the abbey.

In the High Street is Paisley Museum and Art Gallery, which houses a collection of Paisley shawls and traces the development of weaving techniques. Local history, natural history, ceramics and Scottish painting are also covered. Paisley is an industrialized town which has suffered from the recent depression but faces the future with optimism. There are two fine parks – Barshaw and Robertson – and a 1000-acre countryside park at Gleniffer. The Lagoon Leisure Centre is an attractive recent development.

Paisley Town Hall, a Renaissance-style building featuring a slim clock tower by the River Cart, houses a tourist information centre. It is also available for conferences and local functions. The Place of Paisley, adjacent to the abbey, was once the town house of the Earls of Dundonald. It is open to the public. The Old Paisley Society Sma'Shot Cottages, 11–17 George Place, is a fully restored and furnished artisan's dwelling of the Victorian era. There is an 18th-century weaver's loomshop, with combined living quarters and an exhibition room. The Paisley Arts Centre, housed in an 18th-century church building, provides venues for plays, theatre workshops and musical evenings.

The town is strongly associated with the Coats family, who made their fortune from the cotton industry. The Thomas Coats Memorial Church in the High Street was built by them in 1894 and presented to the town. Constructed in red sandstone, it is considered one of the finest Baptist churches in the country. In Oakshaw Street is the Coats Observatory and Weather Station. Continuing a tradition of astronomical observation and meteorological recording dating back to 1882 when it was built, this observatory has been updated with the installation of a satellite picture receiver, making it one of the best-equipped in Britain.

On the outskirts of Paisley is another link with the past: Elderslie, traditionally the birthplace of Sir William Wallace (1270–1305), the younger son of Sir Malcolm Wallace and Scotland's great hero. A modern memorial has been erected near an old house believed to occupy the site of the patriot's former home.

Five miles west of Paisley is **Kilbarchan**, named for St Barchan. The reformer John Knox was descended from the Knox family who lived at Ranfurly Castle here. In the 18th century Kilbarchan was a thriving centre for handloom weaving. A weaver's cottage has been preserved as a typical home of this type of craftsman of the period, with looms, weaving equipment and domestic utensils. Situated in an attractive cottage garden, it is open to the public.

Pathhead, *Lothian* (3/B2)

A village consisting essentially of one long and broad street. One mile to the north stands Oxenfoord Castle, built by Robert Adam round an older castle belonging to the Dalrymple family who became Earls of Stair. It was later added to by William Burn. Oxenfoord Castle, with its attractive grounds and pretty Cranston parish church (built in 1894), now belongs to a girls' boarding school. The main LAUDER road here crosses a fine bridge with five arches, each 80 ft in height, designed by Thomas Telford. Turning off this road, you come to **Humbie**, set at the foot of the Lammermuir Hills. In 1886 Mrs Stirling Boyd created a children's village here; this has continued as a charitable foundation, now known as the Algrade Organization for the Mentally Handicapped. Eighteenth-century Johnstounburn House, once the home of the Usher family, is now a hotel.

Weaver's cottage at Kilbarchan

The Borders: The Buffer Counties

ALASTAIR DUNNETT

As a Highlander, I have reason, along with my clan and kin, to be historically grateful to the Borders and its men. For many a century they kept the incessantly invading English out or, at worst, confined to the south of Scotland, so that we in the north and west could get on with our own small clan feuds and battles, and with the setting-up of our brief precarious Jacobite kingdom. In doing so they, like the Israelites of old, forged themselves into a fighting force whose renown, whatever they might claim for themselves, was proclaimed even by their bitterest enemies.

Holinshed, a 16th-century English historian and propagandist whose countrymen had taken their swords into the endless invasion thrusts into Scotland, said of these Border Scots: 'Thereunto we find them to be hardy and couragious [*sic*], lending themselves to the uttermost perils with great assurance, so that a man may pronounce nothing to be overhard or past their power to perform.' There was one of the famous Douglas line, Sir William, a son of the 'Good Lord James' of Bruce's time, of whom another old writer stated: 'He was terrible in arms, modest and gentle in time of peace, the scourge of England, and the buckler and wall of Scotland; one whom good success never made presumptuous, and whom evil fortune never discouraged.'.

The Borders today are the two and a half counties which separate Scotland from England. Their present names are Berwickshire, Roxburghshire and a part of Dumfriesshire. Not so long ago they were called, respectively, Merse, Teviotdale and Annandale, and you will not travel far in them today before you hear some reference to these old names, if only because people will often cling like anchors to old familiar assurances. And, of all people, Borderers are hard to uproot.

The shape of the border between Scotland and England is worth a study. You would think that, even in ancient times, it would be simple to draw a straight dividing line between our two kingdoms at the narrowest part from west to east. This wasn't how our border took shape. Every yard of it was fought over for centuries and is drenched in blood. At last it was more or less settled, or so we think; but it is far from being a straight line. Broadly, it runs from south-west to north-east through a line of rivers, springs, marches, hilltops, mountain peaks, battle grounds, bogs and sterile parcels of land, each one with the name of its heroes still ringing in the imagination with the clang of swords and the dying words of those who were robbed by death of their small victories. It is a crooked line, pressing in salients into the enemy side for no reason we can now discover, and parts of it seem to run backwards for a time from south-east to north-west. You have to take it as you find it. There are still in the world places where such struggles go on to determine a border, and if people despair that a solution will ever be found, they might do well to ponder that there cannot be anywhere on earth a bloodier border than ours, and that in the end we came to some sort of settlement.

You would think that across such a border, settled now from violence for nigh on four centuries, there would be developing a fusion of custom and thought. Not so. The border is clearly marked at many crossing points, and you hardly pass from England to Scotland and back again without noticing the contrasts in speech, form and accents, in farming practice, in building styles, in social habits and children's games, in religious thinking and attitudes to life generally, as if a defensive national requirement existed to keep the places apart after the long hostility. Of course, the weapons are long since laid aside; but there is a cautious awareness of 'them and us'.

One of the classic crossing places was the ford of the River Tweed at Coldstream, where there is now and has been for many years a fine bridge. Coldstream, on the Scottish side, looks across to the English village of Cornhill, hardly a mile away. An old colleague who was born and brought up in Cornhill has reminded me that in his childhood he was taught that the people in that adjacent kingdom of Scotland could not readily be trusted not to descend upon the English community with murder in their hearts and weapons in their hands. You don't readily get rid of five centuries of invasion in a mere four centuries.

In Scotland – and there is, no doubt, a comparable English school of thought – there is the feeling, and most of the evidence, that this was mainly a one-sided practice. Our southern neighbours had long since persuaded themselves that Scotland was some kind of vassal state of theirs, an attitude that still exists. Moreover, the English felt a need to protect their frontiers by reducing any strong people looking across at them. In other parts of the world this still goes on. It is also clever, if you want to fight a war, to en-

Near Carter Bar (see p. 34)

sure that it is on somebody else's territory. Accordingly, there was a great deal of marching north.

Apart from the Tweed ford, the other great crossing into Scotland was, and still is, Carter Bar, high on the Cheviot Hills. From there, looking north, the whole rich south of Scotland plain is invitingly spread out, so that many an English commander and his troops must have drooled at the prospect of the rich pickings lying almost within their grasp, provided they could subdue the hard men who lived down there. This they would try to do, and would keep trying.

The contrast of this area of Scotland with neighbouring parts of England made it irresistible to invaders. The farmlands were unsurpassed, developed under the monkish genius of the great abbeys set up at such a cost by an early Scottish king that he impoverished the throne for several rulers who followed him and who perhaps prayed for his soul but were scathing about his inroads upon the treasury. The invaders would remember that the last few days' march, upon the soil of northern England, had been through a bleak and boggy treeless land with little worth plundering. Across the border, however, in addition to the farms and their crops, and the improved breeds of sheep and cattle that could be driven south, there were wealthy little towns down there, with trade going busily, and well-built houses, streets and bridges, and of course many a strong castle, peel tower and rallying point.

It was almost too easy. Hawick was only 12 miles away; Jedburgh was 11 miles; Langholm, Eyemouth and Duns were 7 or 8 miles and Kelso was hardly that; Ayton was less than 5 miles. Even the farther off places like Selkirk, Melrose and Galashiels were barely 20 miles. And from all of these places it was just a short march to Edinburgh itself. These were great prizes, and many a gleeful dispatch went off from the commanders to the King of England, telling of triumphal sackings and rapine and riches. When the time came to mount a retaliatory raid into the enemy territory, the Scots had to contemplate that there were such meagre settlements as Morpeth 30 miles away, or Wooler or Carlisle bristling with defences, or even Durham, 50 footsore miles distant, and great battlements to contend with at the finish.

So the warfare was mainly a defence by the inhabitants against a fierce and acquisitive enemy. The Borderers whom these invaders met were much like the Borderers of today – passionate and proud people, immensely independent, especially in defence of their own; and many an invader had to draw back badly stung. The general pattern, though, was that the townspeople would be much

Greenknowe Tower, near Gordon

outnumbered and, after fighting from house to house and street to street, would eventually have to retreat, burning their crops and driving their sheep and cattle before them, leaving the 'scorched earth'. The women and children would have long since been led into the welcoming hills. When the enemy had gone south again at last to where he might find supplies and no assaults, the Border men came back and built their homes and their towns again. You will not find many ancient dwellings in the Borders.

Jedburgh seems to have got the worst hammering of all the Border towns. It was burned and gutted by the English more often than any of the other towns, which means it was rebuilt more often too, as you can see when you go there. Peebles was burned, not by the English soldiery, but by a vice-admiral, showing that the senior service wanted to be in on the act. This same town endured one of the later visitations when Cromwell arrived and stabled his horses in the Church of St Andrew. He seems to have been a great stabler of horses in holy places, for this story has pursued him all around Scotland. He was in the vicinity when he made his attempt to reduce Neidpath Castle, on its great eminence towering over the River Tweed. Neidpath is still there, and you can gain entrance to it – but where is Cromwell?

Dumfries was a town of wealth too and, although somewhat out of the main stream of the invasion route, had its share of burning by the English. Duns didn't escape burning either. Ayton was also burned and demolished at an earlier time by the then Earl of Surrey, a name which recurs in the invasion annals, apparently to show that several men of this title took a turn in the Scottish Borders, perhaps to sharpen their swords for the French Wars.

Kelso received a lot of attention too. It was burned by Lord Dacre in 1523; by Norfolk in 1542; and with great zest by Hertford in 1544. The Earl of Somerset turned up in 1547, and by this time the Border Scots were getting adept at anticipating events, for Lord Dacre, who was with that force, wrote ruefully: 'Little or nothing is left upon the frontiers of Scotland without it be part of old houses whereof the thatch and coverings are taken away, by reason whereof they cannot be burned.' Earlier the Earl of Surrey had described the Border towns as 'well built, and containing many fair houses'.

It was the invasion of 1544–5 which made a field day for Hertford, for he burned all the four splendid royal abbeys in one 'season', as it were – Kelso, Jedburgh, Melrose and Dryburgh. So beautiful were they that still today people travel far to see the glory of their ruins. T. Ratcliffe Barnett paid the following tribute to the gallant defenders of the first of these establishments:

> The Kelso monks . . . were mainly fighters. For in that last terrible tulzie with the ruthless Hertford twelve monks and ninety laymen held the Abbey against the English, and when the guns battered down the splendid walls the gallant soldier-monks retreated to the tower, where they held out all night. A dozen Scots escaped by ropes in the darkness, but at dawn the steeple was won, and the last Scot in it died fighting. That was the end.

The town of Kelso was rebuilt, but there were not the resources to rebuild the abbey. Abbey burning, as we have seen, was an old story anyway. Richard II once spent a night in Melrose Abbey; when he got up the next day he was in a bad mood because his invasion plan had largely failed, so he spent the afternoon burning down the abbey. There were also great castles to be put to the torch if they happened to be indifferently defended, which was unlikely. These were also in most cases royal residences, because the Scottish kings were devoted to hunting, setting aside large areas of the Borders for their exclusive use in the sport. At times invading English kings were able to take one of these strongholds and even set up court in it; so that when the rightful occupants returned they deemed it wise to set about demolishing it with their own hands in order that the auld enemy would not be able in the future to win it back again and hole up there for the winter. This is what happened in the case of Roxburgh, said at one time to be the fourth most important town in Scotland in prosperity and population. It had so often been captured and taken back, so often partially destroyed, that, although it had been the scene of much noble and tragic history – one Scottish king was married there; another was born there; another was killed in a gunnery accident – the Borderers felt it was time to be done with the place. They completed the damage done by the latest incursion so thoroughly that the town and the castle were wiped off the map: no walls, no ruins remained – only a few tumbled grass-covered stones, difficult to find now, mark where Roxburgh stood.

Out of these furious events came great tales of valour and prowess, also celebrated in ballad and song. There came also the realization of the opposing strengths. One of the useful legacies north of the Border is the fact that the Scots must be about the only people in the world who have never underestimated the English.

Kelso Abbey (see p. 127)

Floors Castle, Kelso (see p. 127)

An early move towards peace came when the English and the Scottish monarchs agreed each to provide three wardens of the Marches, who would, with their followers, act as a kind of state police and so attempt to diminish the endless hostility. These were powerful appointments; the wardens met regularly to sort out problems, and sometimes even these meetings led to fighting and bloodshed.

An early warden for Scotland, appointed by Mary Queen of Scots, was Bothwell. When she was staying in Jedburgh, she learned that Bothwell had fallen ill in his castle of Hermitage, and on a wet October day she made the 50-mile ride to see him. Arriving back at Jedburgh, she went down with a violent fever and almost died. Later, in her long English captivity, she used to say: 'Would that I had died at Jedburgh!'

As a great power, England's excuse for the raids and invasions was that they were necessary to protect her frontiers, an explanation still advanced by the powerful in other parts of the world today. There were spoils of war as well, if the attempt had been successful. When the victorious army of 1544 marched south again, they drove before them 800 prisoners, 10,000

head of cattle, 12,500 sheep, 1300 horses and much 'inside gear and plenishing'.

There was, however, a constant flux in the warlike scene, and it would have been unwise to regard these transfers as permanent. Raiding parties were continually mounted on the Scottish side, and some of the plundering hordes would be cut off before they had got far. So the cattle and other captives would often be turned back to where they came from, and some of the animals must have crossed the Border both ways many times in their lives. In a countryside of ballads and verses an appreciation of this bovine predicament was not lacking, as this plaint shows:

Lament of the Border Cow

I've hiked, in years o' rivin'
  Ilk weary border track.
Ae nicht the Scots are drivin'
  Then southmen herd us back.
When reivers' scabbards rattle
  And roof-trees light the howes –
Think on the spoils of battle,
  The footsore border cows.

The Border lands that witnessed these events were not much different in appearance from how they look today. The rounded grassy hills still run green to the tops, so that you might think a ploughman could drive his share over the top and furrow down the other side. For centuries the farming men had beaten back the scrub and small brakes of trees and had won the acres to pass them on as unrivalled pasture land for sheep and cattle. It is a braw and beautiful land. There are few wild crags and escarpments; the fine, slow-moving rivers do not brawl or dash. Tweed, Ettrick and Yarrow, teeming with game fish, all join in the small space. Ettrick and Yarrow meet 2 miles west of Selkirk, and the joint waters meet Tweed 3 miles further on. Selkirkshire has also for long been reckoned a true Border county, and with every step you walk between the Lammermuirs and the Cheviots you are treading upon history – history made by the people who are still there and who remain passionately devoted to every feature of the land. Thinking of the Lammermuirs in winter, Lady Jane Scott said: 'Heaven won't seem Heaven if I don't see those benty fields and tufts of rushes there.'

Unlike so many parts of embattled Scotland, the Borders have not been abandoned by the old families who gave leadership and zest to former ways of life. The Scotts (Dukes of Buccleuch) are still at Bowhill; one branch of the Kers (Marquises of Lothian) is at Monteviot and the other (Dukes of Roxburghe) at Floors Castle; the Stuarts are still at Traquair after twenty generations; the Homes are at The Hirsel, and the Haigs at Bemersyde; the Scotts of Harden (Lords Polwarth) are still at Harden. The continuity of some of these names goes back a thousand years; and if you happen to find yourself in the neighbourhood of one of their great houses, you are likely to find that some will invite you in and show you their treasures.

It's not all 'old forgotten far-off things, And battles long ago'. The fighting may have stopped four and a half centuries ago, and the men of the Borders may have long since forgiven their invaders, but they have taken robust steps to make sure that what they did is not forgotten. Each year, in early summer, these Border towns erupt in a welter of ceremonial rejoicing known as

Statue commemorating Hawick Common Riding

the Common Ridings. In former times the independent people of these towns developed the custom of riding round the boundaries of common lands as a reminder to the adjacent landowners that they knew what the town's privileges consisted of. One hears that in parts of England a similar custom exists, but it takes a genteel form. The folk march to the boundaries of the borough's land, and there the breeches of a number of small boys are smacked, so that in later life they will remember the place.

As the centuries passed, there came to be added to the annual Borders helter-skelter certain episodes of the people's long struggle, and these are enacted with passion and fury, although with mostly good humour, in the jolly or solemn uproars of the Common Ridings. Probably the most ancient of these annual flings occur at Selkirk and at Hawick, while the spectacular display at Galashiels dates only from earlier this century. It would not be wise to remind any Gala man that you know about this; for he would be entitled to tell you that the events they celebrate are as ancient and as dour as anybody's.

At Selkirk a young man is selected each year to lead the ceremonies and the chases. There is a hushed and moving moment when, as standard bearer, he casts the colours. Standing gallant and alone on a stage in the main concourse of the town, he represents the only survivor of the many men that Selkirk sent to the disaster of Flodden. In a series of rehearsed movements he streams out the flag on its pole – the flag is a replica of a captured English standard – and we strangers in the crowd, who will never know this burghal immortality, can attach to each furl of the cloth the name of some flower of the forest, wede awa'.

Hawick has its own different ceremonies. The man chosen to lead the revels is the cornet, and each year he chooses to accompany him on the three-day exertions the cornet's lass. From that time, as a rule, she becomes his lass for life. It is a sentimental kind of public courtship. But there are many expected duties to be performed: endless ceremonial rides in and around the town, each commemorating some incident of the old wars. There is a wild gallop up the Nip Knowes, led by the cornet carrying a famous flag; it is a copy of the one captured from an English raiding party in the year after Flodden by a small group of callants (or youths), few of the grown men of Hawick having come back from the stricken field of 1513.

On the racecourse there is a cornet's race – and woe betide any contestant who tries to outride the cornet and win. I believe that there is a longbowman somewhere behind a hedge, ready to shoot down the usurper.

And of course, there is the cornet's ball where, at midnight, the cornet's reel is danced. I have never heard of nor seen anything like it anywhere else. The men and the women line up in rows opposite each other, with the cornet at the top of the row and his lass opposite him. Next to them are last year's cornet and his lass; and then the previous year's cornet and his lass; and so on down the long lines. Here and there near the top of the women's line there will be gaps left by lasses off on childbirth duties or other women's business. Towards the end of the lines there are the gaps which the years have made by taking away partners forever, and at the very end there are the old couples who carried the hopes and the flags as long as sixty years ago.

When they die, these old people will never be forgotten: in Hawick they can tell you the names of the cornets for the last three centuries, and their names are written in the annual Common Riding programme. Visitors, however, might well wonder whether they themselves will be remembered in even a hundred years from now. No one brought up in this expectation of responsibility and continuity could fail to be stirred by the whole meaning of what they are taking part in. I hope that the dancing days of the cornets and their lasses will never be over.

Of course, everything is done with style in Hawick. Not so long ago, if you ordered a gill of whisky there, they poured you twice as much as you would get anywhere else. And today, if you go into one of the woollen mills of this boom town, which has imposed a style of twin-sets and cardigans upon the world, you can first ask for the garment to be specially modelled for you. A model will be produced to wear and parade the garment, but she will not be a professional model, with the usual dreary hair and the 'Bride of Frankenstein' facial make-up; she will be one of the 'bright-eyed daughters' of the town, brought straight for the purpose from the looms or the office, and as eager as they all are to take Hawick's part in the thrust for the auld town's undoubted renown.

There might be no better way of ending this outside tribute to the Borders than to remember the greatest riposte of all time. Samuel Johnson, no great friend of Scotland but one who at least came to have a look, grumbled scathingly of porridge, which he rightly guessed to be our staple: 'Oats! The food of horses in England and of men in Scotland.' To this Lord Elibank (one of the scholarly Murrays) responded: 'True, Sir. But where will you find such horses – and such men!'

Peebles, *Borders* (3/A4)
King David II granted this attractive town a charter nominating it a royal burgh in 1367. Before regionalization in 1974, this was the county town of Peeblesshire; its main industry, in common with most of the neighbouring towns and villages, was wool. Peebles, they say, is for pleasure, and the town remains an enormously popular holiday resort – the Hydro being the largest hotel in the Borders. There are facilities for golf, tennis, pony trekking and angling on the River Tweed.

In the High Street, housed in the Chambers Institution – the gift of William Chambers, the publisher, in 1859 – is the Tweeddale Museum. Various themes from Tweeddale's heritage and culture are shown in changing exhibitions. The remains of a Trinitarian friary, founded by King Alexander III and known as Cross Kirk, are of interest, though all that remain are the nave and west tower. Nearby are the ruins of St Andrew's Church which was founded in 1195 and became a Collegiate Church in 1543. An intriguing venture in Peebles High Street is the Cornice Museum of Ornamental Plasterwork, where a plasterer's casting shop of 1900 has been recreated.

William and Robert Chambers, the well-known Edinburgh publishers, were both born in Peebles at the beginning of the 19th century. The novelist and governor general of Canada, John Buchan, and his sister, who wrote under the name of O. Douglas, were brought up in the town, although a good deal of their time was spent at BROUGHTON where their grandfather was minister.

West of the town is Neidpath Castle, raised in the 13th century and held by the Frasers, the Hays of Yester, the Dukes of Queensberry and currently by the Earl of Wemyss. Standing dramatically above the River Tweed among wooded hills, it was visited by Mary Queen of Scots and King James II and attacked by Oliver Cromwell. The walls are nearly 12 ft thick and there is a rock-hewn well and pit prison.

Two miles south-east of Peebles are **Kailzie Gardens**, the inspiration of Mrs Angela Richard. Seventeen acres of garden surrounded by mature timber are open to the public. There is a walled garden dated 1812 with extensive greenhouses, a laburnum alley, shrub borders and collections of shrub roses. Woodland and burnside walks have been created, and the estate is populated with owls, pheasant and waterfowl. An art gallery is an additional attraction, and there is a shop and a tearoom.

Pencaitland, *Lothian* (3/C2)
The Tyne Water flows through this village, where it is crossed by a bridge dating from 1510. Pencaitland is in the centre of rich farming country and there are a number of fine houses in the area. Fountainhall, once called Woodhead and then Penkaet, is a fine 17th-century mansion built for the Pringle family. Winton Castle has been a seat of the Ogilvies of Winton since 1885. The original castle, built for the 1st Lord Seton in 1480, was destroyed by the English in 1544 and rebuilt in 1619 by the 8th Lord Seton, who was also 3rd Earl of Winton. A gem of Scottish Renaissance architecture, it has beautiful plaster ceilings, carved stone chimneys and fine pictures. Personally conducted tours are available by prior arrangement.

At **East Saltoun** is Saltoun Hall where Andrew Fletcher, the great Scottish patriot who opposed the Act of Union in 1707, was born in 1653. This has now been converted into flats. Nearby is Saltoun Mill which dates from the 17th century.

Penicuik, *Lothian* (3/A2)
The original hamlet was situated to the west of the present town, now the fourth largest in Lothian Region, before it was planned and laid out on its present site in 1770 by Sir John Clerk. Penicuik grew with the paper-making industry and the driving of ironstone pits. A hamlet was built at Kirkhill to house cotton spinners from Eskmill. Paper making has now virtually disappeared from the area, but a number of manufacturing companies were established here in the late 1960s and early 1970s, notably Edinburgh Crystal which opens for guided tours so that visitors can see the entire manufacturing process from molten to engraved glass. Penicuik has become a dormitory town for people working in EDINBURGH and a new town centre redevelopment has been completed with leisure centre, sheltered housing and a new high school.

Glencorse Barracks, for many years the depot of the Royal Scots Regiment, the oldest regiment in Britain, is now the Scottish Infantry Depot, housing seven regiments. Robert Louis Stevenson once worshipped at the now ruined Old Glencorse Kirk, north of Milton Bridge. The grounds of Penicuik House, which belong to the Clerk family, are accessible for walking. This fine Adam-designed mansion was severely damaged by a fire in 1900 and the Clerks live in

Neidpath Castle

the adapted stable block. Penicuik is twinned with L'Isle sur la Sorgue, a town in Vaucluse, southern France.

South-east of Penicuik is Auchendinny House, the last work of the architect Sir William Bruce; the author Henry Mackenzie lived here in the late 18th century. The pretty village of **Howgate** has an inn which dates from the days when this was a post on the main road from EDINBURGH to PEEBLES.

On the edge of the Pentland Hills is Rullion Green, scene of secret meetings held by Covenanters and of a battle between them and the troops of King Charles II in 1666 which ended in their defeat.

Polwarth (4/A4) *see* Greenlaw

Port Glasgow (1/C1) *see* Greenock

Port Logan, *Dumfries and Galloway* (5/B6)
A fishing village on Logan Bay in the Rhinns of Galloway. On the bay is a tidal pool in the rocks, 30 ft deep and 53 ft in circumference, completed in 1800 as a fresh-fish larder for Logan House, home of the McDouall family for many centuries. Damaged by a mine in 1942, it was reopened in 1955. It holds up to thirty fish, mainly cod, so tame that they can be fed by hand, coming to the surface when a bell is rung.

The climate here is the mildest in Scotland, and at Logan Botanic Gardens plants from the warm and temperate regions of the world thrive. There are tree ferns and cabbage palms, and visitors can enjoy the food from the salad bar in or out of doors from April until September.

North of Port Logan and south-west of Sandhead is the medieval church of Kirkmadrine, restored in the 19th century. It houses three of the earliest Christian memorial stones discovered in Britain, dating from the 5th or early 6th century. Ardwell House, which once belonged to the McCulloch family, has beautiful gardens which are open to the public. Visitors are encouraged to walk around the two attractive ponds and enjoy the fine views out to sea.

Portpatrick, *Dumfries and Galloway* (5/B5)
Named after St Patrick, this large village became established because of its proximity to Donaghadee on the Irish coast. Although shielded by cliffs, it is nevertheless very exposed to the sea. John Rennie built an artificial harbour here

Opposite: Dunskey Castle (see p. 162)
Below: Logan Botanic Gardens

in 1821, but this was eventually abandoned in favour of STRANRAER as a safer ferry haven. Today Portpatrick is an attractive and popular holiday village.

Half a mile to the south is the substantial ruin of Dunskey Castle, built in the 15th century by the Adair family. Improvements to the original castle were made in the 17th century and the estate was acquired by the parish minister, the Revd James Blair. Unfortunately, he moved away in 1648 and by 1684 the castle had become a ruin.

Port William, *Dumfries and Galloway* (5/E6)

This part of the world was enchantingly portrayed in the author Gavin Maxwell's autobiographical book, *The House at Elrig*. Port William, which lies on Luce Bay, was founded by Sir William Maxwell of Monreith in 1770. Monreith House, built in 1799, lies to the east and has lovely gardens, a park and the White Loch which never entirely freezes over. In Monreith Bay, which has fine sands, a small otter statue has been erected overlooking the water in memory of Gavin Maxwell who died in the north-west of Scotland.

The area is full of prehistoric sites. Two miles north-east of Port William are two groups of well-defined cup-and-ring marks on bedrock, probably carved in the Bronze Age. Four hundred yards south of the cup-and-ring-marked stones is an alignment of three stones, one of which has fallen. These are well known as the Drumtroddan Stones. Three hundred yards west of Blairbuy Farm is a large stone known as the 'Wren's Egg', deposited here by a glacier. On the edge of a promontory above Barsalloch Point, three-quarters of a mile from Monreith, is an Iron Age fort, defended by a deep ditch in horseshoe form.

Five miles north-west of Port William lies Chapel Finian, a small chapel or oratory probably dating from the 10th or 11th century, in an enclosure about 50 ft wide.

Prestongrange (3/B1) *see* Prestonpans

Prestonpans, *Lothian* (3/B1)

In the 12th century monks from NEWBATTLE founded a salt-panning industry here, and there was later coal mining in the vicinity. Coal was transported from the harbour which was known

Statue commemorating Gavin Maxwell, Monreith Bay

as Morrisonhaven or, alternatively, Acheson's Haven.

One and a half miles south-west lies **Prestongrange**, a former colliery site with eight hundred years of mining history, now a Scottish Mining Museum. The visitor centre provides audio-visual programmes plus walk-through exhibitions and displays. There is a Cornish Beam Pumping Engine House and Exhibition Hall containing mining artefacts. A self-drive Coal Heritage Trail leads to Lady Victoria Colliery at NEWTONGRANGE; on view are three steam locomotives, a steam navvy, a colliery winding engine and the remains of a Hoffman Kiln. From April until October, on the first Sunday of each month, there are special 'Steam Days'.

The National Trust for Scotland has restored Hamilton House, built in 1628 for Sir John Hamilton, brother of the 1st Earl of Haddington. Nearby is Northfield House, built in about the same period, which has fine painted ceilings. Preston House, the home of Lord and Lady Grange, no longer exists. After twenty years of marriage, Lord Grange agreed to pay Lady Grange £100 a year to stay as far away from him as possible. She returned to EDINBURGH on the pretext of seeing her children, whereupon a party of Highlanders seized and gagged her and transported her to the remote island of St Kilda. There she was imprisoned for six years until a letter from her reached the lord advocate who, after some deliberation, had her moved to the Isle of Skye, where she died in 1745.

Preston Tower, now ruined, was the home of the Hamilton family in the 15th century. It was attacked by the Earl of Hertford in 1544 and by Oliver Cromwell in 1650. Preston Market Cross, standing half a mile south of Prestonpans, is the only example of a mercat cross in Scotland standing where and as it was built. The tall shaft, surmounted by a unicorn, stands on a circular structure with niches and a parapet.

East of Prestonpans a cairn commemorates the famous victory of Prince Charles Edward Stuart over General John Cope and his govern-

Below left: Winding engine at the Scottish Mining Museum
Below right: Pit-head winding wheel at the Mining Museum

Seton Collegiate Church

ment forces in 1745. Nearby **Cockenzie**, an old fishing village, is now dominated by the electricity-generating station which can be seen from miles around. Port Seton, also once a fishing village, is now considered part of Cockenzie. It is in fact more of a holiday resort with attractive sands, safe (if chilly) bathing and camping facilities.

Seton Castle, the work of Robert Adam, was built in 1790 on the site of what had been Seton Palace, owned by the Seton family, staunch supporters of Mary Queen of Scots. Mary fled here after the murder of her secretary, Rizzio. Close by is Seton Collegiate Church, an important ecclesiastical monument of the late 15th century, with a splendid vaulted chancel.

Prestwick, *Strathclyde* (1/C6)

The site of Scotland's International Airport, Prestwick is one of the oldest baronial burghs in the country. The ruined Church of St Nicholas, believed to date from 1163, was built by Walter, high steward of Scotland, ancestor of the Stuart kings. In the churchyard are the graves of several provosts and many freemen of the town. Situated behind the Episcopal Church of St Ninian is a well where King Robert I came to drink the water as a cure for a skin ailment, almost certainly leprosy. The ancient mercat cross, where proclamations were made and public floggings took place, was moved in 1963 to help traffic flow. It was re-erected on a traffic island opposite the post office.

The shore here boasts 3 miles of clean sand, and skirting this are putting courses, crazy golf layouts and a go-kart circuit. There are three major golf courses (the Prestwick Golf Club was founded in 1851), bowling rinks and an enthusiastic sailing club. Other sporting pastimes for visitors including angling, tennis and outdoor bowling, and swimming in a modern indoor pool. At Boydfield Gardens band concerts are held regularly in the summer months.

Renfrew, *Strathclyde* (1/E2)

A charter was given to this country town in 1396 by King Robert III, and one of the titles held by the Prince of Wales is that of Baron Renfrew. In 1164 King Malcolm IV confronted and killed Somerled, Lord of the Isles and ancestor of Clan Donald, in a great battle here.

In the High Street is the Old Kirk, a gift from King David I, but since three times rebuilt. The last ferry to operate on the upper Clyde travels between Renfrew and Yoker for foot passengers only.

A wide range of manufacturing industries have found a home in Renfrew which has expanded to such an extent that it joins almost imperceptibly on to PAISLEY. GLASGOW's Abbotsinch Airport lies to the south-west.

Near the confluence of the Black Cart Water and the White Cart Water is a swing bridge. Close by is the Argyll Stone, which commemorates the fact that the Earl of Argyll was captured in 1685 at Blytheswood House, west of Renfrew Ferry, and later tried and executed in Edinburgh for his part in the Duke of Monmouth's rebellion.

Rosewell, *Lothian* (3/A2)

South-west of BONNYRIGG, this is one of the best remaining examples of a company village set up in the 19th century around the local coal mine (which closed in 1961). The village housing illustrates the various strata of employees.

The larger part of the old village has been designated a Conservation Area; on the outskirts is St Joseph's Hospital, which cares for handicapped people and which was visited by Pope John Paul during his tour of Britain in 1982.

Roslin Glen, *Lothian* (3/A2)

A public park consisting of 51 acres owned by Midlothian district council. Gunpowder was manufactured at Roslin Mill, but the works closed down in 1954. Above the River North Esk stands Roslin Castle, believed to have been founded by Sir William St Clair and expanded by William Sinclair, 3rd Earl of Orkney, who founded the nearby chapel in 1446. The story goes that Sir William wagered his head against the lands of Pentland that two of his hounds would pull down a deer before it reached a certain spot. The deer was killed just before it reached the spot and King Robert I awarded the estate to St Clair. The castle today is beautiful, but dilapidated, although much repair and conservation work has been taking place under the supervision of the district council and the Manpower Services Commission. Another legend concerning the castle is that if a trumpet is blown and the sound heard in the lower apartments, a sleeping lady will awake and point out where a treasure worth several million pounds is hidden.

Also in the glen is Hawthornden Castle, built in the 15th century, although it is said that in

1341 Alexander de Ramsay built a fortress in the caves which lie behind the main castle block. William Drummond, the poet (1585–1649), was born here and it remained in the Drummond family until the mid-1970s. It is now a retreat for poets and writers.

Ruthwell (6/D5) *see* Annan

St Boswells, *Borders* (3/D5)
Roads from Selkirk, Jedburgh, Melrose, Kelso and Galashiels meet at this small town which retains a village green where once large Border fairs took place. For years, St Boswells has housed the kennels of the Duke of Buccleuch's foxhounds. Nearby is Lessuden House which takes its name from the ancient name of this village before it expanded.

Two miles to the east is Mertoun House, designed by Sir William Bruce in 1703. It became the home of the 6th Duke of Sutherland and twenty acres of beautiful grounds with delightful walks and views of the River Tweed are open to the public. There is a walled garden and a well-preserved dovecot, thought to be the oldest in the county.

Borders Regional Council has its headquarters at **Newton St Boswells** which lies to the north-west. Two miles to the west is the tiny village of **Bowden** which has a 12th-century church which was restored in 1909. A 16th-century mercat cross is now a war memorial.

Four and a half miles to the north is **Earlston** in the valley of Lauderdale and situated close to the Leader Water. Thomas the Rhymer, the shadowy 13th-century poet and prophet, was also known as Thomas of Ercildoune, from which the name Earlston derives. Just south of the present-day town are the ruins of his tower.

St John's Town of Dalry (5/H2) *see* New Galloway

Saltcoats (1/B4) *see* Ardrossan

Sanquhar, *Dumfries and Galloway* (2/B9)
Two famous Covenanting declarations were signed at this village on the bank of the River Nith, the most celebrated being in 1680 by the Reverend Richard Cameron, whose supporters later formed the Cameronians Regiment, although Cameron himself was killed soon after. James Renwick made the second declaration in 1685; a granite obelisk replaces the mercat cross on which they were displayed.

Sanquhar was made a royal burgh in 1484 under the protection of the then powerful Crichton family. The castle was subsequently acquired by the 1st Duke of Queensberry who, having built himself a palace at DRUMLANRIG, still preferred to stay in this humbler accommodation.

The Tolbooth dates from 1735 and was designed by William Adam. One room serves as a Sanquhar Museum, displaying items of local interest. Sanquhar Post Office is the oldest in Britain, functioning since 1763, twenty years before the introduction of the regular mail coach service.

Selkirk, *Borders* (3/C6)
Overlooking the Ettrick Water, this royal burgh was the site of a Tyronesian abbey founded by King David I in 1113 but later transferred to KELSO. King William the Lion held a parliament here in 1204 and a royal castle once existed. Strategically, however, Selkirk suffered repeatedly from the English invasions and the town was destroyed by the English army after

Sanquhar Town Hall

The Post Office at Sanquhar, Britain's oldest, which is still operational

the Battle of Flodden in 1513. The Common Riding which takes place each year recalls that event when the standard bearer, representing the town's sole survivor, casts the colours into the market place. The 400th anniversary statue shows him with the captured English standard.

Sir Walter Scott was sheriff of the county in the early 18th century and there is a statue of him in the market place. The courthouse where he dispensed justice can be visited. At the end of the High Street is a statue of the explorer Mungo Park (1771–1806) who was born in a cottage at nearby Foulshiels. Maternal ancestors of the American president, Franklin D. Roosevelt, lie buried in Kirk o' the Forest. The noble Marquis of Montrose stayed in the town before the Battle of Philiphaugh in 1645 at which he was defeated. Halliwell's House Museum and Gallery, situated off the main square, consists of a row of 18th-century dwelling houses extensively renovated to house a museum of Selkirk's history. The building's links with the ironmongery trade have been recreated and the Robson Gallery here has constantly changing exhibitions.

Selkirk is a centre for tweed and woollen goods, and some of the mills can be visited. Visitors are also welcome at the factory of Selkirk Glass, where they can see craftsmen at work.

Four miles to the south-west is **Bowhill**, home of the Scotts of Buccleuch. This fine mansion was erected by the 3rd Duke of Buccleuch in 1795. It is open to the public during the summer months. Within is an impressive collection of French furniture and paintings, including works by Van Dyck, Reynolds, Raeburn and Claude Lorraine. Through marriage the Buccleuchs acquired the dukedom of Queensberry, and Bowhill is one of the four splendid homes owned by the present Duke of Buccleuch and Queensberry. He encourages riding and pony trekking and the involvement of local schoolchildren in activities which familiarize them with the countryside. His other homes are Drumlanrig near DUMFRIES, Dalkeith Palace near Edinburgh, and Boughton which is in Northamptonshire.

On the same estate is Newark Castle, where the 1st Duchess of Buccleuch (she held this title in her own right) came to live after the execution of her husband, the Duke of Monmouth, natural son of King Charles II. Newark (or New Wark)

Newark Castle (see p. 167)

was so called to distinguish it from the older Auldwark Castle which stood nearby. This five-storey oblong tower house was a royal hunting seat for the Forest of Ettrick; the royal arms of King James I can be seen on the west gable. The courtyard here was the scene of a vile incident in 1645 when some hundred prisoners captured after the Battle of Philiphaugh were executed on the orders of General Leslie. Walter Scott and William Wordsworth visited the castle together.

Five miles south-east of Selkirk is **Lilliesleaf**, a quiet little village on the Ale Water. The original font of the church here dates from the 12th century, but the building has been much altered. To the south-west once stood Riddell House, burnt down in 1954, a former seat of the Riddell family who held sway in the district for seven centuries.

Shotts (2/C3) *see* Motherwell

Skateraw (4/A2) *see* Innerwick

Smailholm (3/E5) *see* Kelso

South Queensferry, *Lothian* (2/F2)
An ancient royal burgh standing below the Forth Rail Bridge, opened in 1890, and the Forth Road Bridge, opened by Her Majesty the Queen in 1964. King Malcolm IV gave the monks of Dunfermline a grant of land here, and this was later confirmed by King Robert I. Tradition has it that Saint Margaret, Queen to King Malcolm III, used this place for her crossing over to Fife and the royal court at Dunfermline, hence the name 'Queen's Ferry'.

A Carmelite chapel was founded in 1330, but the existing building was restored as an Episcopalian church in 1890 on the site of a 15th-century building. The Hawes Inn is an ancient hostelry where many famous travellers have stopped for the night. Dundas Castle was built for Sir James Dundas in 1424, and the Dalmeny Estate is the home of the Primrose family who became Earls of Rosebery. The family first lived at nearby Barnbougle, but later built Dalmeny House; this was the home of the 5th Earl, who became British prime minister in 1893. Dalmeny House is open to the public and should not be missed; its many features of interest include the 5th Earl's wonderful library, Goya tapestries, superb French furniture from the Roseberys' former English home, Mentmore, and an intriguing collection of Napoleonic memorabilia.

On the other side of South Queensferry is Hopetoun House, seat of the Marquises of Linlithgow. The 1st Earl of Hopetoun commissioned Sir William Bruce to build him his stately home at the end of the 17th century. Thereafter William Adam and his sons, John and Robert, all contributed to create the spectacular building which exists today. The grounds include a nature trail and there is a Museum of Horse. The great Ballroom at Hopetoun is regularly used for concerts, hunt balls and other social occasions. Paintings in the main house include Van Dycks and a Rubens.

From South Queensferry, **Inchcolm Island** is also accessible by cruise ship; the island is the site of the 12th-century St Colm's Abbey, built by Alexander I.

Sprouston (4/A6) *see* Kelso

The spectacular Forth Rail Bridge, one of the greatest engineering feats of its day, was opened in 1890

Stenton, *Lothian* (3/E1)
A conservation village which has consequently retained its character. The name is of Saxon origin. Near the village green stood the Tron (or wool stone) on which wool was weighed at the annual local fair. It was restored in 1970. The present church, designed by William Burn, replaced an earlier one in 1829; 300 yd away is the Rood Well, said to have been placed there by the monks of MELROSE in medieval times. In 1659 Bessie Knox and four other women were convicted of witchcraft by their own confession and met the customary grisly end.

The lands of Biel, Stenton, Pitcox and Belton were once part of the estates of the Earls of Dunbar. Biel passed through the Lauders to the Hamiltons who were created Lords Belhaven and Stenton. A stone bridge at Biel carries the Belhaven arms and name.

Stevenston (1/B4) *see* Ardrossan

Stewarton, *Strathclyde* (1/D4)
On the Annick Water in rich dairy-farming country, this town was once famous for the manufacture of 'Tam O'Shanter' bonnets. David Dale, the GLASGOW industrialist who founded NEW LANARK, was born here in 1793.

Nearer to KILMARNOCK is **Kilmaurs**, originally Cunninghame, but renamed after St Maure. It was created a burgh of barony by the 3rd Earl of Glencairn in 1527. The parish church was rebuilt in 1888 and the Glencairn burial aisle nearby was erected in 1600 in the grounds of the original 1404 church; it was restored in 1844. There is a memorial to the 9th Earl of Glencairn, Lord High Chancellor of Scotland, who died in 1664. Across the moors towards FENWICK is Rowallan Castle, originally the home of the Mures of Rowallan, then owned by the Corbett family. The castle has been developed over several centuries as can be seen in the 13th–15th and 16th-century architecture; there are two imposing circular towers.

Stobo (2/F6) *see* Drumelzier

Straiton (1/C8) *see* Maybole

Stranraer, *Dumfries and Galloway* (5/B4)
A royal and municipal burgh with regular ferry services to Larne in Northern Ireland. At the head of Loch Ryan, this is a busy seaport and a popular holiday resort into the bargain. Stranraer Castle, built in the 16th century, was used by John Graham of Claverhouse during his persecution of the Covenanters. The Wigtown District Museum, which is in the Old Town Hall in George Street, has items of local history interest and changing exhibitions.

To the north-east stands Craigcaffie Castle built in the 16th century. It was a stronghold of the Neilsons, who were granted their lands here by King Robert I. Three miles east of Stranraer, the gardens of Castle Kennedy are open to the public. They are famous for rhododendrons,

The Tron (or wool stone) at Stenton

azaleas, magnolias and embothriums. The pinetum here was the first in Scotland. The adjoining Lochinch Castle to the north is the home of the Earls of Stair. Ferry services to Larne also operate from CAIRNRYAN, 3 miles north of Stranraer.

Strathaven, *Strathclyde* (2/A5)
Once a weaving town, Strathaven is fringed by Calderglen Country Park which consists of 300 acres of wooded gorge and parkland. There is an extensive path system, woodland and a river with waterfalls, picnic sites, and a visitor centre providing a history of the area. In addition visitors can enjoy a children's zoo, an ornamental garden and an adventure playground. In Strathaven Park is the John Hastie Museum of local history, and a popular local theatre, club and arts centre occupy the attractively converted Town Mill and Granary, a three-hundred-year-

old grain mill, originally owned by the Dukes of Hamilton.

Strathaven Castle, once called Avondale Castle and now a ruin, was built in the 15th century by a natural son of the 2nd Duke of Albany. It passed to the Hamilton family, who left in the 18th century.

Strathaven is a largely residential area, being within commuting distance of GLASGOW. For fifteen years the immortal Scottish music-hall comedian Sir Harry Lauder had his home here at Lauder Ha'.

Symington, *Strathclyde* (1/C5)
A rural village where the small restored church has a trio of round-headed Norman windows dating from the 12th century. The roof is of exposed timber and the piscina is still preserved in the south wall. This is one of the few pre-Reformation buildings still in regular use in Scotland.

Not far from the village of Symington can be seen the ruins of Barnweil church. One of the oldest churches in Ayrshire, it was closed in 1673. A tower in memory of William Wallace was erected here in 1855.

Tarbolton, *Strathclyde* (1/D6)
Robert Burns founded a literary and debating society here which became known as the Bachelors' Club. Founded in 1780, it had six founder members, including the poet's brother. Burns lived and worked with his father at Lochlea Farm for seven years, attended dancing lessons at Tarbolton and was initiated into freemasonry. The Bachelors' Club met in a 17th-century house which has been restored by the National Trust for Scotland and is open to visitors.

On the B744 road is the Enterkine Nature Trail, running through natural woodland with badgers' setts, ponds and varied birdlife.

Temple (3/B3) *see* Gorebridge

Thankerton (2/D6) *see* Carstairs

Thornhill, *Dumfries and Galloway* (6/B2)
In the middle of spectacular Dumfriesshire landscape, this is a pretty town in close proximity to the great Queensberry house of DRUMLANRIG. The Queensberry mountain (2,285 ft) dominates the town on the east and within walking distance is the great Forest of Ae. To the north is Morton Castle, standing beside a small loch. Randolph, 1st Earl of Moray, lived here when he was regent for King David II. The castle passed to the Douglas family and is now ruined.

South-west of Thornhill lies **Keir** which has a curious claim to celebrity. On the smithy is an inscription announcing that Kirkpatrick Macmillan was born here. He invented the bicycle in 1839, and when he rode his invention to GLASGOW, he was fined for knocking over a pedestrian.

Torhouse Stone Circle (5/E5) *see* Wigtown

Torthorwald, *Dumfries and Galloway* (6/D4)
A small agricultural village elevated to a burgh of barony in 1473. Torthorwald Castle was a late 14th-century stronghold of the Kirkpatrick family, but passed to the Carlyles and is now ruined after various family feuds in the 16th century. William Paterson, founder of the Bank of Scotland, was born in Torthorwald, and there is a memorial in the shape of a cairn to John Paton, the missionary.

Town Yetholm (4/B7) *see* Kelso

Tranent, *Lothian* (3/C1)
Tranent derives its name from the ancient British *Trew-er-nent*, meaning 'a village in a ravine or river'. The Romans came here in the 3rd century, the Anglo-Saxons in the 5th, and in 1020 Eaduf, the Saxon Earl of Northumberland, ceded the district to King Malcolm II.

The old parish church certainly dates from early times, possibly the 11th century; only a ruin now remains. The present church is 19th-century and nearby is a dovecot dating from the 16th century.

In 1544 the Earl of Hertford with his English army burnt Tranent. In 1745, after the Battle of Prestonpans, Colonel Gardiner, immortalized in Sir Walter Scott's *Waverley*, died here from wounds and was buried in the old church. In August 1797 the Militia Riot (or Tranent Mob) took place, a particularly bloody riot over balloting for the Scots Militia in which eleven people were shot dead.

Inland at **Ormiston** there is a 15th-century cross. The Ormiston estates were originally possessed by a family of the name of Orme. They then belonged to the Lindsays until 1368, when they passed by marriage to the second son

Mercat cross, Ormiston

of Sir Alexander Cockburn of Clerkington, hereditary sheriff of HADDINGTON. In 1545 the reformer George Wishart sheltered at Ormiston Hall as the guest of Alexander Cockburn. During the night the Earl of Bothwell with a party of men, at the instigation of Cardinal Beaton who was living at the time at nearby Elphinston Tower, came to the house and abducted Wishart. Cardinal Beaton then transported the unfortunate man to St Andrews where he was tried and burned at the stake on 1 March 1546.

John Cockburn of Ormiston (1685–1758) was a notable agrarian 'improver'. A member of the last Scottish parliament, and then a British member of parliament, he believed in planting trees and hedges in order to control land use and encouraged the open discussion of farming topics among his neighbours and contemporaries.

Troon, *Strathclyde* (1/D5)
A residential town with harbour and popular yachting marina, this is a favoured resort for holiday makers. It is best known for its five eighteen-hole golf courses, including the Royal Troon, formed in 1878 and regular host to the British Open. There are over 2 miles of soft, sandy beaches with safe bathing.

Troon Harbour was begun in the 18th century by the 4th Duke of Portland and Troon Sailing Club invites visitors to take advantage of its extensive facilities at North Beach. Other tourist diversions are putting, crazy golf, bowling, tennis and trampolining. The principal buildings of Troon, including the Concert Hall and fine Municipal Buildings, are 20th-century. The Troon and Kilmarnock Railway was the first regular passenger railway in Scotland and a silver model of 'The Duke', the first engine, can be seen in Troon Town Buildings. On the edge of the town is the Fullerton Estate, once owned by the Dukes of Portland and now accessible to the public for walks and picnics.

Turnberry, *Strathclyde* (1/B8)
This spot on the south-west coast is renowned the world over for its spectacular hotel and championship golf course, often host of the British Open. Turnberry was originally part of the Marquis of Ailsa's Culzean estate, but by 1902 golf had taken over. During the First and Second World Wars the links were requisitioned by the military, but after the reclamation of the land the courses were re-built.

The scant remains of Turnberry Castle, the childhood home of Robert the Bruce, can still be seen: it is claimed that Bruce landed here in 1307 to begin his campaign to liberate Scotland from King Edward I of England. There is a right of way on foot across the golf course, and access to the lamp room of the lighthouse is at the discretion of the keeper.

Tweedsmuir (2/E7) *see* Broughton

The golf course and hotel at Turnberry

Tyninghame, *Lothian* (4/E1)
An attractive village planned for the estate which belonged to the Earls of Haddington. The original church was founded in the 8th century by St Baldred, but destroyed in the 10th century by invading Vikings. What remains today dates from Norman times.

The lands at Tyninghame were granted to the Hamilton family (who became Earls of Haddington) in 1628, and the great house was enlarged in 1829. Through marriage, the family also became owners of Mellerstain where the present Earl now lives. For tax reasons, Tyninghame has been converted into flats and the contents sold; the house and colourful gardens are therefore no longer open to the public. Binning Woods, planted by the 6th Earl of Haddington in 1705 on what had previously been moorland, were spectacular, although much of the timber disappeared during the Second World War. Queen

Miner's cottage, Wanlockhead

Victoria, on visiting Tyninghame, remarked that the grounds reminded her of those at Windsor.

Walkerburn (3/B5) *see* Innerleithen

Wanlockhead, *Dumfries and Galloway* (2/C8)
This is the highest village in the Lowlands, standing in isolation among the Lowther Hills. Because of the remoteness of the surrounding moors, it was a popular refuge for Covenanters in the 17th century.

The Romans were probably the first people to find lead here, and lead mining was carried on around Wanlockhead from 1264 until recent times. Gold was also mined locally; the largest piece found weighed over 4 oz. The village has the second oldest subscription library in Britain (the oldest is at nearby Leadhills) founded by a group of miners in 1756. Their first purpose-built library was erected in 1788, and the present larger building dates from 1850.

The mines closed in 1928, but the Scottish Lead Mining Museum can be visited in Goldscaur Road. There is an indoor museum with mining and social relics and a replica lead mine. The Miners' Reading Society Library has some interesting editions, and there is a local gold, silver and mineral collection. Outside is an early 19th-century wooden water-balance pump for lead mining with the track of a horse engine beside it.

West Calder (2/E3) *see* Mid Calder

West Kilbride, *Strathclyde* (1/B4)
The arrival in 1964 of a nuclear electricity-generating station at Hunterston Bay, combined with projects associated with the offshore deep-water facilities for ships, dramatically altered the appearance of West Kilbride and neighbouring Seamill. Portencross remains unchanged. The Hunterston 'B' is an advanced gas-cooled reactor nuclear power station with an installed generating capacity of 1320 megawatts – about enough continuous electricity for a city of the size of EDINBURGH. Visitors can see an audio-visual presentation on how the station operates and there are guided tours to key operational areas. The massive bulk of the nuclear power station makes it a landmark on this particularly beautiful stretch of coastline which faces over towards the ISLES OF CUMBRAE, Arran and Bute.

The lands of Hunter at West Kilbride were granted to William Hunter by King Robert II in 1374, and the ancient castle of Hunterston stands in the grounds of Hunterston House, the Victorian family home. The Hunter Family Association has plans to develop a clan centre here for its members throughout the world.

Law Castle is a tower house which once was a stronghold of the Boyd family. The gunloops in the walls and the corbelling of the battlements help to date it to the 15th century. Another 15th-century keep is Portencross Castle, used by early Stuart kings as an occasional stopping-off place *en route* to their castle at Rothesay. Near the castle is a cannon from the Spanish Armada; there is a legend that it was a local witch who caused the sinking of an Armada ship off the coast here. Nearby Blackshaw Farm is a working farm open to visitors.

West Linton, *Borders* (2/F4)
A village on the Lyne Water in the shadow of the Pentland Hills, now popular with commuters to EDINBURGH. Important sheep markets used to take place here four times a year. The village was also well-known for its stonemasons. The figure on Lady Gifford's Well, the village pump, was carved in 1666 by James Gifford and is said to represent his wife. There are other carvings, probably by the same hand, on a house across the road, dated 1660 and 1678. A village information and exhibition centre in Raemartin Square is open from April until October.

White Coomb, *Dumfries and Galloway* (2/F8)
The White Coomb is a hill rising to 2696 ft at the summit of Birkhill Pass. Nearby is a waterfall called Dob's Linn, once a refuge for Covenanters. To the east is the Grey Mare's Tail Waterfall, 200 ft high and believed by some to be the location of the Holy Grail of Arthurian legend. The Tail Burn flows into the Moffat Water.

Whitekirk (4/D1) *see* Haddington

Whithorn, *Dumfries and Galloway* (5/F6)
Mentioned by Ptolemy in the 2nd century, Whithorn is one of the oldest Christian centres in Britain. Here, around 400 AD, St Ninian first introduced Christianity to Scotland and built what is believed to be the first stone-built church in Scotland. The church became known in Latin as *Candida Casa* (or White House). The present priory ruins date from the 12th century, and a museum here displays early Christian crosses, some carved in rock, others indoors, including the famous Monreith Cross. King Robert I created Whithorn an ecclesiastical burgh and, ill with leprosy, made a pilgrimage here a few months before he died in 1329. Many of the Stuart monarchs followed his example, notably King James IV (who came on foot from EDINBURGH) and Mary Queen of Scots who made the journey in 1563. An Act of Parliament in 1581 declared such practice illegal.

Chapel of St Ninian, Isle of Whithorn

The area is rich in archaeological sites. One mile to the west is Rispain Camp, a rectangular settlement defended by a bank and ditch and dating from the 1st or 2nd century. Discoveries of rings, pottery and weaponry have been made. Three miles to the south-east is **Isle of Whithorn**, standing on what was once an island. The 13th-century chapel is dedicated to St Ninian and was probably used by pilgrims on their way to Whithorn. Isle of Whithorn has an enthusiastic yachting community and has become a busy summer holiday resort. On the coast, 4

Above: Mural in Whithorn
Preceding pages: Glen below the Grey Mare's Tail (see p. 177)

miles away at Physgill, is St Ninian's Cave, reputedly used by the saint on a retreat. There are early Christian crosses carved in the rock, but others found here are now in Whithorn Museum. The Whithorn Trust, under the initiative of the Church of Scotland, has undertaken extensive excavations at Glebelands where deposits discovered in 1984 and subsequent finds have indicated that there was intensive occupation here from the 5th century onwards. The dig is open to visitors and guided tours of the site are provided. A visitor centre with interpretative displays is also being developed.

Wigtown, *Dumfries and Galloway* (5/F5)
Chartered in the 13th century, this is the former county town of Wigtownshire, located on the west side of Wigtown Bay. An old town cross dates from 1748 and another commemorates the Battle of Waterloo. The ruined church was originally dedicated to St Machitis, and the parish church adjoining the ruin was erected in 1853. In the churchyard is a stone in memory of the 'Wigtown Martyrs', two women aged eighteen and sixty-three who were tied to stakes and drowned for their religious beliefs during the persecution of the Covenanters in 1685, a period known as 'the Killing Times'. There is also a monument to them on the hill and a pillar on the shore of Wigtown Bay. The malt whisky distillery at nearby Bladnoch is open to visitors.

Four miles west of Wigtown is **Torhouse Stone Circle**, a Bronze Age circle of nineteen boulders on the edge of a low mound.

Fronting on to the bay further down the coast is the little port of **Garlieston**, founded in the 18th century by Lord Garlies, later 7th Earl of Galloway. His father, the 6th Earl, had built nearby Galloway House in 1740, and this was later enlarged by William Burn and the hall decorated by Sir Robert Lorimer. The gardens, though not the house itself, are open to the public and cover 30 acres leading down to the sea and a sandy beach. Fine old trees and seasonal snowdrops and daffodils, rhododendrons and azaleas grace the area and there is a walled garden with greenhouses and a camellia house.

South of Garlieston is the little church of Cruggleton, dating from Norman times. The

Norman arch, Whithorn Priory (see p. 177)

Torhouse Stone Circle (see p. 180)

chancel arch and doors and windows are 12th-century. Close by, ruined Cruggleton Castle was once a stronghold of Fergus of Galloway and later held by the Comyns. Such was the strength and reputation of this remote castle that Queen Elizabeth I of England sent spies to report back to her on its potential. Seven miles south of Wigtown is Sorbie Tower, a stronghold of the Hannays until they were outlawed in the 17th century for their behaviour towards the Murrays. It has recently been impressively restored by the Hannay Society.

Wishaw (2/B4) *see* Motherwell

Bibliography

There are numerous books covering the south of Scotland and dealing with every aspect of socio-economic history, topography and culture. The books listed below have been published in the past twenty years and update much of what was written before, although there are many classic early works, now of antiquarian value, which have not been surpassed. For those readers who seek further detailed information, the following are recommended:

Daiches, David. *Glasgow.* Andre Deutsch, London 1977

Grimble, Ian. *Castles of Scotland.* BBC Books, London 1987

Hanley, Cliff. *History of Scotland.* Hamlyn, London 1987

Macaulay, James. *The Classical Country House in Scotland 1660–1800.* Faber & Faber, London 1987

Martine, Roddy. *Homelands of the Scots.* Spur, Edinburgh 1981

Martine, Roddy. *Scottish Clan and Family Names.* Bartholomew, Edinburgh 1987

Moffat, Alistair. *Kelsae – A History of Kelso from Earliest Times.* Mainstream, Edinburgh 1987

Prebble, John. *Scotland.* Secker & Warburg, London 1984

Smith, Roger. *The Scottish Borders and Edinburgh.* Moorland, London 1983

Scottish Tourist Board *1001 Things to See.* Edinburgh, 1987

Steel, David. *Border Country.* Weidenfeld & Nicolson, London 1987

Tranter, Nigel. *The Illustrated Portrait of the Border Country.* Robert Hale, London 1972

Ward, Robin. *The Spirit of Glasgow.* Richard Drew, Glasgow 1984

Key to Maps

MOTORWAYS with interchanges numbered on principal motorways
Autoroutes échangeurs numérotés sur principales autoroutes
Autobahn mit Anschluss

M1 — Interchanges / Echangeurs / Autobahnenschluss — Service areas / Station Service / Raststätte

Limited interchange
Access or exit from motorway only in direction of arrow
Entrée ou sortie de l'autoroute dans le sens des flèches
Autobahnauf oder abfahrt nur in Richtung des Pfeils
Access ← exit ←

M25 **Motorways under construction**
Autoroutes en construction
Autobahn im Bau

M20 **Motorways projected**
Autoroutes en projet
geplante Autobahn

40 **PRIMARY ROUTES**
Routes principales
Hauptverbindungsstrasse

RING ROADS
Routes de ceinture
Ringstrasse

498 **Other A (1st class) roads**
Routes principales (première classe)
Strasse 1 Ordnung A

Narrow roads with passing places
Routes etroites avec places de croisement
Schmale strassen mit ausweichstellen

6238 **Other B (2nd class) roads**
Routes secondaires (seconde classe)
Strasse 2 Ordnung B

Minor roads
Routes départementales
Nebenstrasse

Projected by-pass roads
Routes de contournements en projet
Geplante Umgenungsstrasse

Dual carriageways
Routes à chaussées séparées
Zweibahnige Schnellstrasse

2 **Mileage distances**
Distances en milles
Entfernung in Meilen

Sea par bateau See / hovercraft **Car Ferries**
Transports de voitures
Autofahren

PRESTWICK **Principal Airports**
Principaux Aéroports
Verkehrsflughafen

Railways, Stations
Chemins de fer, Gares
Eisenbahnen Bahnhofe

Internal Car Ferries
Bacs intérieurs pour voitures
Autofahren innerhalb GBs

Level crossings
Passages à niveau
Bahnubergange

AYR **Primary route destinations**
Destination des routes principales
Hauptstreckenziel

Steep gradients
Fortes dénivellations
Steigung

Tourist information centre
Bureau du Syndicat d'Initiative
Fremdenverkehrsamt

Picturesque Locality — Viewpoint — Historic building — Other places including antiquities
Places of interest
Endroits remarquables
Besondere Sehenswurdigkeiten

National Parks and areas of outstanding natural beauty
Parcs Nationaux et régions de grande beauté naturelle
Nationalparks und Gebiete von aussergewohnlich landschaftlicher Schonheit

National Forest Parks
Parcs forestiers Nationaux
Nationale Waldparks

BRANDS HATCH **Motor race circuits**
Circuits automobiles
Motorrennstrecke

Wooded areas
Régions boisees
Bewaldete Gegenden

Golf courses
Terrains de Golf
Golfplatz

YES TOR 2027 **Principal heights** (in feet)
Altitudes
Höchste Erhebungen (in Fuss)

Sand Shingle **Beaches**
Plages
Strand

County and Regional boundaries
Limites de Comtés et regions
Landergrenzen

Recognised by the Countryside Commission

PENNINE WAY **Long distance footpaths**
Sentiers a grande randonnee
Langstreckenwanderwege

GOODWOOD **Country Parks**
Parcs naturels regionaux
Naturschutzparke

Picnic Areas
Endroits pour piqueniquer
Picknickplatze

RAC approved caravan and camping sites
Terrains de camping et de caravaning conseillés par le RAC
Vom RAC empfohlene Wohnwagen- und Campingplatze

WOOLER **Youth Hostels**
Auberge de jeunesse
Jugendherberger

RAC/AA Telephone boxes
Cabines téléphoniques du RAC/AA
RAC/AA Telefonzellen

Scale 5¼ miles to 1 inch
0 5 10 15 miles
0 24 kilometres

Based upon the Ordnance Survey Maps with the sanction of the Controller of H M Stationery Office

1
A
B
C
D
E
F
Dunoon
Greenock
Port Glasgow
Dumbarton
Kilpatrick Hills
Lennoxtown
Milton of Campsie
Milngavie
Kirkintilloch
Langbank
Bowling
Erskine Bridge
Duntocher
Bearsden
Bishopbriggs
Inverkip
Wemyss Bay
Skelmorlie
Kilmacolm
Bishopton
Clydebank
Renfrew
Glasgow
Houston
Bridge of Weir
Kilbarchan
Johnstone
Paisley
Largs
Lochwinnoch
Barrhead
Rutherglen
Cambuslang
Millport
Fairlie
Kilbirnie
Beith
Neilston
East Kilbride
Hamilton
Dalry
Eaglesham
West Kilbride
Stewarton
Strathaven
Ardrossan
Saltcoats
Stevenston
Kilwinning
Kilmaurs
Irvine
Kilmarnock
Newmilns
Darvel
Galston
Troon
Monkton
Prestwick
Mauchline
Tarbolton
Catrine
Ayr
Auchinleck
Cumnock
Drongan
Maybole
Culzean
Patna
Dalmellington
New Cumnock
Girvan
Dailly
Turnberry
Kirkoswald
Straiton
Cunninghame
Kyle
2
3
4
5
6
7
8
9

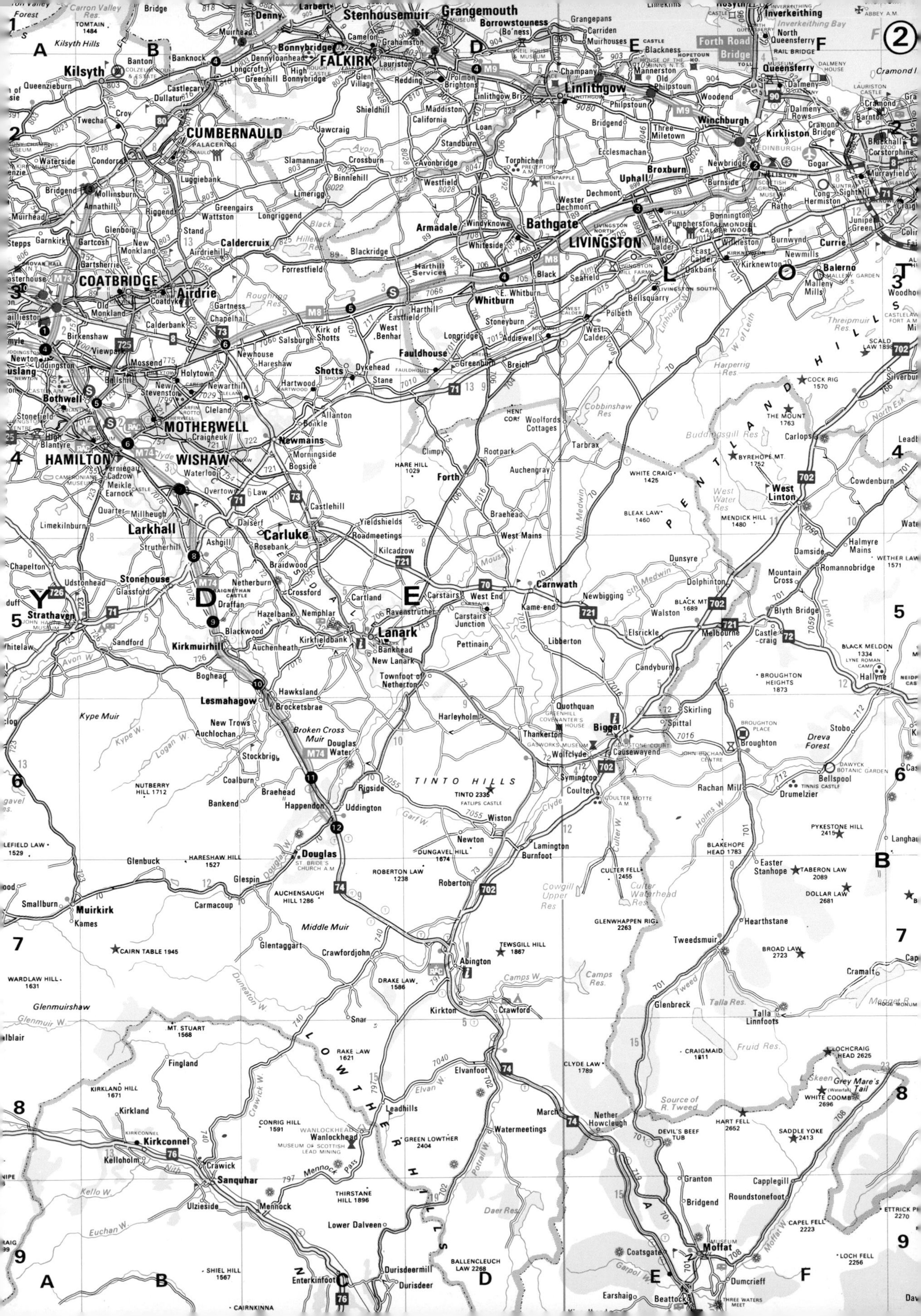

2
Denny
Larbert
Stenhousemuir
Grangemouth
Borrowstounness (Bo'ness)
Grangepans
Carriden
Inverkeithing
Inverkeithing Bay
North Queensferry
Forth Road Bridge
Kilsyth Hills
Banton
Banknock
Bonnybridge
Camelon
Grahamston
FALKIRK
Muirhouses
Blackness
Kilsyth
Dennyloanhead
Longcroft
Laurieston
Polmont
Queensferry
Dalmeny
Cramond
Queenzieburn
Castlecary
Dullatur
Greenhill
High Bonnybridge
Glen Village
Redding
Brightons
Linlithgow Bridge
Linlithgow
Champany
Old Philpstoun
Philpstoun
Woodend
Twechar
Croy
Shieldhill
Maddiston
California
Bridgend
Three Miletown
Winchburgh
Kirkliston
Dalmeny Rows
Barnton
CUMBERNAULD
Jawcraig
Standburn
Loan
Ecclesmachan
Cramond Bridge
Blackhall
Corstorphine
Waterside
Condorrat
Slamannan
Crossburn
Avonbridge
Torphichen
Newbridge
Broxburn
Gogar
Murrayfield
Luggiebank
Binniehill
Westfield
Uphall
Dechmont
Burnside
Ratho
Hermiston
Sighthill
Bridgend
Mollinsburn
Annathill
Limerigg
Wester Dechmont
Riggend
Greengairs
Wattston
Longriggend
Muirhead
Glenboig
Armadale
Windyknowe
Bathgate
Pumpherston
Bonnington
Juniper Green
Currie
Stepps
Garnkirk
Gartcosh
Stand
New Monkland
Caldercruix
Airdriehill
Blackridge
Whiteside
LIVINGSTON
Mid Calder
Wilkieston
Burnwynd
East Calder
Oakbank
Kirknewton
Newmills
Balerno
Malleny Mills
Gartsherrie
Forrestfield
Harthill Services
COATBRIDGE
Airdrie
Coatdyke
Old Monkland
Black
Seafield
E. Whitburn
Whitburn
Livingston South
Bellsquarry
Gartness
Chapelhall
Harthill
Eastfield
Polbeth
Baillieston
Birkenshaw
Calderbank
Kirk of Shotts
West Benhar
Stoneyburn
Longridge
Addiewell
West Calder
Threipmuir Res.
Uddingston
Viewpark
Newhouse
Salsburgh
Hareshaw
Fauldhouse
Greenburn
Breich
Scald Law 1898
Mossend
Holytown
Shotts
Dykehead
Stane
Harperrig Res.
PENTLAND HILLS
Bellshill
New Stevenston
Newarthill
Hartwood
Cock Rig 1570
Bothwell
Cleland
Allanton
Cobbinshaw Res.
Woolfords Cottages
The Mount 1763
MOTHERWELL
Bonkle
Craigneuk
Newmains
Blantyre
HAMILTON
WISHAW
Morningside
Clyde
Tarbrax
Buddingsgill Res
Carlops
Climpy
Rootpark
Byrehope Mt. 1752
Cadzow
Meikle Earnock
Waterloo
Bogside
Hare Hill 1029
Forth
Auchengray
White Craig 1425
West Linton
Cowdenburn
Overtown
Law
Castlehill
West Water Res.
Quarter
Millheugh
Limekilnburn
Larkhall
Dalserf
Carluke
Yieldshields
Braehead
Bleak Law 1460
Mendick Hill 1480
Ashgill
Strutherhill
Rosebank
Roadmeetings
Kilcadzow
West Mains
Halmyre Mains
Chapelton
Braidwood
Dunsyre
Damside
Wether Law 1571
Udstonhead
Stonehouse
Glassford
Netherburn
Crossford
Carnwath
Mountain Cross
Romannobridge
Draffan
Cartland
Carstairs
West End
Newbigging
Dolphinton
Strathaven
Hazelbank
Nemphlar
Ravenstruther
Carstairs Junction
Kame-end
Black Mt 1689
Walston
Blyth Bridge
Sandford
Blackwood
Kirkfieldbank
Lanark
Elsrickle
Melbourne
Castlecraig
Kirkmuirhill
Auchenheath
Bankhead
New Lanark
Pettinain
Libberton
Black Meldon 1334
Avon W.
Boghead
Townfoot of Netherton
Candyburn
Broughton Heights 1873
Hallyne
Lesmahagow
Hawksland
Brocketsbrae
Harleyholm
Quothquan
Skirling
Kype Muir
New Trows
Auchlochan
Thankerton
Biggar
Spittal
Broughton
Stobo
Broken Cross Muir
Douglas Water
Wolfclyde
Causewayend
Dreva Forest
Stockbriggs
Coalburn
TINTO HILLS
Symington
Dawyck Botanic Garden
Nutberry Hill 1712
Braehead
Rigside
Tinto 2335
Coulter
Rachan Mill
Bellspool
Drumelzier
Bankend
Happendon
Uddington
Wiston
Pykestone Hill 2415
Glenbuck
Hareshaw Hill 1527
Douglas
Newton
Lamington
Burnfoot
Blakehope Head 1783
Glespin
Dungavel Hill 1674
Roberton Law 1238
Roberton
Culter Fell 2455
Easter Stanhope
Taberon Law 2089
Muirkirk
Smallburn
Kames
Carmacoup
Auchensaugh Hill 1286
Cowgill Upper Res
Culter Waterhead Res
Dollar Law 2681
Middle Muir
Glenwhappen Rig 2263
Hearthstane
Cairn Table 1945
Glentaggart
Crawfordjohn
Tewsgill Hill 1867
Tweedsmuir
Broad Law 2723
Abington
Wardlaw Hill 1631
Drake Law 1586
Camps Res.
Cramalt
Glenmuirshaw
Kirkton
Crawford
Glenbreck
Talla Res.
Talla Linnfoots
Snar
Mt. Stuart 1568
LOWTHER HILLS
Rake Law 1621
Fruid Res.
Craigmaid 1811
Lochcraig Head 2625
Fingland
Elvanfoot
Clyde Law 1789
Kirkland Hill 1671
Grey Mare's Tail
White Coomb 2696
Source of R. Tweed
Leadhills
Hart Fell 2652
Kirkland
Conrig Hill 1591
Wanlockhead
Museum of Scottish Lead Mining
Green Lowther 2404
March
Nether Howcleugh
Watermeetings
Saddle Yoke 2413
Kirkconnel
Kelloholm
Devil's Beef Tub
Crawick
Sanquhar
Mennock Pass
Granton
Capplegill
Kello W.
Thirstane Hill 1896
Bridgend
Roundstonefoot
Ulzieside
Mennock
Daer Res.
Euchan W.
Lower Dalveen
Ettrick Pen 2270
Capel Fell 2223
Moffat
Coatsgate
Shiel Hill 1567
Durisdeermill
Ballencleuch Law 2268
Loch Fell 2256
Enterkinfoot
Durisdeer
Dumcrieff
Earshaig
Beattock
Three Waters Meet
Cairnkinna

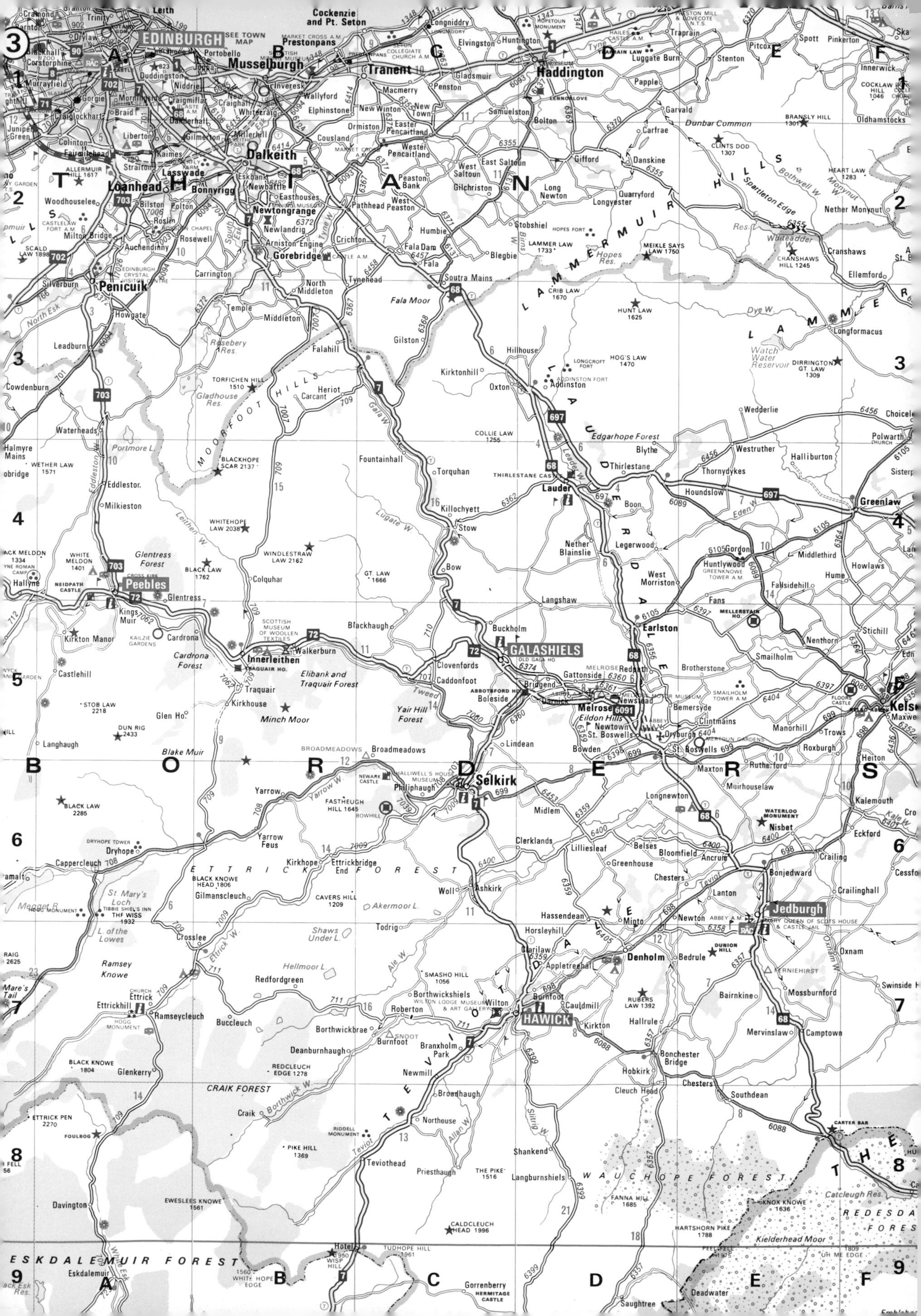

3
EDINBURGH
SEE TOWN MAP
Leith
Cockenzie and Pt. Seton
Prestonpans
Musselburgh
Portobello
Longniddry
Elvingston
Huntington
Haddington
Tranent
Gladsmuir
Penston
Macmerry
Inveresk
Wallyford
Elphinstone
New Winton
Ormiston
Easter Pencaitland
Wester Pencaitland
Samuelston
Bolton
Traprain
Luggate Burn
Stenton
Pitcox
Spott
Pinkerton
Innerwick
Papple
Garvald
Dunbar Common
Oldhamstocks
Carfrae
Danskine
Gifford
Quarryford
Longyester
Long Newton
East Saltoun
West Saltoun
Gilchriston
Pathhead
Peaston Bank
West Peaston
Humbie
Fala Dam
Fala
Blegbie
Soutra Mains
Crichton
Tynehead
North Middleton
Middleton
Temple
Carrington
Gorebridge
Arniston Engine
Newlandrig
Newtongrange
Easthouses
Newbattle
Eskbank
Dalkeith
Bonnyrigg
Lasswade
Loanhead
Polton
Bilston
Roslin
Rosewell
Auchendinny
Penicuik
Howgate
Milton Bridge
Woodhouselee
Silverburn
Colinton
Fairmilehead
Liberton
Gilmerton
Straiton
Kaimes
Dalkeith
Corstorphine
Murrayfield
Gorgie
Craiglockhart
Braid
Morningside
Duddingston
Niddrie
Craigmillar
Danderhall
Craighall
Whitecraig
Millerhill
Cousland
LOTHIAN
LAMMERMUIR HILLS
Lammer Law 1733
Meikle Says Law 1750
Hopes Res.
Crib Law 1670
Hunt Law 1625
Clints Dod 1307
Bransly Hill 1301
Heart Law 1283
Nether Monynut
Cranshaws
Ellemford
Longformacus
Dye W.
Watch Water Reservoir
Dirrington Gt. Law 1309
Wedderlie
Choicelee
Polwarth
Westruther
Halliburton
Thornydykes
Houndslow
Greenlaw
Blythe
Thirlestane
Edgarhope Forest
Lauder
Boon
Legerwood
Nether Blainslie
West Morriston
Gordon
Huntlywood
Middlethird
Howlaws
Hume
Fallsidehill
Fans
Mellerstain Ho.
Earlston
Stichill
Nenthorn
Smailholm
Brotherstone
Redpath
Kelso
Floors Castle
Clintmains
Bemersyde
Dryburgh
Newstead
Melrose
Eildon Hills
Newtown St. Boswells
St. Boswells
Bowden
Maxton
Rutherford
Roxburgh
Manorhill
Trows
Heiton
Kalemouth
Eckford
Nisbet
Waterloo Monument
Muirhouselaw
Longnewton
Ancrum
Bloomfield
Belses
Lilliesleaf
Greenhouse
Chesters
Crailing
Bonjedward
Crailinghall
Lanton
Jedburgh
Mary Queen of Scots House & Castle Jail
Oxnam
Ferniehirst
Mossburnford
Swinside Hall
Bedrule
Dunion Hill
Denholm
Minto
Hassendean
Horsleyhill
Clarilaw
Appletreehall
Cauldmill
Hallrule
Bairnkine
Rubers Law 1392
Kirkton
Hawick
Wilton
Wilton Lodge Museum & Art Gallery
Burnfoot
Mervinslaw
Camptown
Bonchester Bridge
Hobkirk
Chesters
Southdean
Cleuch Head
Carter Bar
Catcleugh Res.
Knox Knowe 1636
Redesdale Forest
Kielderhead Moor
Hartshorn Pike 1788
Peel Fell 1975
Deadwater
Saughtree
Wauchope Forest
Fanna Hill 1685
Shankend
Langburnshiels
The Pike 1516
Caldcleuch Head 1996
Priesthaugh
Teviothead
Northouse
Broadhaugh
Newmill
Branxholm Park
Teviot
Allen W.
Slitrig W.
Riddell Monument
Pike Hill 1369
Craik
Craik Forest
Borthwick W.
Redcleuch Edge 1278
Deanburnhaugh
Burnfoot
Snoot
Roberton
Borthwickbrae
Borthwickshiels
Smasho Hill 1056
Redfordgreen
Hellmoor L.
Buccleuch
Ettrick
Ettrickhill
Hogg Monument
Ramseycleuch
Ramsey Knowe
Crosslee
Ettrick W.
Glenkerry
Black Knowe 1804
Ettrick Pen 2270
Foulbog
Davington
Eweslees Knowe 1561
Eskdalemuir Forest
Eskdalemuir
Black Esk Res.
White Hope Edge 1560
Wisp Hill 1950
Hotel
Tudhope Hill 1961
Gorrenberry
Hermitage Castle
L. of the Lowes
St Mary's Loch
Tibbie Shiel's Inn
The Wiss 1932
Hogg Monument
Megget R.
Cappercleuch
Dryhope
Dryhope Tower
Black Law 2285
Black Knowe Head 1806
Gilmanscleuch
Ettrick Forest
Kirkhope
Ettrickbridge End
Cavers Hill 1209
Akermoor L.
Shaws Under L.
Todrig
Ale W.
Woll
Ashkirk
Clerklands
Midlem
Yarrow
Yarrow Feus
Yarrow W.
Fastheugh Hill 1645
Bowhill
Newark Castle
Philiphaugh
Halliwell's House Museum
Selkirk
Broadmeadows
Lindean
Yair Hill Forest
Caddonfoot
Clovenfords
Tweed
Boleside
Abbotsford Ho.
Bridgend
Darnick
Gattonside
Galashiels
Old Gala Ho.
Buckholm
Langshaw
Blackhaugh
Bow
Stow
Killochyett
Lugate W.
Gt. Law 1666
Torquhan
Fountainhall
Gala W.
Heriot
Carcant
Falahill
Gilston
Fala Moor
Hillhouse
Kirktonhill
Oxton
Addinston
Addinston Fort
Longcroft Fort
Hog's Law 1470
Collie Law 1255
Thirlestane Castle
Leader W.
LAUDERDALE
Moorfoot Hills
Rosebery Res.
Gladhouse Res.
Torfichen Hill 1510
Blackhope Scar 2137
Whitehope Law 2038
Windlestraw Law 2162
Black Law 1762
Colquhar
Leithen W.
Glentress Forest
Glentress
Peebles
Neidpath Castle
Cross Kirk
Hallyne
Kings Muir
Kirkton Manor
Kailzie Gardens
Cardrona
Cardrona Forest
Innerleithen
Traquair Ho.
Walkerburn
Scottish Museum of Woollen Textiles
Elibank and Traquair Forest
Traquair
Kirkhouse
Minch Moor
Glen Ho.
Blake Muir
Stob Law 2218
Dun Rig 2433
Castlehill
Langhaugh
BORDERS
Eddleston
Milkieston
Portmore L.
Waterheads
Cowdenburn
Leadburn
North Esk
Halmyre Mains
Wether Law 1571
White Meldon 1401
Allermuir Hill 1617
Castlelaw Fort
Scald Law 1898
Edinburgh Crystal Visitor Centre
Ettrick Pen

4
A
B
C
D
E
F
G
1
2
3
4
5
6
7
8
9
North Berwick
Bass Rock
Craigleith
Fidra
Eyebroughy
Tantallon Castle A.M.
Auldhame
Scoughall
Gullane Bay
Dirleton
Gullane
Castle & Gardens A.M.
Museum
Black dykes
Kingston
Whitekirk
West Fenton
Fenton Barns
Aberlady Bay
Myreton Motor Museum
Aberlady
Craigielaw
Drem
Tyninghame Gardens
Tyne Mouth
John Muir
Tyninghame
Gosford Bay
Gosford House
The Chesters Fort A.M.
Museum of Flight
Preston
Ballencrieff
Athelstaneford
East Linton
West Barns
Dunbar
Broxburn
Spittal
Longniddry
Hopetoun Monument
Preston Mill & Dovecote N.T.S.
Traprain
Hailes
©1989 George Philip Ltd., London
Dunbar
Broxburn
Barns Ness
Skateraw
Spott
Pinkerton
Thorntonloch
Innerwick
Cocklaw Hill 1046
Dunglass Collegiate Church A.M.
Cockburnspath
Reed Pt.
Cove
Siccar Pt.
Wheat Stack
Fast Castle
Ransly Hill 1301
Oldhamstocks
Lumsdaine
St. Abb's Head
Earn's Heugh
Ecclaw
Northfield
St. Abb's
St. Abb's Haven
Heart Law 1283
Grantshouse
Huxton
Coldingham
Priory
Coldingham
Monynut W.
Butterdean
Museum
Nether Monynut
Duns Forest
Eye W.
Houndwood
Eyemouth
Cairncross
Ale W.
Abbey St. Bathans
Abbey St. Bathans Trout Farm
Cranshaws
Cranshaws Hill 1245
Auchencrow
Reston
Burnmouth
Ayton
Ayton Castle
Ellemford
Marygold
Edin's Hall Broch A.M.
Prenderguest
Whiterig
Lamberton Beach
Longformacus
Lintlaw
Chirnside
Lamberton
Preston
Chirnsidebridge
Clappers
Edrom
Norman Arch A.M.
Foulden
Halidon Hill
Duns Law
Dirrington Gt. Law 1309
Jim Clark Room
Duns
Buxley
Manderston
Whiteadder W.
Allanton
Highfields
Castle, Town Walls
Berwick
Berwick upon Tweed
Clockmill
West Blackadder
Hutton
Paxton
Tweedmouth
Choicelee
Gavinton
Tweed
Loanend
Spittal
Polwarth Church
Sinclair's Hill
Fishwick
East Ord
Redshin Cove
Whitsome
Horncliffe
Halliburton
Blackadder W.
Fogo
Bogend
Horndean
Sisterpath
Norham Castle
Thorntonpark
Murton
Scremerston
Fogorig
Swinton
Ladykirk
Thornton
West Allerdean
Cheswick
Greenlaw
Swintonmill
Norham
Shoreswood
Shoresdean
Simprim
Grindon
Ancroft
Goswick
Haggerston
Beal
Keel Hd.
Holy Island (Lindisfarne)
Causeway
Holy I. Sands
Holy Island
Castle Pt.
Lindisfarne Castle & Priory
Burrows Hole
Middlethird
Lambden
Leitholm
Shellacres
Felkington
Berrington
Howlaws
Orange Lane
Castle Heaton
Duddo
Hume
Dundock Wood (The Hirsel)
Lennel
Bowsden
Fenham
Eccles
Coldstream
Cornhill-on-Tweed
Birgham
Etal
Lowick
Kyloe
Fenwick
Kyloe Hills
Stichill
Carham
Wark
Castle
Crookham
Lady Waterford Hall
Ford
Buckton
Northumberland
Elwick
Ross
Farne Islands
Staple I.
Nenthorn
Ednam
W. & E. Learmouth
Branxton
Budle Bay
Inner Sd.
Hadden
Kerchesters
Pressen
Flodden
Kimmerston
Holburn
Detchant
Middleton
Easington
Budle
Bamburgh
Bamburgh Castle
Grace Darling Museum
Sprouston
Holefield
Downham
Hetton Steads
Nth. Hazelrigg
Belford
Waren Mill
Floors Castle
Kelso
Windywalls
Milfield
Nesbit
Spindlestone
Burton
Coast
Maxwellheugh
Lempitlaw
Mindrum
Pawston
Fenton Town
Doddington
Trows
Hoselaw
Kilham
Glen
Lanton
Newtown
Dod Law
W. & E. Horton
Sth. Hazelrigg
Bradford
Elford
Seahouses
Roxburgh
Heiton
Blakelaw
Longknowe
Westnewton
Coupland
Bellshill
Warenton
Lucker
North Sunderland
Shotton
Kirknewton
Akeld
Adderstone
Yeavering Bell (Camp)
Humbleton
Chatton
Warenford
Newham
Swinhoe
Fleetham
Kalemouth
Frogden
Kirk Yetholm
Hethpool
Wooler
Greendikes
Newstead
Chathill
Crookhouse
Town Yetholm
Kirk Yetholm
Church
Linton
Earle
Haugh Head
Rosebrough
Ellingham
Kale W.
Eckford
Chillingham
Chillingham Wild Cattle
Newtown
Lilburn Tower
Preston
Preston Tower
Brunton
Crailing
Morebattle
N. Middleton
Cold Law 1484
Ros Castle
Hepburn
Brockdam
Cessford
Cliftoncote
S. Middleton
East Lilburn
North Charlton
Doxford
Christon Bank
Crailinghall
The Schil 1985
Hownam Law 1472
Hownam Mains
Mowhaugh
Langleeford
Ilderton
Roseden
Old Bewick
West Ditchburn
South Charlton
Jedburgh
Queen of Scots House
Castle Jail
Sourhope
The Cheviot 2676
Harthorpe Burn
Roddam
Harehope
Auchope Cairn 2382
Wooperton
New Bewick
Eglingham
Rock
Rock Hall
Oxnam
Hownam
Craik Moor
Dunmoor Hill 1860
Rennington
Oxnam W.
Chatto
National Park Inf. Centre
Brandon
Beanley
Ferniehirst
Swinside Hall
Greensidehill
Ingram
Powburn
Shipley
Littlehoughton
Mossburnford
Beefstand Hill 1842
Windy Gyle 2036
Shill Moor
Branton
Titlington
Hulne Priory
Longhoughton
Glanton
Glanton Pike
Hulne Park & Brizlee Tower
Abbey
Castle
Denwick
Camptown
Pennine Way
Cheviot Hills
Cushat Law 2020
Great Ryle
Bolton
Alnwick
Woden Law 1388
Kale W.
Prendwick
Abberwick
Aln
Alnmouth
Bilton
Hindhope
Barrowburn
Alnham
Whittingham
Blindburn
Little Ryle
Yetlington
Callaly Castle
Thrunton
Callaly
Thrunton Wood
Brownhart Law 1664
Scrainwood
Coquet
Alwin
Biddlestone
Shilbottle
Netherton
Edlingham
Carter Bar
Shillmoor
Low Buston
High Buston

5
DUMFRIES
GALLOWAY
THE GLENKENS
THE RHINNS
THE MACHARS
CARRICK FOREST
LUCE BAY
WIGTOWN BAY
STRANRAER
Newton Stewart
Kirkcudbright
Gatehouse of Fleet
Wigtown
Creetown
Glenluce
Portpatrick
Port William
Whithorn
Isle of Whithorn
Garlieston
Kirkcowan
New Galloway
St. John's Town of Dalry
Carsphairn
Ballantrae
Colmonell
Barrhill
Cairnryan
Kirkcolm
Drummore
Twynholm
Minnigaff
Glentrool Village
Glen Trool Lodge
Bargrennan
Sorbie
Kirkinner
Port Logan
Sandhead
Mochrum
Loch Ryan
Loch Ken
Glentrool Forest Park
Kirroughtree Forest
Cairn Edward Forest
Merrick 2765
Rhinns of Kells
Cairnsmore of Fleet 2329
Clints of Dromore
Artfield Fell
Braid Fell
Kennedy's Pass
Corsewall Pt.
Black Head

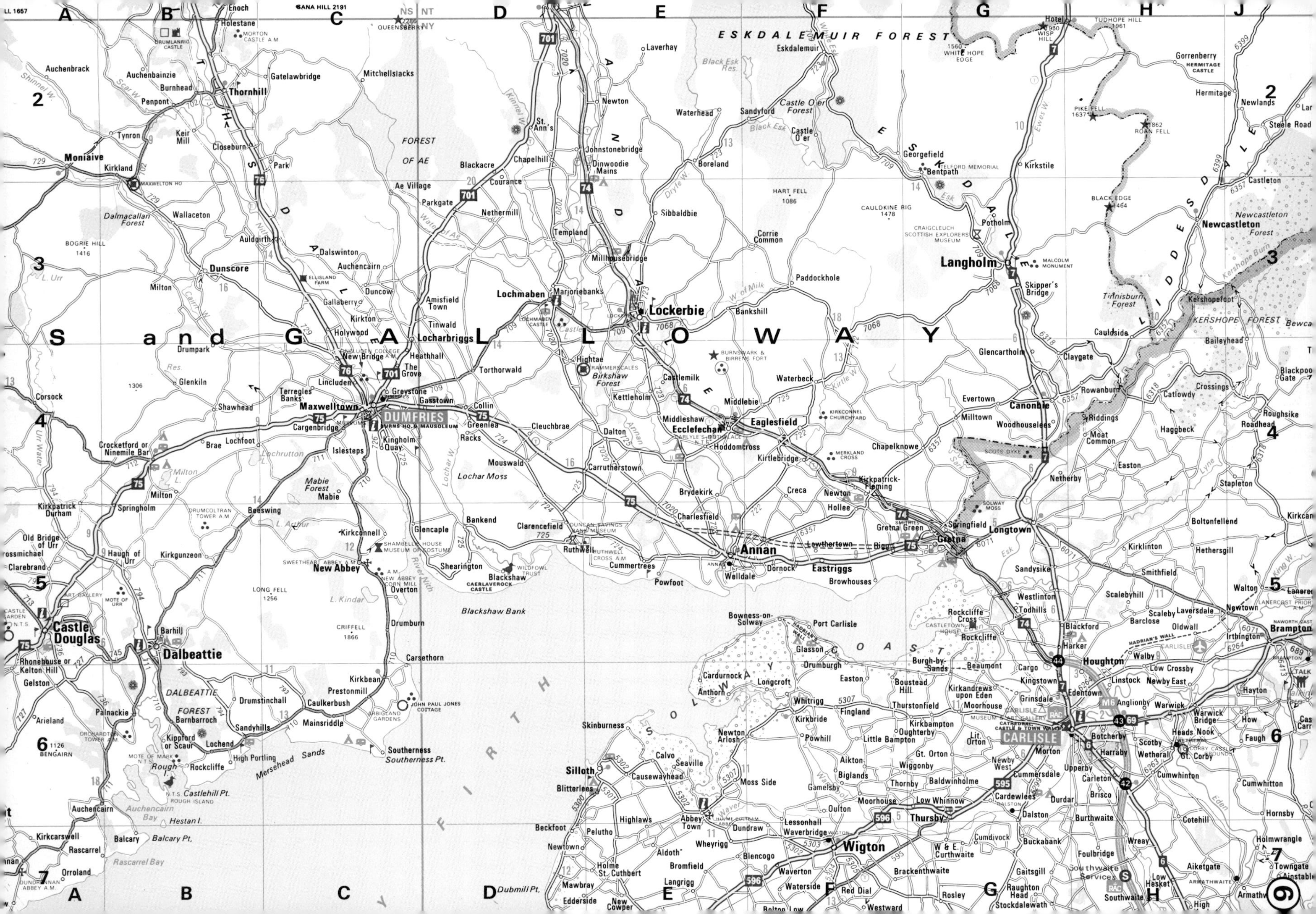

ESKDALEMUIR FOREST
DUMFRIES and GALLOWAY
ESKDALE
LIDDESDALE
SOLWAY COAST
SOLWAY FIRTH
FOREST OF AE
KERSHOPE FOREST
DALBEATTIE FOREST
Lockerbie
Langholm
Newcastleton
Dumfries
Maxwelltown
Annan
Gretna
Longtown
Carlisle
Wigton
Silloth
Castle Douglas
Dalbeattie
Moniaive
Thornhill
Dunscore
Lochmaben
Ecclefechan
Eaglesfield
Canonbie
Brampton
Houghton
Thursby
New Abbey
Locharbriggs
Blackshaw Bank
Lochar Moss
Southerness Pt.
Balcary Pt.
Rascarrel Bay
Hestan I.
Auchencairn Bay
Dubmill Pt.
Mersehead Sands

Index

Numbers in *italics* refer to illustrations